Exam Ref 70-743
Upgrading Your Skills
to MCSA: Windows
Server 2016

Charles Pluta

Exam Ref 70-743 Upgrading Your Skills to MCSA: Windows Server 2016

Published with the authorization of Microsoft Corporation by:
Pearson Education, Inc.

Copyright © 2017 by Pearson Education, Inc.

ISBN-13: 978-0-7356-9743-0

ISBN-10: 0-7356-9743-4

Library of Congress Control Number: 2016959957

1 16

Trademarks

Microsoft and the trademarks listed at https://www.microsoft.com on the "Trademarks" webpage are trademarks of the Microsoft group of companies. All other marks are property of their respective owners.

Warning and Disclaimer

Every effort has been made to make this book as complete and as accurate as possible, but no warranty or fitness is implied. The information provided is on an "as is" basis. The author, the publisher, and Microsoft Corporation shall have neither liability nor responsibility to any person or entity with respect to any loss or damages arising from the information contained in this book or programs accompanying it.

Special Sales

For information about buying this title in bulk quantities, or for special sales opportunities (which may include electronic versions; custom cover designs; and content particular to your business, training goals, marketing focus, or branding interests), please contact our corporate sales department at corpsales@pearsoned.com or (800) 382-3419.

For government sales inquiries, please contact governmentsales@pearsoned.com.

For questions about sales outside the U.S., please contact intlcs@pearson.com.

Editor-in-Chief	Greg Wiegand
Acquisitions Editor	Trina MacDonald
Development Editor	Rick Kughen
Managing Editor	Sandra Schroeder
Senior Project Editor	Tracey Croom
Editorial Production	Backstop Media, Troy Mott
Copy Editor	Jordan Severn
Indexer	Julie Grady
Proofreader	Christina Rudloff
Technical Editor	Ron Handlon
Cover Designer	Twist Creative, Seattle

Contents at a glance

Contents

What do you think of this book? We want to hear from you!

Microsoft is interested in hearing your feedback so we can continually improve our books and learning resources for you. To participate in a brief online survey, please visit:

https://aka.ms/tellpress

Chapter 4   Implement Windows Containers   93

Chapter 10 Install and configure Active Directory Domain Services   243

What do you think of this book? We want to hear from you!

Microsoft is interested in hearing your feedback so we can continually improve our
books and learning resources for you. To participate in a brief online survey, please visit:

https://aka.ms/tellpress

Introduction

With each release of Windows Server, more and more features are added or modified that makes knowing the product inside and out more and more difficult. The 70-743 exam "Upgrading your skills to Windows Server 2016" is for administrators that have previously achieved the MCSA certification for Windows Server 2008, or Windows Server 2012, and plan to achieve the latest certification offering.

Understanding that the exam is geared specifically towards administrators with existing knowledge, this Exam Ref book assumes you remember and know the knowledge that is necessary to pass the previous versions of the exam. Therefore, we focus solely on the skills that are measured in the 70-743 exam, sometimes skipping the basics of the skill. A lot of these skills build on the knowledge you've retained from Windows Server 2008 or Windows Server 2012. However, some of the skills are brand new to Windows Server 2016, and are expected to be highlighted on the exam.

The goal of this book is to act as a reference to give you the tools and knowledge that you need to succeed in passing the exam. While we cover every skill that the exam measures and focus on real-world examples of how to use the technologies that are listed, there is no way of guaranteeing that you will pass the exam simply by using this book. As you are well aware as an existing MCSA credential holder, nothing is better than getting hands-on experience with each of the roles and features in Windows Server 2016 before taking the exam. It is recommended that you use the information in this book, combined with a hands-on approach of trying each role or feature discussed by using both graphical and Windows PowerShell (or command-line) tools. This will ensure that you have the best opportunity to succeed when taking the exam.

This book covers every major topic area found on the exam, but it does not cover every exam question. Only the Microsoft exam team has access to the exam questions, and Microsoft regularly adds new questions to the exam, making it impossible to cover specific questions. You should consider this book a supplement to your relevant real-world experience and other study materials. If you encounter a topic in this book that you do not feel completely comfortable with, use the "Need more review?" links you'll find in the text to find more information and take the time to research and study the topic. Great information is available on MSDN, TechNet, MVA, and in blogs and forums.

Organization of this book

This book is organized by the "Skills measured" list published for the exam. The "Skills measured" list is available for each exam on the Microsoft Learning website: *https://aka.ms/examlist*. Each chapter in this book corresponds to a major topic area in the list, and the technical tasks in each topic area determine a chapter's organization. If an exam covers six major topic areas, for example, the book will contain six chapters.

Microsoft certifications

Microsoft certifications distinguish you by proving your command of a broad set of skills and experience with current Microsoft products and technologies. The exams and corresponding certifications are developed to validate your mastery of critical competencies as you design and develop, or implement and support, solutions with Microsoft products and technologies both on-premises and in the cloud. Certification brings a variety of benefits to the individual and to employers and organizations.

> **MORE INFO   ALL MICROSOFT CERTIFICATIONS**
>
> For information about Microsoft certifications, including a full list of available certifications, go to *https://www.microsoft.com/learning*.

Acknowledgments

Charles Pluta I would like to thank my wife Jen for her love and support throughout all of my projects. I would also like to thank Greg Baker for giving me the opportunity to succeed from the beginning of my career. I would also like to thank Brian Svidergol, Elias Mereb, and Mike Corkery, who have provided their continued friendship and technical expertise throughout the years. Finally, I would like to thank Trina, Troy, and all of the editors and reviewers behind the scenes that dedicated their time to making this book happen.

Free ebooks from Microsoft Press

From technical overviews to in-depth information on special topics, the free ebooks from Microsoft Press cover a wide range of topics. These ebooks are available in PDF, EPUB, and Mobi for Kindle formats, ready for you to download at:

https://aka.ms/mspressfree

Check back often to see what is new!

Microsoft Virtual Academy

Build your knowledge of Microsoft technologies with free expert-led online training from Microsoft Virtual Academy (MVA). MVA offers a comprehensive library of videos, live events, and more to help you learn the latest technologies and prepare for certification exams. You'll find what you need here:

https://www.microsoftvirtualacademy.com

Quick access to online references

Throughout this book are addresses to webpages that the author has recommended you visit for more information. Some of these addresses (also known as URLs) can be painstaking to type into a web browser, so we've compiled all of them into a single list that readers of the print edition can refer to while they read.

Download the list at *https://aka.ms/examref743/downloads*.

The URLs are organized by chapter and heading. Every time you come across a URL in the book, find the hyperlink in the list to go directly to the webpage.

Errata, updates, & book support

We've made every effort to ensure the accuracy of this book and its companion content. You can access updates to this book—in the form of a list of submitted errata and their related corrections—at:

https://aka.ms/examref743/errata

If you discover an error that is not already listed, please submit it to us at the same page.

If you need additional support, email Microsoft Press Book Support at *mspinput@microsoft.com.*

Please note that product support for Microsoft software and hardware is not offered through the previous addresses. For help with Microsoft software or hardware, go to *https://support.microsoft.com.*

We want to hear from you

At Microsoft Press, your satisfaction is our top priority, and your feedback our most valuable asset. Please tell us what you think of this book at:

https://aka.ms/tellpress

We know you're busy, so we've kept it short with just a few questions. Your answers go directly to the editors at Microsoft Press. (No personal information will be requested.) Thanks in advance for your input!

Stay in touch

Let's keep the conversation going! We're on Twitter: *http://twitter.com/MicrosoftPress.*

Important: How to use this book to study for the exam

Certification exams validate your on-the-job experience and product knowledge. To gauge your readiness to take an exam, use this Exam Ref to help you check your understanding of the skills tested by the exam. Determine the topics you know well and the areas in which you need more experience. To help you refresh your skills in specific areas, we have also provided "Need more review?" pointers, which direct you to more in-depth information outside the book.

The Exam Ref is not a substitute for hands-on experience. This book is not designed to teach you new skills.

We recommend that you round out your exam preparation by using a combination of available study materials and courses. Learn more about available classroom training at *https://www.microsoft.com/learning*. Microsoft Official Practice Tests are available for many exams at *https://aka.ms/practicetests*. You can also find free online courses and live events from Microsoft Virtual Academy at *https://www.microsoftvirtualacademy.com*.

This book is organized by the "Skills measured" list published for the exam. The "Skills measured" list for each exam is available on the Microsoft Learning website: *https://aka.ms/examlist*.

Note that this Exam Ref is based on this publicly available information and the author's experience. To safeguard the integrity of the exam, authors do not have access to the exam questions.

CHAPTER 1

Install Windows Servers in host and compute environments

In this chapter we discuss the requirements for installing, upgrading, and migrating servers to Windows Server 2016. We'll also cover Nano Server, the new version of Windows Server. Finally, we will discuss how to create, manage, and maintain images that can be used for Windows Server deployments.

Windows Server 2016 introduces several new features compared to Windows Server 2012. These features include:

- **Nano Server**   Offers a new installation type that does not provide a graphical or command prompt experience and must be managed remotely.

> **IMPORTANT**
> *Have you read page xxiii?*
> It contains valuable information regarding the skills you need to pass the exam.

- **Containers**   Isolates applications from the operating system. Each container is isolated, but runs on the base operating system. You can further isolate a container by running it as a virtual machine with Hyper-V.

- **Docker**   Provides a method of managing containers, and is supported for Windows Server 2016 and Hyper-V.

- **Rolling upgrades**   Enables you to add Windows Server 2016 nodes to an existing Windows Server 2012 R2 failover cluster and continue to operate the cluster until all nodes have been upgraded.

- **Hyper-V memory enhancements**   Enables you to dynamically add or remove virtual memory and networking adapters from running virtual machines (VM).

- **Nested virtualization**   Provides a method of running a nested Hyper-V installation within a VM.

- **Shielded virtual machines**   Shields using a virtual machine that provides protection for the data that is stored on the VM.

- **PowerShell Direct**   Enables you to run PowerShell on a VM without additional security policies, network, or firewall settings.

- **Windows Defender**   Enables by default that Windows Server 2016 installations and anti-malware patterns are automatically kept up-to-date.

- **Storage Spaces Direct**   Enables you to build a highly-available storage set with direct attached storage by using Server Message Block version 3.0 (SMB 3.0).

- **Storage Replica** Enables you to replicate volumes at the block level for additional redundancy.
- **Microsoft Passport** Enables you to use two-factor authentication by using an enrolled device with Windows Hello or a PIN.
- **Remote Desktop Services** Allows an Azure Structured Query Language (SQL) database to be used, creating a highly available environment with the Remote Desktop Connection Broker.
- **Active Directory Domain Services (AD DS)** Enables AD DS improvements to support privileged access management, Azure AD Join, and Microsoft Passport.

Skills in this chapter:

- Install, upgrade, and migrate servers and workloads
- Install and configure Nano Server
- Create, manage, and maintain images for deployment

Skill 1.1: Install, upgrade, and migrate servers and workloads

Windows Server 2016 offers similar editions and installation options compared to Windows Server 2008 and 2012. In this section, we discuss the installation requirements for the base installation of Windows Server, and outline how Windows Server 2016 differs from previous versions. We discuss the differences in the installation process, server roles, and features.

> **This section covers how to:**
> - Determine Windows Server 2016 installation requirements
> - Determine appropriate Windows Server 2016 editions per workload
> - Install Windows Server 2016
> - Install Windows Server 2016 features and roles
> - Install and configure Windows Server Core
> - Manage Windows Server Core installations using Windows PowerShell, command line, and remote management capabilities
> - Implement Windows PowerShell Desired State Configuration to install and maintain integrity of installed environments
> - Perform upgrades and migrations of servers and core workloads from Windows Server 2008 and Windows Server 2012 to Windows Server 2016
> - Determine the appropriate activation model for server installation, such as Automatic Virtual Machine Activation, Key Management Service, and Active Directory-based Activation

Determine Windows Server 2016 installation requirements

A set of minimum requirements have been published by Microsoft in order to define the bare essentials that are needed to install Windows Server 2016. These are simply minimums, meaning that you may encounter an error during or after installation if your computer doesn't meet them. The minimum requirements are:

- 1.4 GHz 64-bit processor
- 512 MB RAM (Error Correcting Code, or ECC type)
- 32 GB disk space

Note that if installing Windows Server 2016 as a virtual machine, it might initially fail with only 512 MB of RAM. A workaround is to initially assign 800 MB, and then reduce it to 512 MB after installation. 32 GB of storage space is also a bare minimum, and should only be used for Server Core installations. A server with a Graphic User Interface (GUI) installation uses approximately 4 GB of additional space. Additionally, be aware that network installations and servers with more than 16 GB of RAM need additional disk space.

EXAM TIP

If you need to install the Server Core option, be aware that no GUI components are installed—you can't enable a GUI from Server Manager. If you need a full GUI on the server, use the Server with Desktop Experience option.

If you plan to use BitLocker Drive Encryption, then the physical server hardware must also have a Trusted Platform Module (TPM) chip that is version 2.0 or newer. The TPM chip must have an Endorsement Key certificate that is pre-provisioned or can be obtained by the device during the boot process.

NEED MORE REVIEW? LEARN MORE ABOUT TPM CHIPS

For more information regarding TPM chips and TPM Key Attestation, visit *https://technet. microsoft.com/windows-server-docs/identity/ad-ds/manage/component-updates/tpm-key-attestation.*

While some previous versions of Windows Server have listed a recommended set of system requirements, Windows Server 2016 has no such list. The recommended hardware varies significantly between the different editions that can be deployed, as well as the server roles or applications that can be installed. Instead of relying on a recommended number of requirements, perform test deployments in the scenario that you need to obtain a good baseline for your environment.

Determine appropriate Windows Server 2016 editions per workload

Microsoft offers several versions of Windows Server 2016. Selecting the appropriate version for your environment depends on the size or functionality that you expect to receive from the server. Table 1-1 lists the Windows Server 2016 editions that are available.

TABLE 1-1 Comparing Windows Server 2016 Editions

Edition	Description	License model	Client access license
Windows Server 2016 Datacenter	Highly virtualized environments	Per core	Windows Server
Windows Server 2016 Standard	Physical or minimally virtualized environments	Per core	Windows Server
Windows Server 2016 Essentials	Small businesses	Per processor	N/A
Windows Server 2016 MultiPoint Premium Server	Academic volume licensing	Per processor	Windows Server and Remote Desktop Services
Windows Storage Server 2016	OEM channel	Per processor	N/A
Microsoft Hyper-V Server 2016	Free hypervisor	N/A	N/A

Another installation option of Windows Server is Nano Server, which is discussed later in this chapter in "Skill 1.2: Install and configure Nano Server."

Install Windows Server 2016

Although there are a few different editions of Windows Server 2016, the installation process is fairly similar in each of them. Manually installing Windows Server is as simple as completing the GUI wizard and selecting the options. The most important aspect of the installation process is selecting the type of installation that you prefer:

- Server Core (Default)
- Server with Desktop Experience

In previous versions of Windows Server, you can use Server Manager or Windows PowerShell to adjust whether the server has a GUI. With Windows Server 2016, once the installation type has been selected, it cannot be changed. Figure 1-1 shows the available options when manually installing Windows Server 2016.

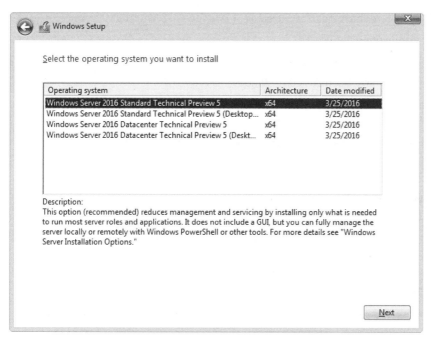

FIGURE 1-1 Windows Setup

Install Windows Server 2016 features and roles

- Windows Server 2016 introduces two new server roles that can be installed:

  - **Device Health Attestation** Works with TPM chips and Mobile Device Management (MDM) to assess mobile device health. DHA enables organizations to raise the security of their mobile devices and monitor mobile device health.

  - **MultiPoint Services** Originally designed for classroom and lab environments, MultiPoint (previously called Windows MultiPoint Server 2012) enables multiple users to share one computer while still receiving individual desktops. Unlike Remote Desktop Services, MultiPoint does not create a separate Remote Desktop Broker or Gateway.

> **NEED MORE REVIEW?**
>
> For more information regarding DHA with Windows 10, visit *https://technet.microsoft.com/en-us/library/mt750346.aspx.*

The following features have been removed as of Windows Server 2016:

- Ink and Handwriting Services
- User Interfaces and Infrastructure

Three new features have been added to Windows Server 2016:

- **Setup and Boot Event Collection**   Enables you to collect and log the setup and boot events from other computers on the network.
- **VM Shielding Tools for Fabric Management**   Provides shielding tools for the Fabric Management server on a network. For the upgrade exam, Fabric Management is not specifically called out in the skills measured.
- **Windows Defender Features**   Comes pre-installed and provides malware protection for the server.

Remember that in addition to using Server Manager, you can also install server roles and features by using the `Install-WindowsFeature` cmdlet. To obtain the list of available features that can be installed, use the `Get-WindowsFeature` cmdlet. For example, to see the available server roles and features that relate to Active Directory, run the following command:

```
Get-WindowsFeature -Name AD* | FT Name
```

Windows returns a list of server roles and features similar to the following:

```
Name

----

AD-CertificateADCS-Cert-Authority

ADCS-Enroll-Web-Pol

ADCS-Enroll-Web-Svc

ADCS-Web-Enrollment

ADCS-Device-Enrollment

ADCS-Online-Cert

AD-Domain-Services

ADFS-Federation

ADLDS

ADRMS

ADRMS-Server

ADRMS-Identity
```

Install and configure Windows Server Core

Performing a default installation by using the GUI to install Windows Server creates a Server Core installation. The default settings for installing Windows Server do not include the Desktop Experience features. Figure 1-2 shows the initial logon screen after performing a Server Core installation.

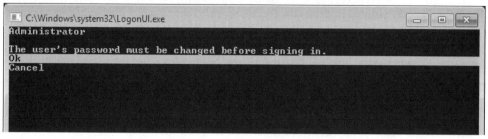

FIGURE 1-2 Server Core log on screen

As Figure 1-2 shows, there is no graphical element to the installation. Unlike some previous versions, you cannot switch from a Server Core installation to an installation with a GUI. The Desktop Experience installation option must be selected during installation to add these specific features.

After changing the password or logging in for the first time, you are simply presented with a blank command prompt. To make any configuration changes locally on the server, run the **sconfig.cmd** command from the command prompt. Figure 1-3 shows the available configuration options by running sconfig.

FIGURE 1-3 sconfig.cmd

Most any task that you can complete from Server Manager can also be completed by running sconfig. Note that sconfig is not restricted just to Server Core, it can also be used to configure a full server installation with the Desktop Experience.

> **NOTE MORE ON SCONFIG**
>
> After options 10 and 11, the improve product opt-in and Windows Activation have been configured, they are removed from the sconfig menu.

Manage Windows Server Core installations using Windows PowerShell, command line, and remote management capabilities

Remote Management is enabled by default in a Server Core installation. There are a few different options for managing a Server Core installation remotely:

- Server Manager
- Windows PowerShell
- Remote Server Administration Tools (RSAT)
- Remote Desktop
- Group Policy (Not supported on Nano Server)

Server Manager can be used from a Windows Server that has the Desktop Experience features installed. Simply add the Server Core installation to Server Manager to manage it remotely. To use Windows PowerShell, simply specify the server in the command as you typically would a server with a desktop. As of this writing, a specific version of RSAT for Windows Server 2016 has not been released. However, the RSAT tools for Windows 10 can remotely manage a Windows Server 2016 installation. Ensure that you make the appropriate firewall exceptions for remote management to operate as expected. The following built-in exceptions need to be enabled:

- COM+ Network Access (DCOM-In)
- Remote Event Log Management (NP-In)
- Remote Event Log Management (RPC)
- Remote Event Log Management (RPC-EPMAP)

Implement Windows PowerShell Desired State Configuration to install and maintain integrity of installed environments

Desired State Configuration (DSC) extends Windows PowerShell and enables you to deploy and configure a server based on a template or baseline. Using DSC you are able to automate the configuration of several settings, including:

- Server roles and features
- Registry settings
- Files and directories
- Processes and services
- Groups and user accounts
- Environment variables
- PowerShell scripts

In addition to performing the initial configuration, you can also use DSC to identify servers that no longer conform to the desired state. DSC has built-in resources to enable you to determine the actual configuration of a server, and implement changes if necessary. There are three primary components of DSC:

- **Local Configuration Manager (LCM)**   The LCM runs on every server (or target node) being managed. The LCM configures the target node based on the DSC. The LCM also performs other actions for the target node, including the refresh method, determining how frequently to perform refreshes, and making partial configurations.
- **Resources**   Used to implement the changing states of a configuration change. Resources are part of the PowerShell modules, and can be written to mimic a file, process, server, or even a VM.
- **Configuration**   Defined as the scripts that comprise and configure the resources. When running the configuration, DSC and the resources perform the configuration and ensure that the target node is configured as defined.

When building a DSC *Script*, there are a few components of the syntax to be aware of. The Script is composed of:

- **GetScript**   This block of code should return the current state of the node being tested. The value must be a String that is returned as the result.
- **TestScript**   This block of code determines if the node that is being tested needs to be modified based on the returned configuration. If any configuration is found to be out of date, then it is remedied by the SetScript block.
- **SetScript**   This block of code modifies the node to the desired configuration.
- **Credential**   The credentials that are needed for the script, if any are required.
- **DependsOn**   This indicates that another resource must be running before the script can be run and configured.

The following is an example of the syntax for DSC:

```
Script [string] #ResourceName
{
    GetScript = [string]

    SetScript = [string]

    TestScript = [string]

    [ Credential = [PSCredential] ]

    [ DependsOn = [string[]] ]
}
```

> **NEED MORE REVIEW?** **LEARNING MORE ABOUT DSC**
>
> For more information and a demonstration on DSC, visit *https://mva.microsoft.com/en-US/training-courses/getting-started-with-powershell-desired-state-configuration-dsc--8672*.

Perform upgrades and migrations of servers and core workloads from Windows Server 2008 and Windows Server 2012 to Windows Server 2016

Performing an OS upgrade to Windows Server 2016 is not too different from upgrading previous versions of Windows Server. A new feature for upgrading failover clusters is the Cluster OS Rolling Upgrade, which is discussed in detail in Chapter 5. Table 1-2 shows the supported upgrade paths to Windows Server 2016.

TABLE 1-2 Supported upgrade paths

Original operating system and edition	Upgrade edition
Windows Server 2008 R2 Standard or Windows Server 2008 R2 Enterprise	Windows Server 2016 Standard or Windows Server 2016 Datacenter
Windows Server 2008 R2 Datacenter	Windows Server 2016 Datacenter
Windows Web Server 2008 R2	Windows Server 2016 Standard
Windows Server 2008 R2 Datacenter with SP1	Windows Server 2016 Datacenter
Windows Server 2008 R2 Enterprise with SP1	Windows Server 2016 Standard or Windows Server 2016 Datacenter
Windows Server 2008 R2 Standard with SP1	Windows Server 2016 Standard or Windows Server 2016 Datacenter
Windows Web Server 2008 R2 with SP1	Windows Server 2016 Standard
Windows Server 2012 Datacenter or Windows Server 2012 R2 Datacenter	Windows Server 2016 Datacenter
Windows Server 2012 Standard or Windows Server 2012 R2 Standard	Windows Server 2016 Standard or Windows Server 2016 Datacenter

In addition to upgrades, you can also use the Server Migration Tools feature in Windows Server 2016 if you need to move away from a 32-bit operating system. The operating systems that you can migrate from are:

- Windows Server 2003
- Windows Server 2003 R2
- Windows Server 2008
- Windows Server 2008 R2
- Windows Server 2012
- Windows Server 2012 R2

Determine the appropriate activation model for server installation, such as Automatic Virtual Machine Activation, Key Management Service, and Active Directory-based Activation

As the name of the skill implies, there are three alternate methods of Windows activation besides simply activating each server individually. They are as follows:

- Automatic Virtual Machine Activation (AVMA)
- Key Management Service (KMS)
- Active Directory-based Activation

Automatic Virtual Machine Activation

AVMA was added with Windows Server 2012 R2, and enables you to activate a virtual machine (VM) by using the underlying virtualization host. This provides a method for activation, even if the VM is in an offline environment. AVMA binds the activation process to the virtualization host, providing real-time reporting and tracking of the license state for each virtual machine. The reporting and tracking data can be generated from the virtualization server.

EXAM TIP

To use AVMA, the virtualization host must be running the Datacenter edition of Windows Server 2016, and it must be activated. The virtual machines can be running multiple editions of either Windows Server 2012 R2 or Windows Server 2016.

By using AVMA, there are no additional product keys or licenses to keep track of. The VM is activated, and remains so regardless of VM migration across hosts or regions. Service providers who build multi-tenant environments do not have to share product keys with tenants, or even access the tenant's virtual machine to activate it. The activation process is transparent to the VM and does not require any input from within the VM.

To use AVMA, you must configure the virtualization host with an AVMA key using the slmgr tool and the /ipk switch. For example: slmgr /ipk <key>.

The AVMA activation for a VM is only valid for seven days. As the time period gets closer to expiration, the VM communicates with the virtualization host again to activate and reset the time period. To determine if a VM has been activated by AVMA, or to see the latest status, run the slgmgr.vbs /dlv command. Figure 1-4 shows the results of the command.

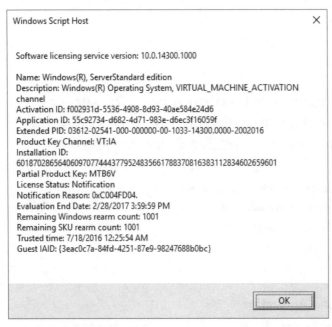

Windows Script Host ×

Software licensing service version: 10.0.14300.1000

Name: Windows(R), ServerStandard edition
Description: Windows(R) Operating System, VIRTUAL_MACHINE_ACTIVATION channel
Activation ID: f002931d-5536-4908-8d93-40ae584e24d6
Application ID: 55c92734-d682-4d71-983e-d6ec3f16059f
Extended PID: 03612-02541-000-000000-00-1033-14300.0000-2002016
Product Key Channel: VT:IA
Installation ID:
6018702865640609707744437795248356617883708163831128346026596 01
Partial Product Key: MTB6V
License Status: Notification
Notification Reason: 0xC004FD04.
Evaluation End Date: 2/28/2017 3:59:59 PM
Remaining Windows rearm count: 1001
Remaining SKU rearm count: 1001
Trusted time: 7/18/2016 12:25:54 AM
Guest IAID: {3eac0c7a-84fd-4251-87e9-98247688b0bc}

OK

FIGURE 1-4 AVMA results

Note that in Figure 1-4, the description field includes the string VIRTUAL_MACHINE_ACTIVATION. This indicates that the virtual machine is activated using AVMA.

If you plan to automate the install of a virtualization host, you can also specify the AVMA key in the Unattended Setup file. Once configured, the registry on the virtualization server provides the following tracking and reporting information for the guest operating system:

- Fully qualified domain name
- Operating system and service packs installed
- Processor architecture
- IPv4 and IPv6 network addresses
- RDP addresses

Key Management Service

To use Key Management Service (KMS) to activate servers on the network, you must first have a server that is running the Volume Activation Services server role. During the server role installation, you can specify whether you want to use KMS or Active Directory-based Activation. When you select KMS, you are prompted to enter the KMS host key, which activates the Microsoft products that contact the server for activation.

After installing and configuring the server role, you can verify that activation is being performed by using KMS clients, which can be servers or computers.

> **NOTE KMS THRESHOLDS**
>
> KMS requires a minimum threshold of 25 servers or computers before it can process the activation requests.

Similar to AVMA, you can use the slmgr.vbs script to provide a KMS key for the clients. For example: slmgr.vbs /ipk <KMSKey>.

After providing the key to the client, you can force an activation attempt by running the slmgr.vbs /ato command. KMS provides an easy method for virtual and physical machines on a network to activate through a central location. A KMS is especially useful if you plan to activate computers that are not on the same domain as the KMS host.

Active Directory-based activation

With AD-based activation, an activation object is created and stored in the schema of the domain. Then, when any non-activated server or computer that has a volume license key defined joins the domain, they access the activation object and areautomatically activated. As long as the device is a member of the domain, it remains activated.

There are three basic steps to using AD-based activation:

1. Install the Volume Activation Services server role.
2. Add a KMS host key to the server.
3. Use a KMS client key on target computers and ensure that they activate.

AD-based activation is extremely useful if all of the computers that you plan to activate are also members of the domain. There is no need for both AD-based activation and KMS hosts in this scenario.

Figure 1-5 shows the activation scenarios when using either Key Management Service or AD-based activation.

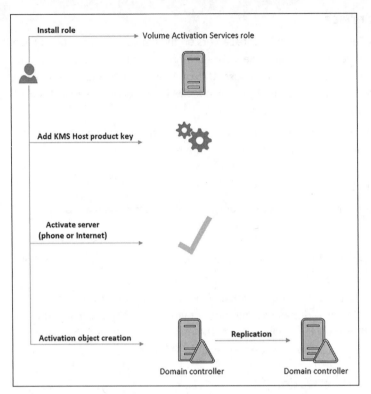

FIGURE 1-5 Activation scenarios

Skill 1.2: Install and configure Nano Server

Nano Server is a new edition of Windows Server that is designed to be lightweight while providing the same services as a full installation. In this section, we discuss the requirements and scenarios in which you can use Nano Server. We also discuss how to install Nano Server, as well as the supported roles and features for Nano Service. Then we explain how to manage and configure a Nano Server installation.

This section covers how to:

- Determine appropriate usage scenarios and requirements for Nano Server
- Install Nano Server
- Implement roles and features on Nano Server
- Manage and configure Nano Server

Determine appropriate usage scenarios and requirements for Nano Server

Nano Server is a new installation option for the Windows Server family. Usage of Nano Server can include multiple scenarios:

- Hyper-V hosts
- Storage hosts for Scale-Out File Servers
- DNS servers
- IIS servers
- Cloud application servers

Nano Server is supported as both a virtual machine and as a physical host. As of this writing, there are no specific hardware requirements for installing Nano Server. The smallest Nano Server configuration is approximately 450 MB with minimal packages and features selected. A VHD with IIS and OEM drivers is more than 500 MB.

Install Nano Server

To install Nano Server, you must first use the Nano Server Image Generator to create the Nano Server image that you use for installation. The image generator is located in the NanoServer folder of the Windows Server 2016 installation media. The steps in creating a Nano Server image are:

1. Copy the NanoServer folder from the installation media to your computer.
2. Using PowerShell, change directories to the copied folder and import the `NanoServerImageGenerator` module.
3. Run the New-NanoServerImage cmdlet to create the installation file.

Importing the PowerShell module is a relatively simple task, but can be troublesome if you use the PowerShell shortcuts. Ensure that you remove the trailing backslash when using tab shortcuts to complete the module name. Figure 1-6 displays successfully importing the image generator PowerShell module.

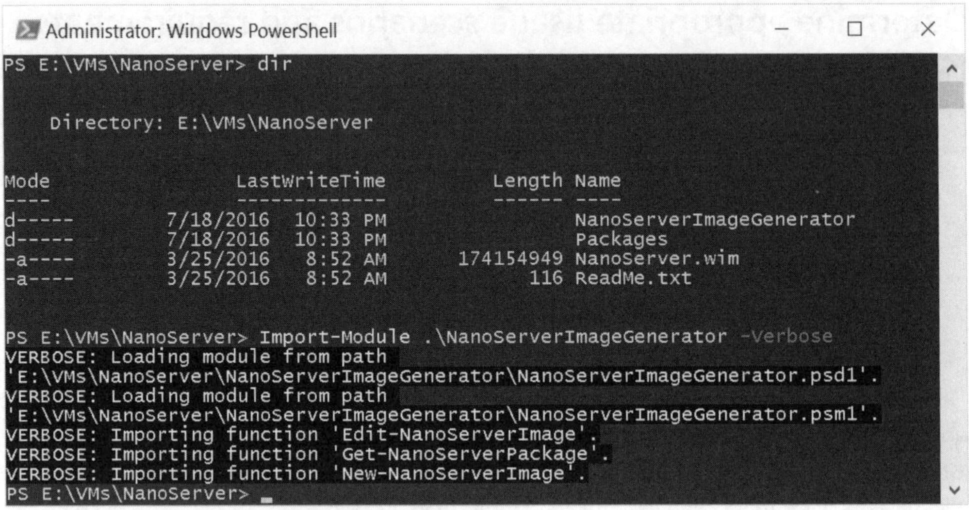

```
Administrator: Windows PowerShell                               —    □    ×

PS E:\VMs\NanoServer> dir


    Directory: E:\VMs\NanoServer


Mode                LastWriteTime         Length Name
----                -------------         ------ ----
d-----        7/18/2016   10:33 PM                NanoServerImageGenerator
d-----        7/18/2016   10:33 PM                Packages
-a----        3/25/2016    8:52 AM      174154949 NanoServer.wim
-a----        3/25/2016    8:52 AM            116 ReadMe.txt


PS E:\VMs\NanoServer> Import-Module .\NanoServerImageGenerator -Verbose
VERBOSE: Loading module from path
'E:\VMs\NanoServer\NanoServerImageGenerator\NanoServerImageGenerator.psd1'.
VERBOSE: Loading module from path
'E:\VMs\NanoServer\NanoServerImageGenerator\NanoServerImageGenerator.psm1'.
VERBOSE: Importing function 'Edit-NanoServerImage'.
VERBOSE: Importing function 'Get-NanoServerPackage'.
VERBOSE: Importing function 'New-NanoServerImage'.
PS E:\VMs\NanoServer> _
```

FIGURE 1-6 Importing the Nano Server Image Generator

The New-NanoServerImage cmdlet has several parameters that are configured when running. For example:

- **Edition** Specifies the edition type of the installation, and can be either Standard or Datacenter.

- **DeploymentType** Specifies whether Nano Server runs as a virtual machine guest, or as a physical host. The accepted values are *Guest* or *Host*.

- **MediaPath** Specifies the location of the installation media for Windows Server 2016. This can be a mounted ISO location, or a copied location.

- **BasePath** This is the directory to which the packages and Windows image are copied.

- **TargetPath** This is the path, filename, and extension where the Nano Server VHD, VHDX, or WIM file is created.

- **ComputerName** This is the hostname of the Nano Server after installation has completed.

For example, to create a Standard Nano Server virtual machine named NanoSvr1 that is located in the current folder, run the following command:

```
New-NanoServerImage -Edition Standard -DeploymentType Guest -MediaPath D:\ -BasePath .\
-TargetPath .\NanoSvr1\NanoSvr.vhdx -ComputerName NanoSvr1
```

You can optionally include the AdministratorPassword parameter during the command, but the password would be plaintext. Omitting the parameter causes PowerShell to prompt

you for the Administrator account password. Figure 1-7 shows running the command successfully, specifying the password separately.

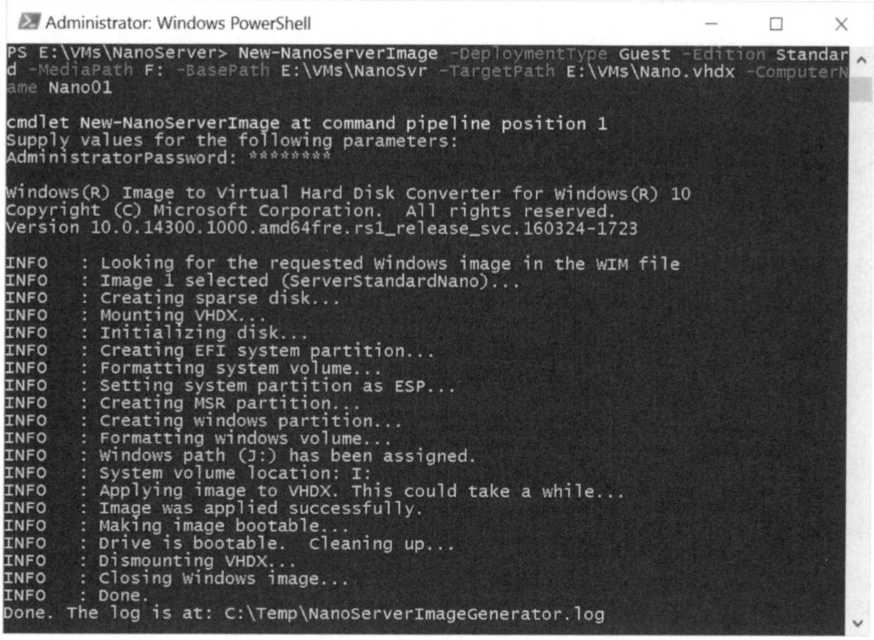

FIGURE 1-7 New-NanoServerImage

Once you have created the image type that you'd like to use, you can mount that image
through Hyper-V, or install it on a physical server. For physical servers, it is recommended that
you also include the OEMDrivers parameter. After the Nano Server image has been generated, this process is not any different than a normal VM or installation.

Implement roles and features on Nano Server

The roles and features for Nano Server can be specified during the image creation to include
these packages within the image. The packages that are built into the base server image can
be included with Nano Server. Simply specify the parameter during the image creation. Some
of the parameters that can be specified include:

- **Storage**   This includes the file server role and other storage components.
- **Compute**   This includes the Hyper-V server role.
- **Defender**   This includes Windows Defender, with a default signature file.
- **Clustering**   This includes the Failover Clustering server role.

After a Nano Server has been installed, you can manage the server roles and features by
using the PackageManagement provider. To install the provider, run the `Install-Package-
Provider NanoServerPackage` command. You can then import the provider by running the
`Import-PackageProvider NanoServerPackage` command.

After you have the package provider installed, you can use the following PowerShell cmdlets to find and add packages to Nano Server:

- Find-nanoServerPackage
- Save-NanoServerPackage
- Install-NanoServerPackage

The InstallNanoServerPackage cmdlet can be used to install packages regardless of whether the Nano Server installation is online or offline. Table 1-3 describes the roles and features that can be installed with Nano Server.

TABLE 1-3 Nano Server Roles and Features

Server role or feature	Option to install
HyperV role	Compute
Failover clustering	Clustering
Drivers for a variety of network adapters and storage controllers (this is the same set of drivers included in a Server Core installation of Windows Server 2016)	OEMDrivers
File Server role and other storage components	Storage
Windows Defender, including a default signature file	Defender
DNS Server role	Packages Microsoft-NanoServer-DNS-Package
Desired State Configuration	Packages Microsoft-NanoServer-DSC-Package
IIS	Packages Microsoft-NanoServer-IIS-Package
Host support for Windows Containers	Containers
System Center Virtual Machine Manager agent	Packages Microsoft-Windows-Server-SCVMM-Package Packages Microsoft-Windows-Server-SCVMM-Compute-Package
Network Performance Diagnostics Service (NPDS)	Packages Microsoft-NanoServer-NPDS-Package
Data Center Bridging	Packages Microsoft-NanoServer-DCB-Package
Boot and run from a RAM disk	Packages Microsoft-NanoServer-Guest-Package
Deploy on a virtual machine	Packages Microsoft-NanoServer-Host-Package
Secure Startup	Packages Microsoft-NanoServer-SecureStartup-Package
Shielded Virtual Machine	Packages Microsoft-NanoServer-ShieldedVM-Package

NEED MORE REVIEW? **NANO SERVER PARAMETERS**

For more information on Nano Server and all of the installation parameters, visit *https://aka.ms/nanoserver.*

Manage and configure Nano Server

After installing and signing into Nano Server, there are limited options for configuring the server directly form the console. The available information from the console includes:

- Computer name
- Workgroup or domain
- Operating system version
- Local data, time, and time zone
- Network configuration

Figure 1-8 displays the local console of a Nano Server installation.

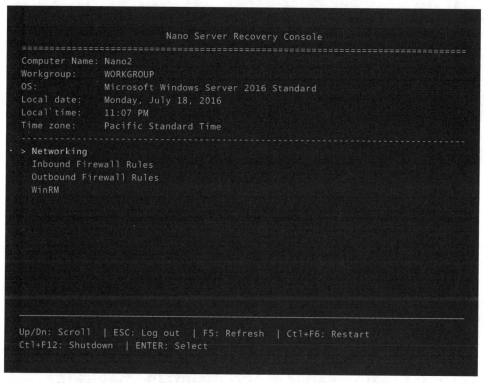

FIGURE 1-8 Nano Server Recovery Console

The basic networking information for the Nano Server machine can be configured through the Networking screen of the Recovery Console. You can configure the desired network adapter from the screen, and then configure the desired network settings. Both IPv4 and IPv6 can be configured from the recovery console. Figure 1-9 displays the networking configuration of a Nano Server through the Recovery Console.

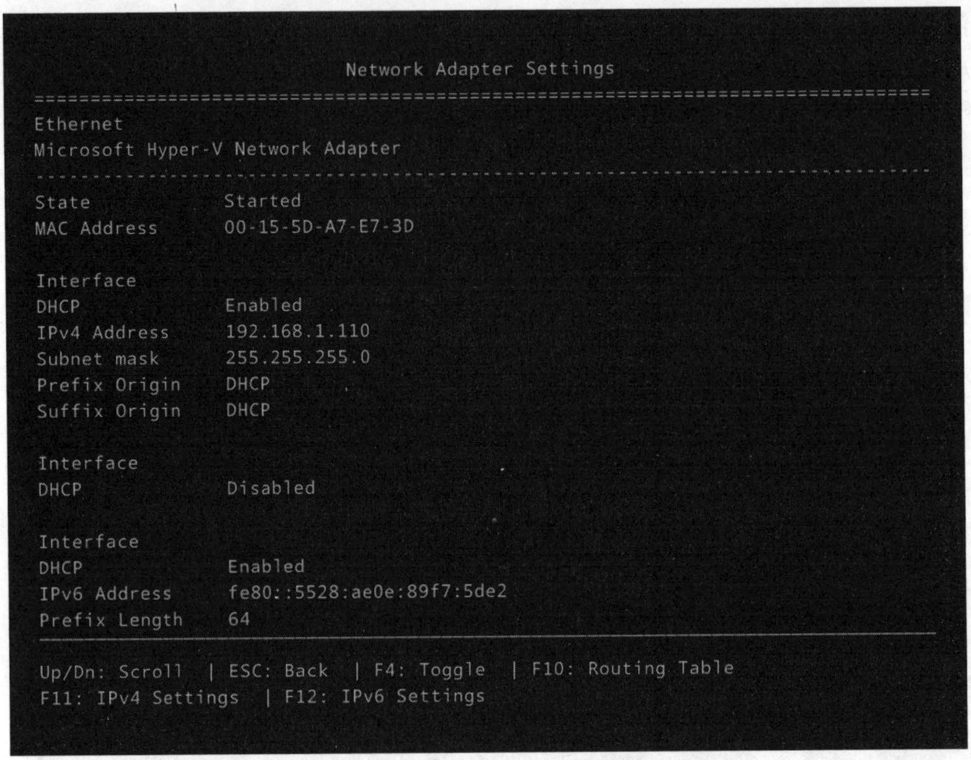

```
                    Network Adapter Settings
=================================================================
Ethernet
Microsoft Hyper-V Network Adapter
- - - - - - - - - - - - - - - - - - - - - - - - - - - - - - - - -

State           Started
MAC Address     00-15-5D-A7-E7-3D

Interface
DHCP            Enabled
IPv4 Address    192.168.1.110
Subnet mask     255.255.255.0
Prefix Origin   DHCP
Suffix Origin   DHCP

Interface
DHCP            Disabled

Interface
DHCP            Enabled
IPv6 Address    fe80::5528:ae0e:89f7:5de2
Prefix Length   64
_____

Up/Dn: Scroll  | ESC: Back  | F4: Toggle  | F10: Routing Table
F11: IPv4 Settings  | F12: IPv6 Settings
```

FIGURE 1-9 Nano Server Network Adapter Settings

The firewall settings must be configured to enable remote management. Remote Management Firewall Settings can be found in the Inbound Firewall Rules screen of the Recovery Console. For additional security, you can also configure outbound firewall rules.

The WinRM screen of the recovery console enables you to reset the firewall and remote management settings for the server back to default. This is useful if you can no longer access the server remotely, but are unaware of any network changes that might be preventing you from connecting.

Skill 1.3: Create, manage, and maintain images for deployment

You can use images to standardize deployments across physical or virtual machines. In this section, we discuss planning for Windows Server virtualization, as well as best practices for Linux and FreeBSD VM deployments. We also explain how to use the Microsoft Assessment and Planning Toolkit to assess an existing environment for upgrading or migrating to a Windows Server 2016 environment. Then we explore other considerations for virtualization, including using and updating deployment images. Finally, we explain how to maintain VHDs for Windows Server Core and Nano Server by using Windows PowerShell.

This section covers how to:

- Plan for Windows Server virtualization
- Plan for Linux and FreeBSD deployments
- Assess virtualization workloads using the Microsoft Assessment and Planning Toolkit and determine considerations for deploying workloads into virtualized environments
- Update images with patches, hotfixes, and drivers and Install roles and features in offline images
- Manage and maintain Windows Server Core, Nano Server images, and VHDs using Windows PowerShell

Plan for Windows Server virtualization

When planning virtualization for Windows Server, there are a few steps that you need to be aware of. Figure 1-10 illustrates nine high-level steps to plan for server virtualization.

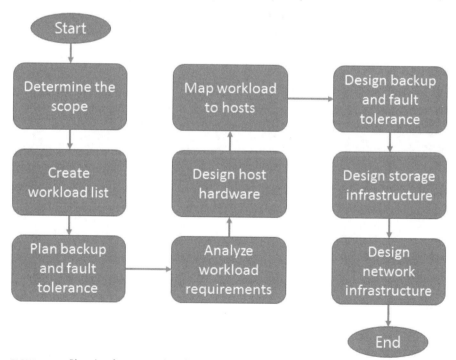

FIGURE 1-10 Planning for server virtualization

- **Determine the scope**   Determine what part of the infrastructure will be virtualized.

- **Create workload list**   Identify the resources that are needed based on the workload.

- **Plan backup and fault tolerance**   Select the approach that will be used to back up the virtualized environment after deployment.

- **Analyze workload requirements**   Identify the requirements for the virtualization solution.

- **Design host hardware**   Identify the hardware requirements for the underlying hardware.

- **Map workload to hosts**   Determine how workloads are placed on each of the virtualization hosts.

- **Design backup and fault tolerance**   Determine the most appropriate approach for performing the backup from the previous planning.

- **Design storage infrastructure**   Design the storage backend for the virtualized environment.

- **Design network infrastructure**   Design the network connectivity for the virtualized environment.

> **NEED MORE REVIEW?** **WINDOWS SERVER 2016 VIRTUALIZATION**
>
> For a deep dive on virtualization with Windows Server 2016, visit *https://mva.microsoft.com/en-us/training-courses/windows-server-2016-virtualization-deep-dive-14094.*

Plan for Linux and FreeBSD deployments

Linux and FreeBSD operating systems have been supported on Hyper-V platforms since Windows Server 2008 R2. The current supported operating system list includes:

- CentOS
- Red Had Enterprise Linux
- Debian
- Oracle Linux
- SUSE
- Ubuntu
- FreeBSD

When using FreeBSD on Hyper-V, there are a few best practices to be aware of to optimize functionality and performance, including:

- **Enable Common Address Redundancy Protocol (CARP)**   When using FreeBSD 10.2, CARP enables multiple hosts on a network to share the same IP address and

Virtual Host ID for high availability. If a host or VM fails, then another active VM can transparently take over the services that were being provided.

- **Add UUIDs** For all devices that are listed in fstab, ensure that the appropriate UUIDs are configured. When Hyper-V storage integration services are installed on a VM, some devices' UUIDs might change, and the entry in fstab will no longer be valid.

- **Disable Fast IDE drivers** The Fast IDE driver conflicts with the Hyper-V IDE driver, and can result in the virtual CD-ROM being unavailable. Disabling Fast IDE enables the use of the virtual CD-ROM.

- **Create GEOM labels** When using FreeBSD 8.x, device nodes are created as discovered during the startup. Device labels can change during this process, which might result in disk mount errors. By creating permanent labels for each IDE partition, you avoid mounting errors.

There are also best practices for using Linux on Hyper-V, including:

- **Tuning file systems** Some Linux file systems use additional disk space, even if the file system is mostly empty. You can reduce the amount of extra space consumption by using a 1 MB block size, and formatting the virtual disk as ext4.

- **Extend boot timeout** Using the Grub boot menu on a Generation 2 virtual machine might cause the countdown timer to end quickly. The default timeout value is set to 5, but is recommended to be set to 100000 for Generation 2 virtual machines.

- **PXE Boot** Generation 2 VMs do not have a PIT timer, and network connections to a PXE TFTP server can be terminated early, preventing the network bootloader from starting. A legacy grub bootloader can be specified to mitigate the timeout issue.

- **Static MAC addresses** Linux virtual machines that are being used in a failover cluster should have static MAC addresses defined. In some versions of Linux, the network configuration details can be lost after a failover. To ensure that all services perform as expected, define a static MAC address.

- **Network adapters** It is recommended that you use the Hyper-V specific network adapters, and not a legacy network adapter. Legacy network adapters might display random values for parameters in ifconfig.

- **I/O Scheduler** For optimized disk I/O performance, use the NOOP I/O scheduled for Linux VMs. This can be changed in the bootloader configuration parameters.

- **NUMA** For Linux VMs that have more than 7 virtual processors or 30 GB of RAM, it is recommended that you disable NUMA in the bootloader configuration.

Assess virtualization workloads using the Microsoft Assessment and Planning Toolkit, determine considerations for deploying workloads into virtualized environments

One tool that is available to assess and plan for a migration—whether it is physical or virtual—is the Microsoft Assessment and Planning (MAP) Toolkit. MAP is classified as a solution accelerator that takes an inventory of your organization's existing infrastructure. Based on the discovered information, MAP provides an assessment and report that you can use for upgrades, migrations, and virtualization workloads. MAP is available for several Microsoft products:

- Windows Server 2016
- Windows Server 2012 R2
- Windows 10
- Windows 8.1
- SQL Server 2014
- Hyper-V

Some of the general tasks that you can use MAP to perform include:

- **Inventory**   Discover devices on the network and generate a detailed report of the servers that can run Windows Server 2016.

- **Reporting**   Generate a report or proposal using the Windows Server 2016 Readiness Assessment. The proposal generates an Executive Overview, Assessment Rules, Next Steps, and a summary of overall readiness for Windows Server 2016.

- **Performance metrics**   Use MAP to capture the performance of the current infrastructure to ensure that the workloads are acceptable for Windows Server 2016.

- **Utilization**   Estimate server utilization before and after virtualization of workloads. You can also determine which physical hosts are specifically suited to become a VM.

Figure 1-11 shows the MAP Toolkit on the server virtualization overview screen.

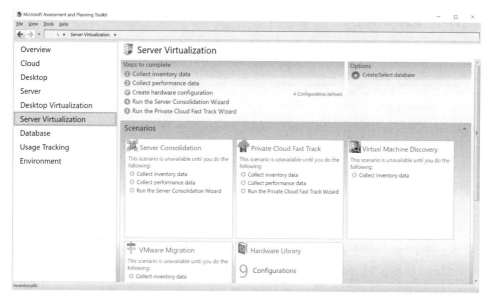

FIGURE 1-11 MAP Toolkit

NEED MORE REVIEW? FINDING MORE ON MAP

For more information on MAP, visit *https://technet.microsoft.com/en-us/solutionaccelera-tors/dd537566.*

Manage and maintain Windows Server Core, Nano Server images, and VHDs using Windows PowerShell, update images with patches, hotfixes, and drivers and install roles and features in offline images

For the purposes of this reference book, we combine the topics of managing, updating, and maintaining images and including roles and features for offline images. The process of using the Deployment Image Services and Management (DISM) platform to manage online and offline images has not significantly changed with Windows Server 2016.

DISM is available both as a command-line utility, and as a PowerShell module. The PowerShell module is built-in to Windows Server, while the command-line utility is a part of the Windows Assessment and Deployment Kit (Windows ADK).

NEED MORE REVIEW? WINDOWS POWERSHELL AND DISM

For more information on using DISM with Windows PowerShell, visit *https://technet. microsoft.com/en-us/library/dn376474.aspx.*

Chapter summary

One of the main features of Windows Server 2016 is the ability to deploy a server without a GUI, as Nano Server. Nano Server provides most of the core server roles and features that a full graphical installation offers, with a much smaller footprint and less attack surface. In this chapter, we discussed:

- Available editions for Windows Server 2016, that include Standard, Datacenter and Nano Server
- Installation options for Windows Server 2016, including the default Server Core or with the Desktop Experience
- Server Core installation and remote management options
- The three primary activation models, including AVMA, KMS, and AD-based activation
- How to generate and use a Nano Server image
- Adding server roles and features to a Nano Server image
- Using DISM to maintain online and offline images

Thought Experiment

You are a consultant for a small healthcare provider, which has two offices and about 75 employees. You plan to deploy two new servers to support the following roles:

- Active Directory Domain Services (AD DS)
- DNS
- DHCP
- Internet Information Services (IIS)

You need to minimize the amount of resources that the servers consume. Which version, edition, and activation method of Windows Server 2016 would you choose?

Thought Experiment Answer

Based on the scenario that is provided, we can deploy one server with a GUI that has the management tools installed, as well as the graphical server roles that are necessary. For the second server, you can use Nano Server to minimize the number of server resources that are needed. Any service or application that the customer has that cannot run on the Nano Server could be installed on the full installation.

There is no additional information in the scenario that would require using the Datacenter edition of Windows Server 2016. However, based on the number of employees, KMS or AD-based activation could be a valid activation type for the server, as well as any future deployment plans. The scenario does not say that the customer is running Hyper-V, so AVMA is not an option. The deciding factor would be if the customer needs to activate computers that are not members of the domain. If so, they should use KMS over AD-based activation.

CHAPTER 2

Implement storage solutions

Storage solutions are a primary aspect of using Windows Server in a production environment. In this chapter, we explain some basic storage options and how to implement these storage options in Windows Server 2016. Then we cover data deduplication, which is a feature of Windows Server that enables you to oversubscribe the capacity of a given storage device by not writing duplicated data.

Skills in this chapter:

- Implement server storage
- Implement data deduplication

Skill 2.1: Implement server storage

Windows Server 2016 offers editions and installation options similar to Windows Server 2008 and 2012. In this section, we explain the installation requirements for the base installation of Windows Server, as well as outline the differences between the editions. We cover the differences in installation process, server roles, and features compared to previous versions of Windows Server.

> **This section covers how to:**
> - Configure storage pools
> - Implement simple, mirror, and parity storage layout options for disks or enclosures
> - Expand storage pools
> - Configure Tiered Storage
> - Configure iSCSI target and initiator
> - Configure iSNS
> - Configure Datacenter Bridging
> - Configure Multi-Path IO
> - Determine usage scenarios for Storage Replica
> - Implement Storage Replica for server-to-server, cluster-to-cluster, and stretch cluster scenarios

Configure storage pools

Storage pools enable you to group physical disks together for more a efficient use of capacity and, in some cases, to increase performance. You can create a storage pool with either Server Manager, or Windows PowerShell. The steps through Server Manager are fairly simple:

1. From Server Manager, navigate to File and Storage Services, and then click Storage Pools.

2. Click Tasks, and then click New Storage Pool.

3. Click Next to bypass the Before You Begin page.

4. On the Storage Pool Name page, shown in Figure 2-1, enter a name for the pool. Ensure that the group of disks that are available to the server are selected.

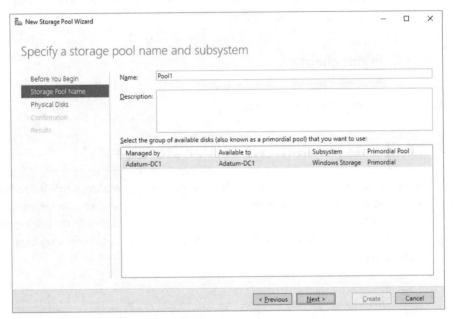

FIGURE 2-1 New Storage Pool Wizard, Storage Pool Name

5. On the Physical Disk page, select the individual disks that make up the pool. Figure 2-2 shows three disks available. Select what you need to allocate to the pool, and then click Next.

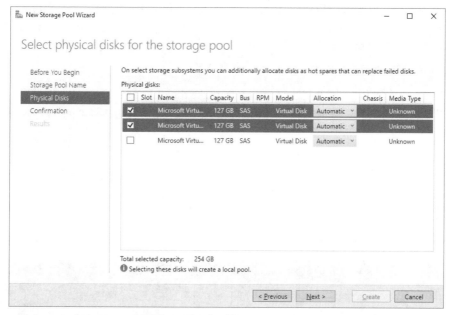

FIGURE 2-2 New Storage Pool Wizard, Physical Disks

6. After selecting the disks, you'll be prompted to review the information on the Confirmation page. Click Create to confirm the details of the storage pool. The summary is shown in Figure 2-3.

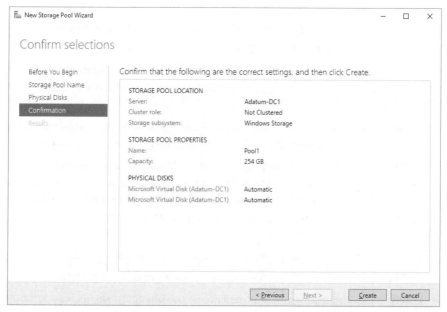

FIGURE 2-3 New Storage Pool Wizard, Confirmation

Using PowerShell to create the storage pool is slightly more complicated, only because you need to identify the physical disks that are available for the pool. First, to identify those disks, run the following command:

```
Get-PhysicalDisk -CanPool $True
```

This returns the available disks to pool. To make the disks easier to pass to the NewStoragePool cmdlet, set the disks to a variable. Then you can create a pool by using the following commands:

```
$Disks = Get-PhysicalDisk -CanPool $True

New-StoragePool -FriendlyName "Pool1" -StorageSubSystemFriendlyName "SubSystemName"
-PhysicalDisks $Disks
```

The results of the commands are shown in Figure 2-4.

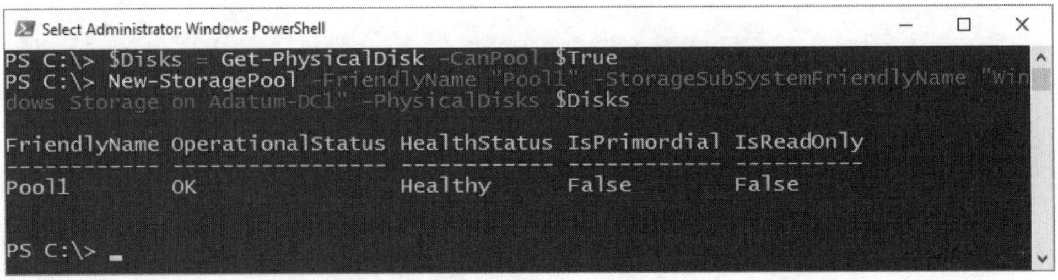

FIGURE 2-4 Creating a storage pool with PowerShell

Implement simple, mirror, and parity storage layout options for disks or enclosures

After a storage pool has been configured, you need to create a virtual disk that uses the pool. Virtual disks enable you to create resilient storage by using the disks in the storage pool. There are three types of resiliency layouts:

- **Simple** Data is striped across the physical disks, enabling you to maximize capacity and throughput. However, a single disk failure causes the pool to be unavailable.

- **Mirror** Data is striped across physical disks, creating two or three copies of the same data. This increases the reliability of the data, ensuring that you can withstand a single (or multiple) disk failures without losing access to the data or the pool. However, storage capacity is diminished because the additional physical drives are being used for redundancy instead of capacity.

  - To protect against a single disk failure, use at least two physical disks in the pool.

  - To protect against two disk failures, use at least five disks in the pool.

- **Parity** Data and a parity bit is striped access the physical disks, increasing both reliability and storage capacity. Storage capacity is not maximized because of the parity data that must also be written, but protects against disk failures.

- To protect against a single disk failure, use at least three disks.
- To protect against two disk failures, use at least seven disks.

Figure 2-5 shows selecting the storage layout from the New Virtual Disk Wizard.

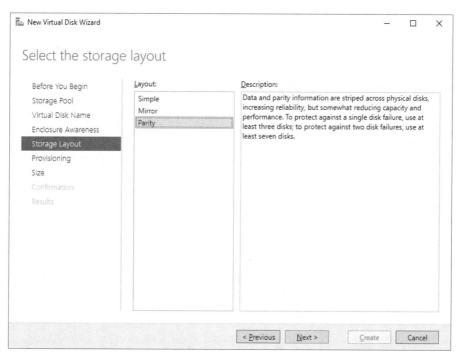

FIGURE 2-5 New Virtual Disk Wizard, Storage Layout

The virtual disk also enables you to select the provisioning type:

- **Thin** Volumes on the virtual disk only uses space as data is being written, up to the maximum size of the volume.
- **Fixed** The volume allocates space from the storage pool immediately, regardless of any actual data written. This ensures that you do not oversubscribe capacity from the pool.

Creating a virtual disk using PowerShell is also straightforward. The New-VirtualDisk cmdlet is used to create the virtual disk. For example, to create a thinly-provisioned disk named vDIsk2 using parity that is 50 GB, run the following command.

```
New-VirtualDisk -StoragePoolFriendlyName Pool1 -FriendlyName vDisk2
-ResiliencySettingName Parity -Size 50GB -ProvisioningType Thin
```

An alternate step to creating a virtual disk is to create a volume. In addition to the settings that you can configure for a virtual disk, a volume is what is actually presented to the server and used by the operating system, accessed by a drive letter. To create a volume in the GUI, use the New Volume Wizard from within Server Manager. You will be asked to specify the following information during the wizard:

- **Virtual disk**   This is the virtual disk that was previously created.
- **Volume size**   This can vary in size, up to the maximum size of the virtual disk. If you presented 50 GB to the virtual disk, you could create two 25 GB volumes.
- **Drive letter or folder**   You can assign a drive letter to the volume. Alternatively, you can mount the volume to a specific folder. For instance, the volume could be mounted in a specific user directory to give users dedicated storage space.
- **File System settings**   These are the typical settings when creating a volume from a physical disk. The file system type, either the resilient filesystem (ReFS) or NTFS. You can also configure the allocation unit size and the volume label at the same time.

To create a volume using similar settings to the virtual disk earlier, run the following command:

```
New-Volume -StoragePoolFriendlyName Pool1 -Size 25GB -AccessPath F: -FriendlyName
Volume1 -ResiliencySettingName Parity -FileSystem NTFS -ProvisioningType Thin
```

In addition to using physical disks, you can also use external storage enclosures with a storage pool. When creating a virtual disk, you can enable enclosure awareness, which increases redundancy depending on the number of enclosures and the resiliency level that you select. This allows you to lose an entire enclosure without losing access to the storage pool. Table 2-1 shows the supported resiliency levels with enclosure awareness.

TABLE 2-1 Enclosure awareness resiliency

Resiliency type	Three enclosures	Four enclosures
Simple	Not supported	Not supported
Two-way mirror	1 enclosure or 1 disk per pool	1 enclosure or 1 disk per pool
Three-way mirror	1 enclosure and 1 disk, or 2 disks	1 enclosure and 1 disk, or 2 disks
Single parity	Not supported	Not supported
Dual parity	Not supported	1 enclosure and 1 disk, or 2 disks

NEED MORE REVIEW?   **WINDOWS SERVER STORAGE POOLS**

For more information on storage pool with Windows Server, visit *https://technet.microsoft.com/en-us/library/hh831739(v=ws.11).aspx.*

Expand storage pools

Expanding a storage pool with additional physical disks is a simple task. From Server Manager, select the storage pool that you intend to expand, right-click and select Add Physical Disk. Figure 2-6 depicts selecting the physical disk that you want to add to the storage pool. Simply place a checkmark next to the disk, and then click OK.

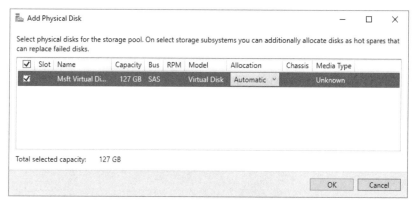

FIGURE 2-6 Add Physical Disk

Similar to creating a storage pool, adding a disk by using PowerShell requires you to first identify the disk to add. To identify and add the available disks to a storage pool, run the following commands:

```
$Disks = Get-PhysicalDisk -CanPool $True

Add-PhysicalDisk -StoragePoolFriendlyName Pool1 -PhysicalDisks $Disks
```

Configure tiered storage

Storage tiers can be enabled on a virtual disk if you have both hard-drive disks (HDD) and solid-state disks (SSD) in the storage pool. Storage tiering automatically moves the most frequently-accessed data to the faster storage type—the SSDs. Data that is not accessed frequently is stored on the spinning HDDs.

Configuring storage tiering is a checkbox during the virtual disk creation. If you do not have a mixture of drive types, then the checkbox is not available during the wizard. If you are using PowerShell, you can specify the StorageTiers and StorageTierSizes parameters as part of the New-VirtualDisk cmdlet.

EXAM TIP

Storage tiers are not supported with thin provisioning. When using storage tiers, you must specify fixed disk sizes.

Configure iSCSI target and initiator

Configuring an iSCSI target or initiator hasn't changed much since Windows Server 2012 R2. And configuring an iSCSI target server enables you to network boot computers from a single boot image that has been provided to the network from a central location. You can use iSCSI targets with Windows Server 2016 to boot hundreds of computers from a single operating system image.

Installing the iSCSI Target Server server role can be performed from both Server Manager and PowerShell. iSCSI Target Server is a part of the File and Storage Services storage role. Installing the server role also installs the management features that are used to configure the server role. After installing the role, you can configure iSCSI virtual disks.

1. To create a new iSCSI virtual disk, launch the wizard from Server Manager. The first screen of the wizard configures where to store the virtual disk. Ensure that the server is selected, select the volume or path of the storage, then click Next. Figure 2-7 shows the C: volume selected for Adatum-DC1.

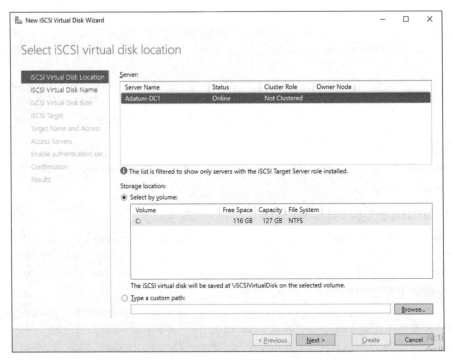

FIGURE 2-7 iSCSI virtual disk location

2. On the iSCSI Virtual Disk Size page, enter a size for the virtual disk. You can also configure whether the disk is fixed, dynamically expanding, or differencing. As shown in

Figure 2-8, the default disk type is set to Dynamically Expanding. Click Next to continue the wizard.

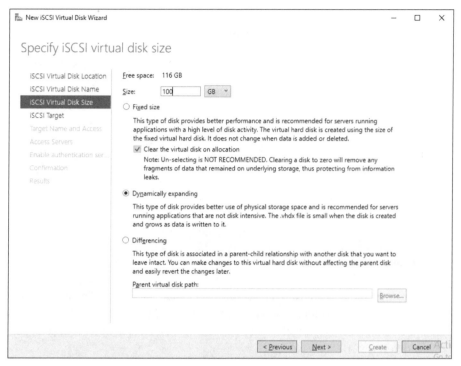

FIGURE 2-8 iSCSI virtual disk size

3. On the iSCSI Target page, select either an existing target or a new target, and then click Next.

4. On the Target Name And Access page, enter a name for the target and then click Next.

5. On the Access Servers page, click Add to specify the iSCSI initiators that access the new virtual disk. Figure 2-9 shows adding the iSCSI initiator.

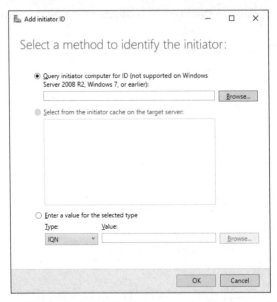

FIGURE 2-9 iSCSI virtual disk size

6. On the Enable Authentication page, select whether you want to Enable CHAP or Enable Reverse CHAP for authentication. These are optional protocols to authenticate the initiator connections or target. Figure 2-10 shows the available options to configure CHAP and Reverse CHAP.

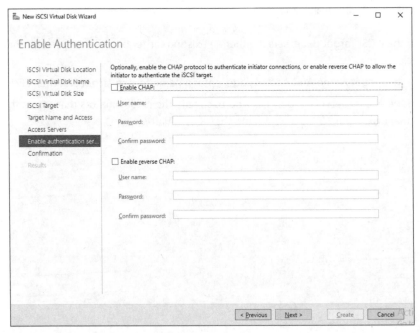

FIGURE 2-10 iSCSI authentication method

7. Click Create to create the virtual disk using the settings that you specified during the wizard.

As with other virtual disks, you can also create an iSCSI virtual disk by using PowerShell with the New-IscsiVirtualDisk cmdlet. For example, to create a 10GB disk, run the following command:

```
New-IscsiVirtualDisk -Path "C:\temp\test.vhdx" -Size 10GB
```

Configure iSNS

The Internet Storage Name Service (iSNS) is a protocol, which can be added to a Windows Server installation, and used to communicate between iSNS servers and clients. iSNS clients are computers, or initiators, that search for storage devices, or targets, on a network. iSNS provides automated discovery, management, and configuration of iSCSI and Fibre Channel devices on a network. Figure 2-11 shows the iSNS Server properties page.

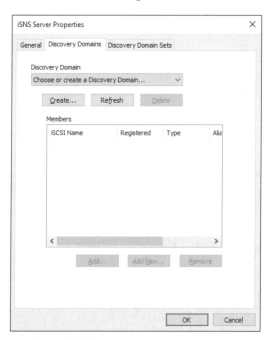

FIGURE 2-11 iSNS Server Properties

By default, when you create an iSNS Server, there are no iSCSI targets listed even if they have been configured already. To ensure that the configured iSCSI targets also appear in the iSNS Server, the iSNS Server must be added to the iSCSI Initiator properties, as shown in Figure 2-12.

FIGURE 2-12 iSCSI Initiator Properties

In the iSNS properties, you can then see the connected devices, and whether they are an initiator or target. iSNS does not have any specific PowerShell cmdlets, but can be configured from the command-line by using the `isnscli.exe` utility.

Configure Datacenter Bridging

Datacenter Bridging (DCB) enhances the Ethernet connectivity between servers on a network. DCB requires DCB-capable network adapters on servers that are providing DCB, as well as DCB-capable network switches that the servers connect to. DCB can be installed by using the `InstallWindowsFeature` cmdlet:

```
Install-WindowsFeature "data-center-bridging"
```

After installing the DCB feature, you can manage DCB on a server by importing three different PowerShell modules:

```
Import-Module netqos
Import-Module dcbqos
Import-Module netadapter
```

Configure Multi-Path IO (MPIO)

MPIO is another feature of Windows Server that can be installed from Server Manager or by using the `Install-WindowsFeature` cmdlet. There are four components that can be managed after installing MPIO:

- **MPIO Devices**   These are the devices that are presented to the server and managed by MPIO. In some cases, a device can be presented, but not specifically added to MPIO. You can manually add additional devices to ensure that they are managed by the service.

- **Discover Multi-Paths**   This enables you to run an algorithm that checks all of the attached devices to the server and ensure that they represent the same Logical Unit Number (LUN) through multiple paths.

- **DSM Install**   This enables you to install DSMs that might be provided by the storage vendor that is being used. Many storage systems are compliant with the Microsoft DSM, but provide their own DSM to work with their architecture.

- **Configuration Snapshot**   This enables you to save the MPIO configuration to a text file. The text file includes DSM information, the number of paths, and the current path state.

In addition to being managed through the MPIO GUI, you can also use `mpclaim` to perform many of the configuration activities.

MPIO is also supported on Nano Server, but with some differences:

- Only the Microsoft DSM is supported
- The load-balancing policy cannot be modified
    - Default: Active/Active Round Robin
    - SAS HDD: LeastBlocks
    - ALUA: RoundRobin with Subset
- Path states are picked up from the target storage system
- Storage devices are claimed by bus type. For example, Fibre channel, iSCSI, or SAS

To enable MPIO for Nano Server, run the following command:

```
Enable-WindowsOptionalFeature -Online -FeatureName MultiPathIO
```

When MPIO is installed on a Nano Server, the disks that are presented are listed as duplicates, with a single disk being available through each path. MPIO must be configured to claim and manage the disks to ensure that only one path is used. A script has been provided by Microsoft to claim and manage the disks, and can be found at: *https://technet.microsoft.com/en-us/windows-server-docs/compute/nano-server/mpio-on-nano-server.*

Determine usage scenarios for Storage Replica

Storage Replica is a new function available with Windows Server 2016 that provides disaster-recovery capabilities. Storage Replica enables you to efficiently use many datacenters by stretching or replicating clusters. If one datacenter goes offline, the workload can be moved to another. Some scenarios where Store Replica can be used include:

- **Stretch Cluster** Enables the configuration of computers and storage as part of a single cluster. In this scenario, some nodes share one set of asymmetric storage, and other nodes share another set, then replicate the data with site awareness. The storage for this scenario can be JBOD, SAN, or iSCSI-attached disks. A stretch cluster can be managed by using Windows PowerShell and the Failover Cluster Manager tool, and can be configured for automated failover. Figure 2-13 illustrates using Storage Replica in a Stretch Cluster.

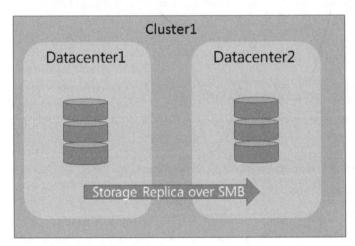

FIGURE 2-13 Stretch Cluster

- **Cluster-to-Cluster** Enables replication between two completely separate clusters, where one cluster copies the data to another cluster. This scenario can also use Storage Spaces on JBOD, SAN, or iSCSI-attached disks as the backend storage. A cluster-to-cluster storage replica can be managed by using PowerShell, but failover must occur manually. Figure 2-14 illustrates using a cluster-to-cluster storage replica.

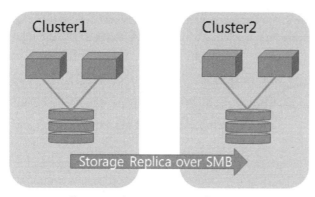

FIGURE 2-14 Cluster-to-cluster storage replica

- **Server-to-server** This enables replication between standalone servers with Storage Spaces on JBOD, SAN, or iSCSI-attached disks. Individual servers can also be managed by PowerShell, and failover must be managed manually. Figure 2-15 illustrates a server-to-server storage replica.

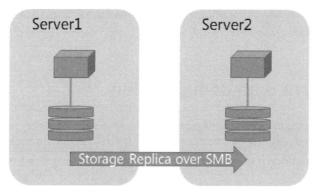

FIGURE 2-15 Server-to-server storage replica

NEED MORE REVIEW? **ACCESS THE STORAGE REPLICA**

For an in-depth look at Storage Replica, visit *https://technet.microsoft.com/en-us/windows-server-docs/storage/storage-replica/storage-replica-overview.*

Implement Storage Replica for server-to-server, cluster-to-cluster, and stretch cluster scenarios

Storage Replica is only available in the Datacenter edition of Windows Server 2016. To install the feature, use the Add Roles and Features Wizard in Server Manager, or run the following command:

```
Install-WindogetwsFeature -Name Storage-Replica -IncludeManagementTools
```

There are 20 different PowerShell options in the Storage Replica module, including:

- **TestSRTopology**   This verifies that the topology meets the requirements for a Storage Replica.
- **NewSRPartnership**   This configures the Storage Replica using the information that you provide. A source and destination name, volume, and replication group must be specified.
- **NewSRGroup**   This can optionally be used on one server in each location in combination with NewSRPartnership to configure the replication in stages.

> **NEED MORE REVIEW?   STORAGE REPLICA**
>
> For walkthroughs on configuring storage replica in a stretch cluster, between clusters, or between servers, visit *https://technet.microsoft.com/en-us/windows-server-docs/storage/storage-replica/storage-replica-windows-server-2016*.

Skill 2.2: Implement data deduplication

Data deduplication enables you to oversubscribe the capacity of a given storage device by not writing the same data twice. For example, if you store multiple documents that contain a majority of the same information, only the difference in data is written to the disk.

> **This section covers how to:**
> - Implement and configure deduplication
> - Determine appropriate usage scenarios for deduplication
> - Monitor deduplication
> - Implement a backup and restore solution with deduplication

Implement and configure deduplication

Data deduplication is another server role that can be installed through the Add Roles and Features Wizard, or by using the `Install-WindowsFeature` cmdlet. The Data Deduplication server role also requires the File Server server role to be installed. Once installed, deduplication can be enabled on specific volumes by running the `Enable-DedupVolume` cmdlet. For example, to enable deduplication on the E drive, and begin an optimization job on that volume, run these commands:

```
Import-Module Deduplication

Enable-DedupVolume E: -UsageType Default -DataAccess

Start-DedupJob E: -Optimization
```

The DataAccess parameter indicates that data access will be enabled as part of the deduplicated volume. There are three possible options for the UsageType parameter when enabling deduplication:

- **Default**   This indicates a general purpose volume as the expected workload for the underlying disk.
- **Hyper-V**   This indicates that the volume stores VHDs for a Hyper-V server.
- **Backup**   This indicates that the volume is optimized for virtualized backup servers.

There are four types of deduplication jobs that run periodically, or can be run manually:

- **Optimization**   This manually starts the process of optimizing the volume for deduplication, and ensures that duplicated data does not consume additional storage.
- **GarbageCollection**   Garbage collection ensures that deleted or modified data is removed from the reference table.
- **Scrubbing**   This starts the data integrity scrubbing on the deduplicated volume.
- **Unoptimization**   This removes the deduplication on a specific volume.

Determine appropriate usage scenarios for deduplication

Typical scenarios for deduplication are file shares that have user documents, software deployment images, or VHD files. These scenarios often generate a large savings of storage space by using deduplication. Table 2-2 shows some common deduplication scenarios.

TABLE 2-2 Deduplication scenarios

Scenario	Content	Typical savings
User documents	Documents and photos	30-50 percent
Deployment shares	Software binaries and images	70-80 percent
Virtualization libraries	VHDs	80-95 percent
General file share	All of the above	50-60 percent

After you have installed the data deduplication feature, you can also use the Deduplication Savings Evaluation Tool. The following output is an example of the ddpeval.exe tool:

```
Data Deduplication Savings Evaluation Tool

Copyright 2011-2012 Microsoft Corporation.  All Rights Reserved.

Evaluated folder: E:

Processed files: 128

Processed files size: 120.03MB

Optimized files size: 40.02MB

Space savings: 80.01MB

Space savings percent: 66

Optimized files size (no compression): 11.47MB

Space savings (no compression): 571.53KB

Space savings percent (no compression): 40

Files with duplication: 20

Files excluded by policy: 20

Files excluded by error: 0
```

Based on the percentage returned by the tool, you can decide whether to implement data deduplication in the environment. With Windows Server 2016, data deduplication introduces the following changes:

- **Increased volume sizes** NTFS volumes up to 64 TB can have deduplication enabled. This has been enhanced by increasing the number of threads working in parallel for individual volumes.

- **Increased file sizes** Individual files up to 1 TB can efficiently be deduplicated on a storage volume.
- **Nano Server support** Deduplication is fully supported on volumes that are presented to a Nano Server installation.

Monitor deduplication

The built-in deduplication jobs support weekly scheduling for optimization, garbage collection, and scrubbing. Additionally, jobs can be configured by using the Windows Task Scheduler. Remember that the garbage collector reclaims space by removing data that is no longer being used. The default weekly schedule can be viewed by running the Get-DedupSchedule cmdlet.

```
Get-DedupSchedule
```

The following output is returned:

```
Enabled     Type                StartTime      Days         Name

-------     ----                ---------      ----         ----


True        Optimization
BackgroundOptimization

True        GarbageCollection   2:45 AM        Saturday
WeeklyGarbageCollection

True        Scrubbing           3:45 AM        Saturday     WeeklyScrubbing
```

The Get-DedupStatus cmdlet can be used to see the overall status of a server.

```
Get-DedupStatus
```

The following output is returned:

```
FreeSpace        SavedSpace   OptimizedFiles    InPolicyFiles    Volume

--------------   ----------   --------------    -------------    ------


140.26 GB        265.94 GB    36124             36125            E:

76.26 GB         42.19 GB     43017             43017            F:
```

To force a refresh of the deduplication service and require it to rescan the available volumes, use the Update-DedupStatus cmdlet.

Implement a backup and restore solution with deduplication

Backup applications that work at the block level should work as expected, as the file system presents the full data to the application. Therefore, the destination media for the backup must be expecting the full data set, as if it was not deduplicated. For example, if a 1 TB volume has 700 GB of raw data that has been deduplicated down to 400 GB, the backup media must be capable of storing 700 GB of data.

Windows Server Backup can back up an optimized volume and retain the deduplicated data without the need for the additional capacity.

> ***NEED MORE REVIEW?*** **BACKUPS WITH DEDUPLICATION**
>
> For more information on performing backups with deduplication, visit *https://technet. microsoft.com/en-us/library/hh831600(v=ws.11).aspx.*

Chapter summary

- Managing storage pools for attached storage
- Using simple, mirror, and parity virtual disks for storage pools
- How to expand storage pools with additional disks
- Configuring tiered storage with HDDs and SSDs
- Configuring iSCSI targets and initiators
- Using iSNS with iSCSI initiators
- Configuring DCB for enhanced SMB functionality
- Using MPIO to optimize multiple paths to attached storage
- Stretched cluster, cluster to cluster, and server to server storage replicas
- Using PowerShell to manage storage replicas
- Installing and configuring data deduplication
- Identifying the best scenarios for using data deduplication
- Monitoring deduplication with PowerShell

Thought Experiment

A company has two datacenters in two different geographic regions. Servers have direct-attached disks that are configured as JBOD. Each direct-attached storage system has a mixture of HDDs and SSDs. The JBOD storage must maximize the storage capacity presented to the server. Servers in each datacenter are members of a failover cluster. The failover cluster is limited to a single datacenter. A group of servers used for marketing contain a file share with marketing documents and photos. Another group of servers use local storage for Hyper-V VHDs.

Using this information, answer the following questions:

1. What type of storage pool should the JBOD storage systems use?
2. Would tiered storage increase the performance of the JBOD array?
3. Which storage replica scenario works best for this company?
4. Would the Marketing servers benefit from using data deduplication?
5. Would the Hyper-V servers benefit from using data deduplication?

Thought Experiment Answers

1. The JBOD storage system should use a parity pool to maximize the amount of storage that is presented to the server.
2. Yes, tiered storage would ensure that data that is frequently accessed is stored on the SSDs, while data that is not accessed frequently is stored on the HDDs.
3. Because the failover clusters are limited to a single datacenter, a cluster to cluster storage replica scenario is the best fit for this environment. A stretch cluster is not feasible because they are not members of the same cluster. This also eliminates individual server to server storage replicas.
4. Yes, documents and photos are a viable storage type for data deduplication.
5. Yes, Hyper-V machines with VHDs are a viable storage type for data deduplication.

CHAPTER 3

Implement Hyper-V

In this chapter, we explore almost all of the settings that can be configured within the Hyper-V role. First we explain how to install or add the role to a server. Then we cover individual virtual machine (VM) settings, including the generation and versions. We also go through configuring the different storage options for Hyper-V, for both individual and shared virtual disks. Finally, we configure the networking capabilities of Hyper-V.

Skills in this chapter:

- Install and configure Hyper-V
- Configure virtual machine settings
- Configure Hyper-V storage
- Configure Hyper-V networking

Skill 3.1: Install and configure Hyper-V

In this section, we cover the requirements and processes for adding the Hyper-V role. We also detail how to install the management tools, and use those tools to manage local and remote Hyper-V hosts. We also highlight is the configuration versions of VMs, and how those versions unlock specific features within Hyper-V. and, finally, we explain two new features in Hyper-V, Windows PowerShell Direct, and nested virtualization.

> **This section covers how to:**
> - Determine hardware and compatibility requirements for installing Hyper-V
> - Install Hyper-V
> - Install management tools
> - Upgrade from existing versions of Hyper-V
> - Delegate virtual machine management
> - Perform remote management of Hyper-V hosts
> - Configure virtual machines using Windows PowerShell Direct
> - Implement nested virtualization

Determine hardware and compatibility requirements for installing Hyper-V

In addition to the system requirements that we discussed in Chapter 1 for Windows Server 2016, the Hyper-V role also has additional hardware requirements. Hyper-V requires a 64-bit processor that uses second-level address translation (SLAT). The virtualization components of Hyper-V will not be installed if the processor does not support SLAT. Note that this is strictly for the virtualization components. The Hyper-V Manager, PowerShell cmdlets, and management tools can be used without SLAT.

You should also ensure that the Hyper-V host has enough memory to support both the Hyper-V OS itself, as well as the virtual machines. As a minimal configuration with the host OS and one VM, you should plan for at least 4 GB of RAM.

Windows Server 2016 also introduces Shielded virtual machines. These VMs rely on virtualization-based security. The Hyper-V host must support UEFI 2.3.1c or later. This is for secure, measured boot. To support optional features, the Hyper-V host should also have a TPM v2.0, and IOMMU so that the host can provide direct memory access protection.

Install Hyper-V

The process for installing Hyper-V has not changed much since Windows Server 2008 and Windows Server 2012. Hyper-V is a server role that can be installed by using the Add Roles and Features Wizard from Server Manager, or by using Windows PowerShell:

```
Install-WindowsFeature -Name Hyper-V -ComputerName Server1 -IncludeManagementTools
-Restart
```

Install management tools

If you only need to install the management tools, this can also be performed by using the Add Roles and Features Wizard from Server Manager, or by using Windows PowerShell. However, there are a few different options when installing only the management tools.

When using Server Manager, the option for installing the management tools is actually part of the Remote Server Administration Tools (RSAT), not Hyper-V. Expanding RSAT shows management tools that can be installed, including tools for Hyper-V.

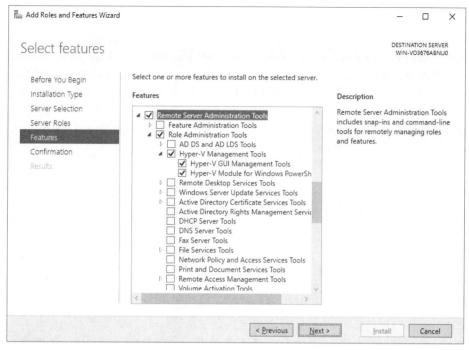

FIGURE 3-1 Add Roles and Features Wizard

Figure 3-1 shows the two components of installing Hyper-V, which are:

- **Hyper-V GUI Management Tools**   This is the Hyper-V Manager and Virtual Machine Connect to manage and view virtual machines.
- **Hyper-V Module for Windows PowerShell**   These are the PowerShell cmdlets that can be used to manage Hyper-V.

When using PowerShell to install the management features, there are a few different options:

- **Microsoft-Hyper-V-All**   This installs Hyper-V itself as well as all of the management tools.
- **Microsoft-Hyper-V-Tools-All**   This installs all of the management tools, including the manager, Virtual Machine Connect, and PowerShell module.
- **Microsoft-Hyper-V-Management-Clients**   This installs only the GUI manager and Virtual Machine Connect.
- **Microsoft-Hyper-V-Management-PowerShell**   This installs only the PowerShell module for Hyper-V.

To use PowerShell to install the management tools, use the following command:

```
Enable-WindowsOptionalFeature -Feature 'Microsoft-Hyper-V-Tools-All' -Online
```

Upgrade from existing versions of Hyper-V

This could mean upgrading the operating system, or upgrading the virtual machine version in Hyper-V. Upgrading the operating system is a separate task that doesn't specifically involve Hyper-V. The only consideration from a Hyper-V perspective is the VMs. You have the option of shutting them down temporarily while the upgrade is performed, or migrating them to a different host.

Certain operating systems only support specific versions of virtual machines. Table 3-1 lists the supported VM versions for each operating system.

TABLE 3-1 Supported VM versions

Hyper-V host operating system	Supported VM version number
Windows 8.1	5.0
Windows Server 2012 R2	5.0
Windows 10 builds earlier than 10565	5.0, 6.2
Windows 10 build 10565 and later	5.0, 6.2, 7.0, 7.1, 8.0
Windows Server 2016	5.0, 6.2, 7.0, 7.1, 8.0

Each configuration represents the VM configuration file, saved state, and snapshots that are associated with the VM on the host. By using a newer virtual machine configuration, you also ensure that the virtual machine supports the latest features. Table 3-2 shows features that are only supported in specific VM configuration versions.

TABLE 3-2 Version-specific features

Feature	Minimum VM version
Hot Add/Remove memory	6.2
Secure Boot for Linux VMs	6.2
Production Checkpoints	6.2
PowerShell Direct	6.2
Virtual Machine Grouping	6.2
Virtual Trusted Platform Module (vTPM)	7.0
Virtual machine multi-queues (VMMQ)	7.1
Nested virtualization	8.0

Delegate virtual machine management

The most simple and effective method of enabling others to manage Hyper-V and virtual machines is to add them to the Hyper-V Administrators local security group for each of the Hyper-V hosts to which you plan to delegate management. However, this might not be the most secure method because doing so gives the new administrators permissions to change virtual switch and host settings in addition to VMs.

To delegate access to individual VMs, you need to modify the Hyper-V Authorization Manager store. This enables you to create task and role definitions to which you can delegate access. The general steps to modifying the Hyper-V services authorization include:

1. Launch a Microsoft Management Console (MMC) session, and add the Authorization Manager to the console, as shown in Figure 3-2.

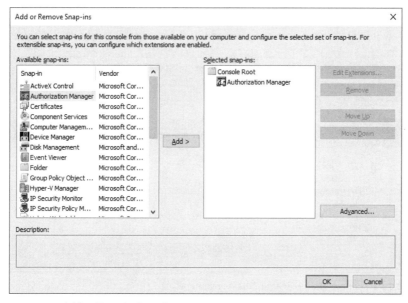

FIGURE 3-2 Add or Remove Snap-ins

2. Right-click the Authorization Manager, and then click Open Authorization Store.

3. In the Open Authorization Store window, ensure that XML File is selected. Click Browse. Navigate to %systemroot%\ProgramData\Microsoft\Windows\Hyper-V\ and select InitialStore.xml, as shown in Figure 3-3. Click OK.

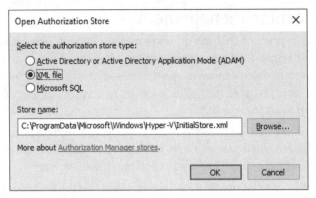

FIGURE 3-3 Open Authorization Store

4. Expand Authorization Manager, Initial Store, Hyper-V services, Role Assignments. Note that by default, the only role assignment is an Administrator, as shown in Figure 3-4.

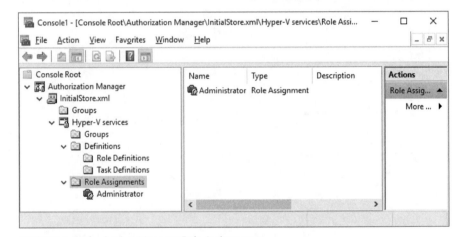

FIGURE 3-4 Authorization Manager Role Assignments

5. Expand Definitions, and then right-click Task Definitions. Click New Task Definition.

6. Name the task definition "VM Managers." In the notification prompt, click OK. In the Add Definition screen, click the Operations tab.

7. Select operations that you would want the VM Managers role to do. In this example, select all operations that are associated with a virtual machine, as shown in Figure 3-5, and then click OK twice.

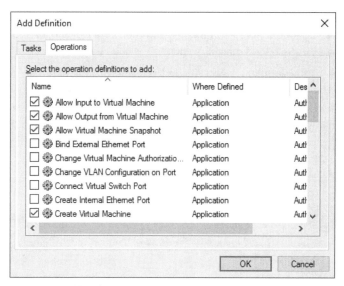

FIGURE 3-5 Add Definition

8. Now that you have created a group of tasks, you can create the role that can use these tasks. Right-click Role Definitions, and then click New Role Definition.

9. Name the Role Definition, such as VM Managers Role, and then click Add. Click the Tasks tab, select VM Managers, and then click OK. There are now be two role definitions, as shown in Figure 3-6.

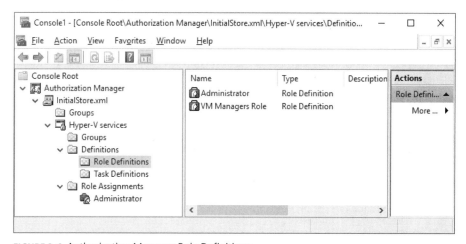

FIGURE 3-6 Authorization Manager Role Definitions

10. Next, you can create the Role Assignment, which is what user accounts are linked to for the permissions. Right-click Role Assignments, and then click New Role Assignment. Select the VM Managers Role, and then click OK.

11. Right-click the new role assignment, select Assign Users and Groups, and then click From Windows and Active Directory. Select a user that you plan to delegate the permissions to, and then click OK. Figure 3-7 shows the final configuration, with the user Admin on a host named Host01 that can manage the tasks assigned as part of the VM Managers Role.

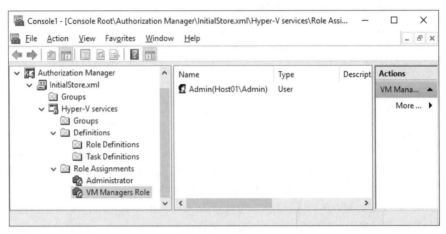

FIGURE 3-7 Authorization Manager Role Assignments

Perform remote management of Hyper-V hosts

Performing remote management within the same domain simply requires the permissions or delegation discussed in the previous section. However, managing a Hyper-V server that is in a workgroup is slightly more complicated.

First, the Hyper-V server must have PowerShell remoting enabled. This is easily accomplished by running the Enable-PSRemoting cmdlet. Note that the network provided on the server must be set to Private. Otherwise, you also need to specify the -SkipNetworkProfileCheck parameter.

The second task on the Hyper-V host is to enable the WSMan credential role as a server. To do this, run the following command:

```
Enable-WSManCredSSP -Role Server
```

The more complicated steps occur on the computer from which you plan to manage the Hyper-V. First, you must trust the Hyper-V server from the remote client. If the Hyper-V host is named Host01, run the following command:

```
Set-Item "WSMan:\localhost\Client\TrustedHosts" -Value "Host01"
```

Then on the remote client, you must also enable the WSMan credential role as a client, and specify the server to manage remotely. For example:

```
Enable-WSManCredSSP -Role Client -DelegateComputer "Host01"
```

Finally, you should also configure the local policy (or a Group Policy if you plan to have multiple remote management points) to allow credentials to be passed. This setting is located at Computer Configuration\Administrative Templates\System\Credentials Delegation. The specific setting is named "Allow delegating fresh credentials with NTML-only server authentication." Enable this setting, and add wsman\Host01 as a server in the list. You should now be able to remotely manage the Hyper-V server that is in a workgroup.

EXAM TIP

For each of the client settings, TrustedHosts, Delegate Computer, and wsman, you can use a wildcard mask (*) as a substitute for specifying multiple Hyper-V hosts.

Beginning with Windows 10 and Windows Server 2016, you also have the option to specify different credentials to manage the Hyper-V host from Hyper-V Manager. Note that the above steps must still be taken if the remote host is in a workgroup. Figure 2-8 shows connecting to a host with different credentials.

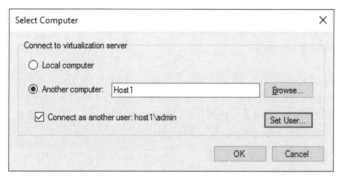

FIGURE 3-8 Select Computer

Configure virtual machines using Windows PowerShell Direct

The name of this skill is slightly misleading, as you don't really configure PowerShell Direct. PowerShell Direct is a new feature which allows you to connect to a VM through PowerShell. From that connection, you can run commands as if you were running them locally. You can perform a connection by using either of the following commands:

```
Enter-PSSession -VMName VMName
```

```
Invoke-Command -VMName -VMName -ScriptBlock { Commands }
```

When making the connection, you are prompted to enter the credentials for the virtual machine, as shown in Figure 3-9.

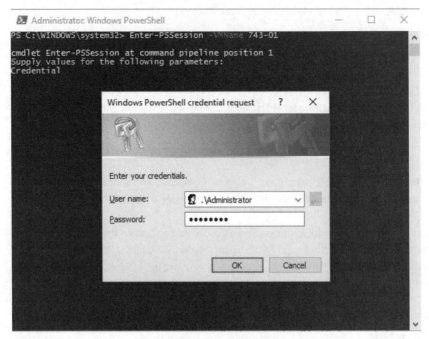

FIGURE 3-9 Windows PowerShell credential request

Using EnterPSSession allows you to interactively manage the virtual machine. You can continue to run commands within the virtual machine until you explicitly exit the session. With InvokeCommand, you are limited to only what is within the ScriptBlock parameter. Once the command is over, you are returned to the local PowerShell session.

In addition to the VMName, you can also use the VMId or the VMGUID to connect to a specific VM. To enter a PowerShell direct session, you must be logged onto the host as a Hyper-V administrator. The VM must be running locally and already booted to the OS.

Implement nested virtualization

Nested virtualization is a new feature that enables you to run Hyper-V inside of a virtual machine that is already running on Hyper-V. This is useful if you plan to use containers, use Hyper-V in a lab environment, or are testing multi-machine scenarios without additional hardware.

The first step to configuring nested virtualization is to ensure that the virtual machine can see the virtualization extensions from the host. This is accomplished from PowerShell by running the following command:

```
Set-VMProcessor -VMName VM1 -ExposeVirtualizationExtensions $True
```

When using nested virtualization, you want to ensure that dynamic memory is turned off for the VM. This can also be configured from PowerShell by running the following command:

```
Set-VMMemory -VMName VM1 -DynamicMemoryEnabled $False
```

Nested virtual switches present a challenge. There are two options to configure the networking in this scenario:

- **MAC address spoofing**   This allows the packets to be routed through two virtual switches.
- **Network Address Translation**   This creates a separate network internally for the virtual host. This is the more likely option, especially in a public cloud environment.

MAC address spoofing is a simple configuration. You can enable spoofing on the VM adapter by running the following command:

```
Get-VMNetworkAdapter -VMName VM1 | Set-VMNetworkAdapter -MacAddressSpoofing On
```

Network Address Translation (NAT) requires a virtual NAT switch to be configured on the virtual Hyper-V host. As part of the NAT configuration, you need to specify the IP address range to use for the translation service.

Note that virtual machines that are being used with nested virtualization no longer support these features:

- Runtime memory resize
- Dynamic memory
- Checkpoints
- Live migration

> **NEED MORE REVIEW?**   **NESTED VIRTUALIZATION**
>
> For more information on nested virtualization, visit *https://msdn.microsoft.com/en-us/virtualization/hyperv_on_windows/user_guide/nesting*.

Skill 3.2: Configure virtual machine settings

In this section, we go through the individual VM settings and options that can be configured. When studying for the exam, you should focus primarily on understanding how these options are configured, and the PowerShell cmdlets to configure them.

This section covers how to:

- Add or remove memory in running a VM
- Configure dynamic memory
- Configure Non-Uniform Memory Access support
- Configure smart paging
- Configure Resource Metering
- Manage Integration Services
- Create and configure generation 1 and 2 VMs and determine appropriate usage scenarios
- Implement enhanced session mode
- Create Linux and FreeBSD VMs, Install and configure Linux Integration Services (LIS), and Install and configure FreeBSD Integration Services
- Implement Secure Boot for Windows and Linux environments
- Move and convert VMs from previous versions of Hyper-V to Windows Server 2016 Hyper-V
- Export and import VMs
- Implement Discrete Device Assignment

Add or remove memory in running a VM

Adding or removing memory—or more accurately, increasing or decreasing the amount of memory that is assigned to a VM—is an easy task. The memory setting in the GUI of the VM settings can be configured even if the VM is running. However, you cannot enable Dynamic Memory if the VM is already running and was not already enabled. To configure VM memory by using PowerShell, use the Set-VMMemory cmdlet. For example, to configure a VM to use 4 GB of memory, run the following command:

```
Set-VMMemory -VMName 743-02 -StartupBytes 4GB
```

Configure dynamic memory

Dynamic memory enables a VM to scale up with additional memory automatically based on the needs of the VM operating system. To enable dynamic memory, the VM must be powered off. Dynamic Memory can be enabled in the GUI by simply placing a checkmark next to the option, and then configuring the Minimum RAM and Maximum RAM. The Startup RAM is the amount of memory assigned to the VM when it is first powered on. Dynamic Memory is also configured by using the Set-VMMemory cmdlet. For example, to enable Dynamic Memory with an initial value and minimum of 4 GB, and a maximum of 8 GB, run the following command:

```
Set-VMMemory -VMName 743-02 -StartupBytes 4GB -DynamicMemoryEnabled $True -MinimumBytes
4GB -MaximumBytes 8GB
```

Configure Non-Uniform Memory Access support

Windows Server 2012 introduced support for virtual NUMA with Hyper-V, ensuring that VMs with large amounts of memory performed as expected. The NUMA topology can be configured in a few ways:

- **Maximum processors per virtual NUMA node**   The maximum number of virtual processors that belong to the same VM, between 1 and 32.
- **Maximum memory per virtual NUMA Node**   The maximum amounts of memory that can be allocated to a VM, up to 256 GB.
- **Maximum virtual NUMA nodes per socket**   The maximum number of VMs that are allowed on a single socket, between 1 and 64.
- **NUMA Spanning**   Allows individual NUMA VMs to access non-local memory, and is enabled by default.

Figure 3-10 shows the default NUMA configuration for a Hyper-V VM.

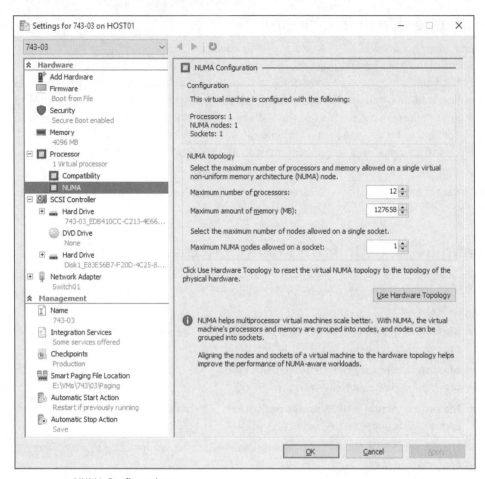

FIGURE 3-10 NUMA Configuration

> **NEED MORE REVIEW?** **NUMA DETAILS**
>
> For more information on NUMA, visit *https://technet.microsoft.com/en-us/library/jj614459.aspx.*

Configure smart paging

Windows Server 2012 introduced Smart Paging, which enhances virtual machine restarts. If a VM has low memory at startup, Hyper-V needs additional memory to start the VM. However, if the host is running several VMs, additional memory might not be available for the VM. Smart Paging is used to provide additional memory to a VM during startup if necessary.

To configure smart paging, simply specify the location where smart paging files should be stored. Figure 3-11 shows the dedicated GUI tab that smart paging is configured from.

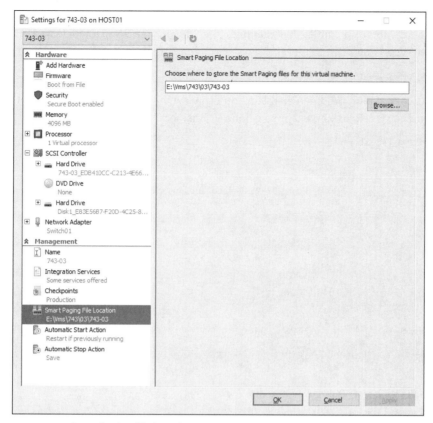

FIGURE 3-11 Smart Paging File Location

Additionally, smart paging can be configured from PowerShell with the Set-VM cmdlet. To set the smart paging file location to E:\VMs\743\03\Paging, run the following command:

```
Set-VM -VMName 743-03 -SmartPagingFilePath "E:\VMs\743\03\Paging"
```

Configure Resource Metering

Resource Metering is a built-in function that enables you to monitor the performance of a VM, including:

- Average CPU usage
- Average memory usage
- Minimum memory usage
- Maximum memory usage
- Maximum amount of allocated disk space
- Total inbound network traffic
- Total outbound network traffic

Resource Metering is not enabled for a VM by default. To enable, run the EnableVMResourceMetering cmdlet. For example, to enable it on a VM named 743-01, run the following command:

```
Enable-VMResourceMetering -VMName 743-01
```

Once Resource Metering has been enabled, you can view the data by running the MeasureVM cmdlet. The following example is for a VM named 743-01.

```
Measure-VM -VMName 743-01 | FL
```

And the output:

```
VMId                              : 85c4c297-9553-41ed-80c5-553b275faf49

VMName                            : 743-01

CimSession                        : CimSession: .

ComputerName                      : HOST01

AverageProcessorUsage             : 9

AverageMemoryUsage                : 2048

MaximumMemoryUsage                : 2048

MinimumMemoryUsage                : 2048

TotalDiskAllocation               : 130048

AggregatedAverageNormalizedIOPS   : 2

AggregatedAverageLatency          : 240

AggregatedDiskDataRead            : 0

AggregatedDiskDataWritten         : 2

AggregatedNormalizedIOCount       : 301

AvgCPU                            : 9

AvgRAM                            : 2048

MinRAM                            : 2048

MaxRAM                            : 2048

TotalDisk                         : 130048
```

Manage Integration Services

With Windows Server 2016, the method of providing integration services has changed. The vmguest.iso file is no longer included with Hyper-V because integration services are provided through Windows Update. The enables you to centralize the management of integration services along with Windows Updates. This is also useful in scenarios where different groups or organizations manage individual VMs. By using Windows Update, the owner of the VM can determine when to upgrade the integration services for their VM.

The available integration services are:

- Guest Service Interface
- Heartbeat
- Key-Value Pair Exchange
- Shutdown
- Time Synchronization
- VSS

You can obtain the current integration services configuration of a VM by running the Get-VMIntegrationService cmdlet. For example:

```
Get-VMIntegrationService -VMName 743-01
```

By default, all integration services except for Guest Service Interface are enabled. To enable a specific service, run the Enable-VMIntegrationService cmdlet. For example:

```
Enable-VMIntegrationService -VMName 743-01 -Name "Guest Service Interface"
```

You can also manage integration services from within the VM itself. To view the list of services from within the VM, run the Get-Service cmdlet. For example:

```
Get-Service -Name VM*
```

The Get-Service cmdlet returns the same list of integration services, but with their service names:

- vmicguestinterface
- vmicheartbeat
- vmickvpexchange
- vmicrdv
- vmishutdown
- vmictimesync
- vmiccvmsession
- vmicvss

From within the VM, you can run Start-Service or Stop-Service to manage the integration services.

Create and configure Generation 1 and 2 VMs and determine appropriate usage scenarios

When creating a VM, you have the option of creating a Generation 1 or a Generation 2 VM. As a whole, Generation 1 VM is more flexible for most scenarios. However, depending on your situation, a Generation 2 VM might be necessary.

A Generation 1 VM is required if the guest operating system is 32-bit, or if you plan on moving the VM to Azure at any point. However, if you're using Azure Site Recovery, a Generation 2 VM automatically converts to a Generation 1 VM when migrated.

A Generation 2 VM provides additional performance and security enhancements:

- PXE support with native Hyper-V adapters
- Faster boot time
- Minimized hardware emulation for devices
- UEFI disk partitions
- Secure Boot ready

You can attempt to convert a Generation 1 VM to Generation 2 by using a Microsoft-built script. However, this script is not supported or guaranteed to reconfigure the VM.

> **NEED MORE REVIEW? VM CONVERSION UTILITY**
>
> The VM conversion utility can be downloaded at: *https://code.msdn.microsoft.com/ConvertVMGeneration.*

Note that when creating disks for use with VMs, Generation 1 VMs use the VHD file extension, while Generation 2 use the VHDX file extension. When installing Nano Server, a key difference is that a VHD is based on a Master Boot Record (MBR), while a Generation 2 VHDX uses GUID Partition Tables (GPT).

Implement enhanced session mode

An enhanced session in Hyper-V enables you to use local resources to connect to a VM. This can include passing flash drives to the virtual machine. Plus, the contents of the clipboard provide the ability to copy and paste files through the connection session.

The local resources can be configured similar to the options that are available through Remote Desktop. Figure 3-12 shows the local resources that can be configured when connecting to a VM with an enhanced session.

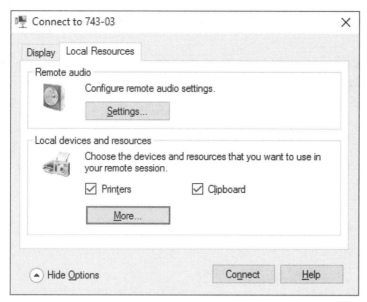

FIGURE 3-12 Enhanced session settings

Create Linux and FreeBSD VMs, install and configure Linux Integration Services, and install and configure FreeBSD Integration Services

For the purpose of this exam, we combined the Linux and FreeBSD topics into one. Hyper-V supports both emulated and specific devices for VMs that run Linux and FreeBSD. When using emulated devices, no additional software is necessary. These emulated devices do not offer high performance or much management compared to specific devices. However, specific devices require additional drivers that are necessary for the devices to work as expected in the VM.

The device drivers for these components are part of the Linux Integration Services and FreeBSD Integration Services. However, only certain versions of each distribution are supported with LIS and BIS. Do not expect to have to memorize the individual versions that are necessary to use Linux or FreeBSD with Hyper-V.

> **NEED MORE REVIEW?** **LIS AND BIS**
>
> For more information on supported distributions for LIS and BIS, visit *https://technet. microsoft.com/en-us/windows-server-docs/compute/hyper-v/supported-linux-and-freebsd- virtual-machines-for-hyper-v-on-windows.*

Implement Secure Boot for Windows and Linux environments

With Windows Server 2016, both Windows and Linux operating systems that are running in a Generation 2 VM can use Secure Boot. Before booting with secure boot, you must configure the Microsoft UEFI Certificate Authority. To configure the VM, run the following command:

```
Set-VMFirmware 743-01 -SecureBootTemplate MicrosoftUEFICertificateAuthority
```

Similar to the integration services, you should not memorize specific versions of operating systems that are supported with Secure Boot. However, you should be aware of the Linux distributions that are supported with secure boot:

- Ubuntu
- SUSE Linux Enterprise
- Red Hat Enterprise
- CentOS

Move and convert VMs from previous versions of Hyper-V to Windows Server 2016 Hyper-V

Moving a VM from one host to another can be accomplished a few different ways:

- **Online migration**   Requires that a Hyper-V cluster be created so that a clustered VM can move from one host to another. The two physical servers should have the same processor to avoid corruption.
- **Storage migration and import**   With this option, you can power off the VM to perform a storage migration. This ensures that all data associated with that VM is moved from the existing platform to the new platform.
- **Export and import**   This option enables you to export the data from the disk, and then import the data back into Hyper-V as a different VM.

An online migration can be performed to move a running VM from one host to another. With Windows Server 2016, the hosts do not have to be members of a failover cluster. Simply add both Hyper-V hosts to the Hyper-V Manager console, and use the Move wizard, or the Move-VM cmdlet. For example:

```
Move-VM 743-01 Host02 -IncludeStorage -DestinationStoragePath D:\743-01
```

An offline method of migration would be to power down the VM and move all of the associated files with the VM, and then import the VM on the new Hyper-V host. We expand on this in the next section.

Once a VM has been migrated from a previous version of Hyper-V, it can be upgraded to the latest version that is available, 8.0. Figure 4-13 shows a portion of the Hyper-V manager, particularly the Upgrade Configuration Version option.

FIGURE 3-13 Hyper-V Management Settings

After the VM has been upgraded, it cannot be downgraded to a previous version of VM.

Export and import VMs

Beginning with Windows Server 2012, performing an export of a VM is not required for it to be imported. The function still exists from the console and PowerShell, and can be an easy way to prepare the VM to be moved, especially if the files are scattered in multiple directories. The files in the export are organized in the following folders:

- **Snapshots** If the VM has any checkpoints, an .XML file for each checkpoint exists with the checkpoint GUID as the name.

- **Virtual Hard Disks** The base VHDX disk and any associated checkpoint AVDHX disk files.

- **Virtual Machines** If the machine is off during the export, only the .XML configuration file is present. If the VM is in a saved state, a subfolder with the VM GUID also exists with a .BIN and .VSV saved state file.

You can also export a VM by using the Export-VM cmdlet. For example:

```
Export-VM -VMName 743-01 -Path F:\Export
```

When importing a VM through the Import Virtual Machine wizard, you are presented with three options:

- **Register** This uses the existing VM ID and registers it in-place. You should choose this option if you already copied the VM files to the desired location.
- **Restore** This uses the original VM ID and copies the files from their current location to the default location that is configured for that specific Hyper-V host.
- **Copy** This creates a new VM ID and copies the files from their current location to the default location that is configured for that specific Hyper-V host.

When importing a VM, you can also use the Import-VM cmdlet. For example:

```
Import-VM -Path "F:\Export\743-01\Virtual Machines\Filename.xml" -Register
```

Note that when importing a VM by using PowerShell, to essentially *restore* a VM, you must use the Copy and GenerateNewId parameters. Restore is not a specific parameter for the cmdlet.

Implement Discrete Device Assignment (DDA)

Windows Server 2016 introduces DDA, a new feature that provides VMs with direct access to PCI Express devices. This is similar to SR-IOV, which was introduced with Windows Server 2012. DDA bypasses the virtualization components and gives VM direct access to the PCIe hardware. There are no DDA configuration options through Hyper-V Manager. As of this writing, managing DDA can only be performed by using the following Powershell cmdlets:

- Get-VMAssignableDevice
- Add-VMAssignableDevice
- Remove-VMAssignableDevice

To add a device to a VM, you must first disable the device for the Hyper-V host. Then using the InstanceId of the device, you can add the device to a specific VM. For example, to add a PCIe non-volatile RAM device to a VM, run this command:

```
Add-VMAssignableDevice -LocationPath "PCIROOT(40)#PCI(0200)#PCI(0000)" -VMName 743-01
```

> *NEED MORE REVIEW?* **DDA DETAILS**
>
> The virtualization team has a blog with several dedicated posts on DDA: *https://blogs.tech-net.microsoft.com/virtualization/2015/11/.*

Skill 3.3: Configure Hyper-V storage

This section covers the details of configuring storage for Hyper-V hosts and virtual machines. Similar to other sections, you should focus on the concepts of how the storage components interact with a host and its VMs, as well as how to complete these actions by using Windows PowerShell.

This section covers how to:
- Create VHDs and VHDX files using Hyper-V Manager
- Create shared VHDX files
- Configure differencing disks
- Modify virtual hard disks
- Configure pass-through disks
- Resize a virtual hard disk
- Manage checkpoints
- Implement production checkpoints
- Implement a virtual Fibre Channel adapter
- Configure storage Quality of Service

Create VHDs and VHDX files using Hyper-V Manager

Creating a disk, whether it is a VHD or VHDX, from Hyper-V Manager is as simple as using the New Virtual Hard Disk Wizard. The steps are:

1. From Hyper-V Manager, Click New, and then click Hard Disk.

2. In the New Virtual Hard Disk Wizard, click Next.

3. The first configuration option is the Choose Disk Format screen where you choose from VHD or VHDX. Another option is VHD Set, which is for shared disks that we cover in the next section. Select VHD or VHDX and click Next.

4. The next configuration is the Choose Disk Type screen, where you select from Fixed Size, Dynamically Expanding, or Differencing. Select Dynamically Expanding and click Next.

   - **Fixed size** This provides the best performance because the full size of the disk is allocated at the time of provisioning. As data changes within the disk, the actual disk size remains the same on the host.

   - **Dynamically expanding** This is a thinly-provisioned disk that only allocates data as the VM needs it. This ensures that you can obtain the most capacity from the host storage, but should be used cautiously.

- **Differencing** A differencing disk uses a parent-child relationship type. In this case, the parent disk contains read-only data that does not change. All changes are written to a different disk—the differencing disk.

5. On the Specify Name and Location screen, provide a filename for the disk, as well as the directory in which you would like to store the disk. This does not specifically have to be with a VM, and can be anywhere that the Hyper-V host has access to. Click Next to continue.

6. Finally, the Configure Disk screen allows you to select from three options, as shown in Figure 3-14. Select Create a New Blank Virtual Hard Disk, and enter 100 in the Size box. Click Finish.

   - **Create A New Blank Virtual Hard Disk** This is simply a blank disk that you can attach to a VM.

   - **Copy The Contents Of The Specified Physical Disk** Any physical disk that is presented to the Hyper-V host can be copied to the virtual disk. After the copy is complete, they are two separate sets of data. Any changes that a VM makes to the virtual disk is independent of the physical storage.

   - **Copy The Contents Of The Specified Virtual Hard Disk** This enables you to select an existing VHD or VHDX and copy the contents of the existing disk to the new disk.

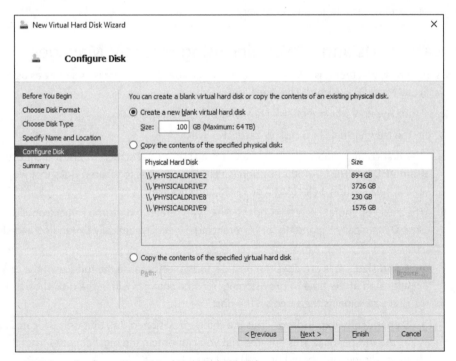

FIGURE 3-14 Configure New Virtual Hard Disk Wizard

Create shared VHDX files

Beginning with Windows Server 2012, a shared VHD can be used to connect a single VHD to multiple VMs. This shared VHD can act as shared storage for cluster configurations without the need for SAN equipment.

A shared VHD is simply a VHD that is being accessed by multiple VMs. After creating a new disk, you can add the drive to a VM with the ShareVirtualDisk parameter. For example:

```
Add-VMHardDiskDrive -VMName 743-01 -Path "\\Host01\Disks\Disk1.vhdx" -ShareVirtualDisk
```

Using a UNC path ensures that even if you move the VM to a different host, it can still access the storage. If you are using Hyper-V Manager, a shared drive can be created by adding a drive from the controller. Figure 3-15 shows the option to add a shared drive to a VM.

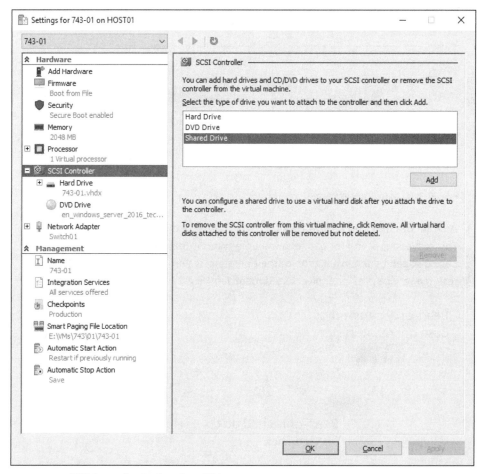

FIGURE 3-15 SCSI Controller Settings for a VM

Configure differencing disks

As we mentioned earlier in this chapter, a differencing disk uses a parent-child relationship type. In this case, the parent disk contains read-only data that does not change. A differencing disk is created using the same methods as a typical VHD, through the wizard or the New-VHD cmdlet, using the Differencing and ParentPath parameters. There are two primary methods of using differencing disks:

- **Many child objects to one parent** In this scenario, a single parent disk is used and many child disks are formed off of this parent. This is useful in lab environments where all VMs share the same image. Only one base VHD is necessary, and then each VM has a differencing disk in the lab for individual changes on that VM. Figure 3-16 illustrates this scenario.

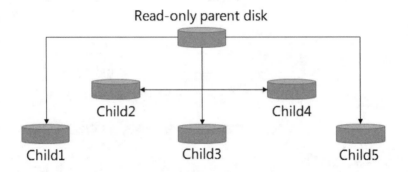

FIGURE 3-16 Many child objects

- **A chain of child and parent disks** In this scenario, disks build on the parent disk. This scenario is useful for patching multiple systems that use differencing disks. The base disk can be the installation of the operating system, and each child disk can represent a service pack or anniversary update. Figure 3-17 illustrates this scenario.

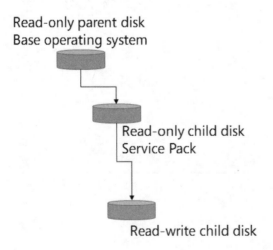

FIGURE 3-17 Chain of disks

Configure pass-through disks

A pass-through disk enables you to present a physical disk on the Hyper-V host and present it directly to a VM. Before presenting a disk to a VM, it must be initialized as either MBR or GPT, but set to offline. Figure 3-18 shows adding an offline physical disk to a VM.

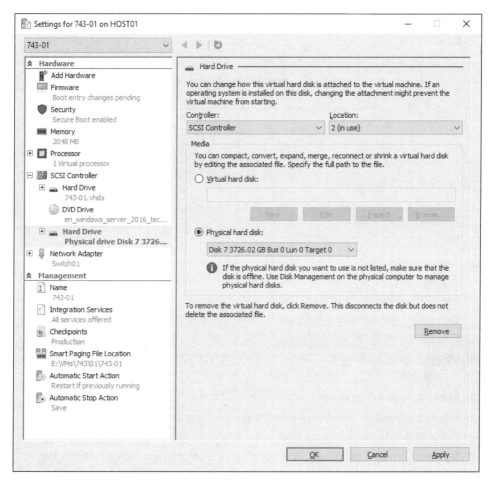

FIGURE 3-18 Adding physical hard disk to a VM

Resize a virtual hard disk

You can resize an existing virtual disk by using the Edit Virtual Hard Disk Wizard, or by using the Resize-VHD cmdlet. Figure 3-19 shows the options to edit a VHD.

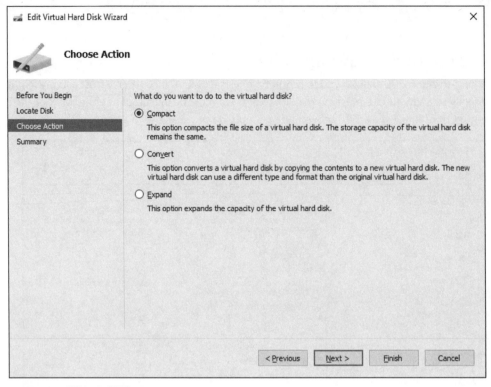

FIGURE 3-19 Editing a VHD

The available options for editing a VHD are:

- **Compact** This optimizes the capacity of a VHD and reduces the overall footprint on the Hyper-V host storage.

- **Convert** This enables you to change the disk type to other types discussed earlier in the chapter.

- **Expand** This simply increases the capacity of the VHD.

When using PowerShell to manage VHDs, there is a separate PowerShell cmdlet to perform each of these actions:

- **Optimize-VHD** Optimizing a VHD provides the same actions as Compact in the wizard.

- **Convert-VHD** This enables you to change the disk type of the VHD.

- **Resize-VHD** This allows you to resize the VHD.

Manage checkpoints

Checkpoints enable you to capture point-in-time snapshots of a VM. This gives you an easy method of quickly restoring to a known working configuration, making them useful before installing or updating an application. When a checkpoint is created, the original VHD becomes read-only, and all changes are captured in an AVHD file. Conversely, when a checkpoint is deleted, the contents of the AVHD are merged with the original disk, which becomes the primary writable file.

Standard checkpoints take a snapshot of both the disk and the memory state at the time that the checkpoint is taken. By default, in Windows Server 2016, snapshots are taken with Production checkpoints. We cover production checkpoints in the next section. The setting for production or standard is configured at the VM level, so you use the Set-VM cmdlet to make this change. For example:

```
Set-VM -Name 743-01 -CheckpointType Standard
```

Implement production checkpoints

Windows Server 2016 introduces production checkpoints, with uses the Volume Shadow Copy Service on Windows guests or File System Freeze on Linux guests. This enables you to take a consistent snapshot of a VM without the running memory. If taking a production checkpoint fails, by default the host attempts to create a standard checkpoint. You can configure the type of checkpoint a VM uses by using the Set-VM cmdlet. For example:

```
Set-VM -Name 743-01 -CheckpointType Production
```

To set the VM to only use production checkpoints, without the ability to fall back to a standard checkpoint, replace the Production option with ProductionOnly. Checkpoints can also be configured from Hyper-V Manager by editing the settings of a VM. Figure 3-20 displays the checkpoint management of a VM.

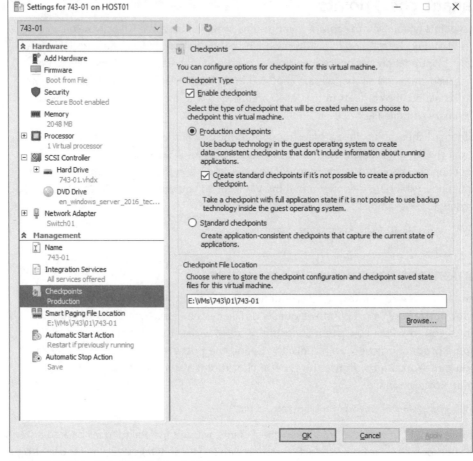

FIGURE 3-20 Virtual Machine Checkpoint Settings

Implement a virtual Fibre Channel adapter

A virtual Fibre Channel (FC) adapter can be used with a virtual SAN to provide direct SAN access to a virtual machine. This enables you to present LUNs from a SAN to a VM by using the virtual World Wide Name (WWN) that is assigned to the adapter. A FC adapter can be added from the settings screen of an individual VM. Figure 3-21 shows the new FC Adapter screen.

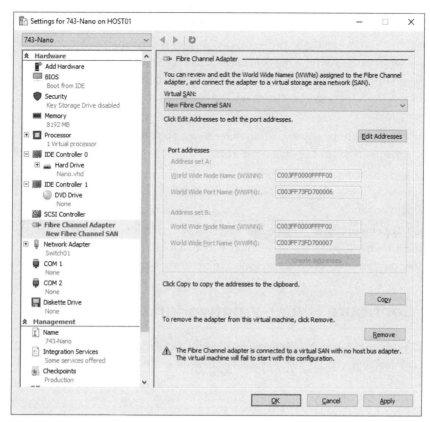

FIGURE 3-21 Virtual Machine Fibre Channel Adapter Settings

Adding a FC adapter can also be accomplished by using PowerShell with the
Add-VMFiberChannelHba cmdlet. For example:

```
Add-VMFibreChannelHba -VMName 743-01 -SanName vSAN1 -GenerateWwn
```

If you need to specify the WWNs that the VM uses the adapter, replace the GenerateWwn
option with the following:

- WorldWideNodeNameSetA
- WorldWideNodeNameSetB
- WorldWidePortNameSetA
- WorldWidePortNameSetB

For example, run the following command to create a FC adapter using these WWNs:

```
Add-VMFibreChannelHba -VMName 743-Nano -SanName vSAN1 -WorldWideNodeNameSetA
C003FF0000FFFF00 -WorldWidePortNameSetA C003FF73FD70000C -WorldWideNodeNameSetB
C003FF0000FFFF00 -WorldWidePortNameSetB C003FF73FD70000D
```

Configure storage Quality of Service (QoS)

Windows Server 2012 introduced the ability to set QoS policies for storage on virtual machines. Windows Server 2016 builds on this functionality and for Scale-Out File Services, and allows you to assign them to one or more VM disks. The storage performance is then readjusted to meet the policies that have been defined. Storage QoS can primarily be used to achieve the following goals:

- **Mitigate noisy neighbor issues** This ensures that a single VM does not use all of the available storage resources and limit other VMs.

- **Monitor end-to-end storage performance** As soon as a virtual machine is started, the performance of the VM is monitored. The details of all running VMs can be viewed from a single location.

- **Manage I/O per workload** The QoS policies that you define ensure that the minimums and maximums meets the application workload for the environment. This helps ensure that performance is consistent, even in different environments.

Skill 3.4: Configure Hyper-V networking

This section will examine the ways in which we use Hyper-V, including how to configure MAC addresses and NIC teaming to configuring virtual machine queues and bandwidth management.

This section covers how to:

- Add and remove virtual network interface cards and configuring network adapters
- Configure Hyper-V virtual switches
- Optimize network performance
- Configure MAC addresses
- Configure network isolation
- Configure NIC teaming in VMs
- Configure virtual machine queue
- Enable Remote Direct Memory Access on network adapters bound to a Hyper-V virtual switch using Switch Embedded Teaming
- Configure bandwidth management

Add and remove virtual network interface cards, configuring network adapters, configuring virtual machine queue, and configuring bandwidth management

A virtual network adapter can be added by a similar method to a drive or Fibre Channel adapter from within Hyper-V Manager. Simply edit the settings of the VM, and select the option to add the network adapter. For Generation 1 VMs, you have the option of creating a standard network adapter, or a legacy network adapter. A standard adapter offers better performance, and a legacy adapter enables PXE boot. Figure 3-22 shows the options after adding a new network adapter.

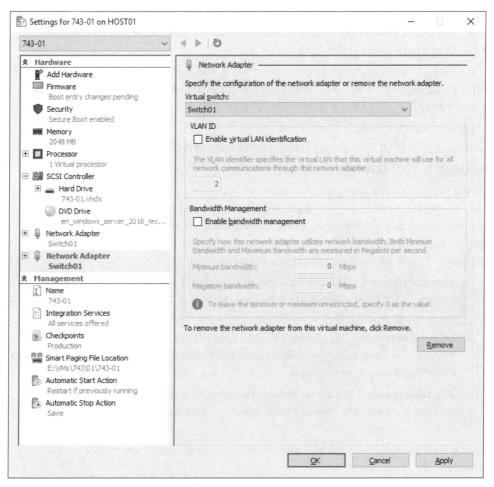

FIGURE 3-22 Virtual Machine Network Adapter Settings

Adding a network adapter can also be accomplished by using PowerShell with the Add-VMNetworkAdapter cmdlet. For example:

```
Add-VMNetworkAdapter -VMName 743-01 -SwitchName Switch01
```

After adding a network adapter to a VM, you can configure the VLAN identification, if necessary, for that adapter. Referring back to Figure 3-22, a synthetic network adapter also supports a few additional features:

- **Bandwidth management** You can configure the minimum and maximum bandwidth targets for the network adapter.

- **Virtual machine queue (VMQ)** If supported by the corresponding physical adapter, VMQ can be enabled on the virtual adapter.

- **IPsec task offloading** If supported by the corresponding physical adapter, IPsec tasks can be offloaded to hardware.

A legacy network adapter does not support these features, and can only be configured with a particular VLAN. Regardless of the adapter type, you can manage the adapter with PowerShell by using the Set-VMNetworkAdapter cmdlet.

Configure Hyper-V virtual switches and configure network isolation

For the purpose of preparing for the exam, we've combined configuring virtual switches and network isolation. Hyper-V virtual switches enable connection from the VM to the Hyper-V, depending on the connection type of the switch. Network isolation can be configured on a VM based on the network adapter and switch settings. There are three options to choose from when creating a virtual switch:

- **External network** This connects the virtual switch to the selected physical network adapter of the Hyper-V host. This physical adapter can be dedicated to the VMs that are running, or it can be shared with the host operating system.

- **Internal network** This connects the VM only to the Hyper-V host and other VMs that have a network adapter connected to this switch. The VM does not have access to the physical adapter on the host.

- **Private network** This simply provides a connection to the VM, although it cannot communicate with the host or with other VMs on the same switch on other Hyper-V hosts.

Figure 3-23 shows the configuration options for a virtual switch from the Virtual Switch Manager.

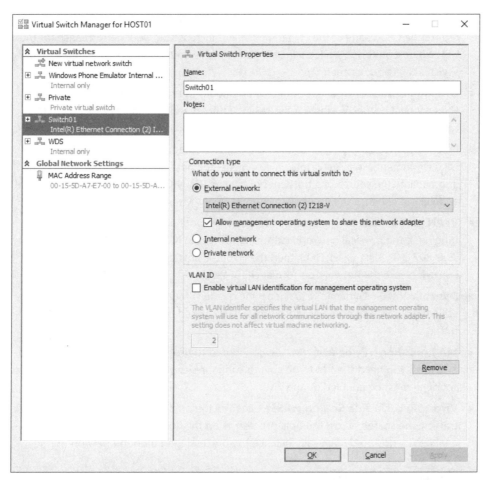

FIGURE 3-23 Virtual Switch Manager

Virtual switches can be added from PowerShell by using the New-VMSwitch cmdlet. For example, to create a new internal virtual switch, run the following command:

```
New-VMSwitch -Name Internal1 -SwitchType Internal
```

Optimize network performance

Optimizing network performance can be achieved from both a Hyper-V host perspective, as well as an individual VM perspective. When preparing for the exam, some performance options to be aware of include:

- **Synthetic network adapter** The Hyper-V-specific network adapter is optimized to reduce the CPU usage of the Hyper-V host and increase network performance for the VM. When monitoring performance, a performance counter is available under \Hyper-V Virtual Network Adapter (*)*.

- **Offload hardware** You can configure offloading to reduce the CPU usage of the Hyper-V host. Hyper-V supports LargeSend Offload and TCP checksum offload if the capabilities have been enabled in the drivers for the physical network adapter.

- **Network switch topology** Similar to designing an appropriate topology for physical environments, in large virtual environments the network switch configuration can also become the source of a bottleneck. You can use NIC teaming on multiple physical adapters to enhance the network performance of VMs.

- **VLAN performance** The synthetic Hyper-V network adapter supports VLAN tagging. If the physical network adapter supports the NDIS_ENCAPSULATION_IEEE_802_3_P_AND_Q_IN_OOB, then the Hyper-V host can also use hardware offloading to increase the network performance for VMs.

- **Dynamic VMQ** Dynamic virtual machine queue (VMQ) enables you to automatically scale the number of processors used for a VMQ, based on the volume of the network traffic.

- **MAC spoofing** By default, VMs are configured to protect against duplicate MAC addresses. If you need the VM to be able to configure its own MAC address, MAC address spoofing must be enabled on the VM.

- **Virtual Receive Side Scaling (vRSS)** Enables the processing for ingress VM network traffic to be shared across multiple processors on the host and virtual machine. vRSS enables the host to dynamically balance the processing of inbound network traffic.

NEED MORE REVIEW? **PERFORMANCE TUNING**

For more information on performance tuning, visit *https://msdn.microsoft.com/en-us/library/windows/hardware/dn567656(v=vs.85).aspx*.

Configure MAC addresses

By default, the network adapter in a VM uses a dynamic MAC address that is assigned from the pool of MAC addresses on the Hyper-V host. The pool of MAC addresses can be configured from the Virtual Switch Manager, as shown in Figure 3-24.

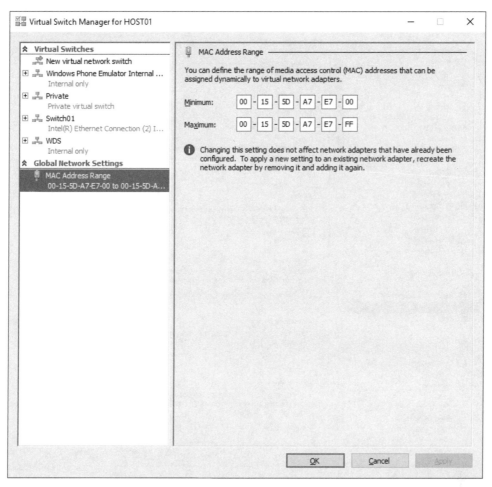

FIGURE 3-24 Virtual Switch Manager- MAC Address Range

Although is it managed from the Virtual Switch Manager, it is configured from PowerShell by using the Set-VMHost cmdlet. For example:

```
Set-VMHost -MacAddressMinimum 00155DA7E700 -MacAddressMaximum 00155DA7E7FF
```

Configuring the MAC address on an individual network adapter is accomplished from the settings of the VM, as shown in Figure 3-25.

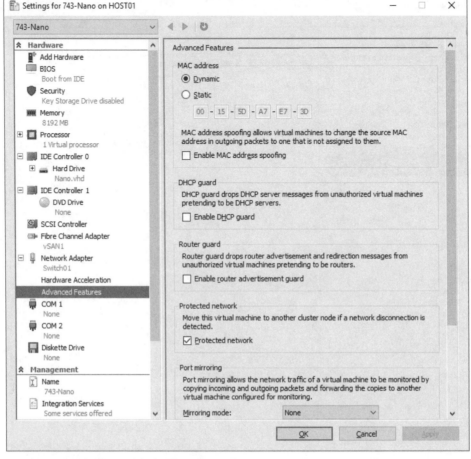

FIGURE 3-25 VM Settings – Advanced Features

The MAC address settings for a virtual network adapter can be configured with PowerShell by using the Set-VMNetworkAdapter cmdlet. For example, to assign a static MAC address, run the following command:

```
Set-VMNetworkAdapter -VMName 743-01 -StaticMacAddress 00155DA7E73B
```

Configure NIC teaming in VMs

If you present multiple network adapters to a VM, you can configure them to be teamed within the VM. However, you must also enable the network adapter to be a member of the team from the Hyper-V host. Figure 3-26 shows the Advanced Features of a network adapter, where NIC teaming can be enabled.

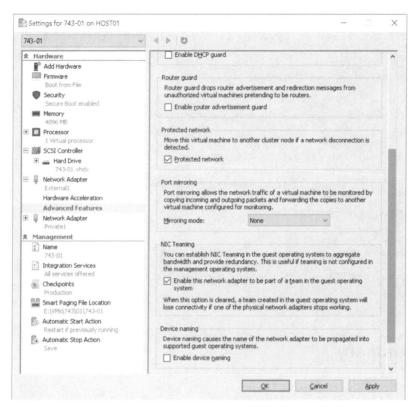

FIGURE 3-26 Advanced Features of a Virtual Network Adapter

Enabling NIC teaming for a virtual network adapter can also be performed through PowerShell by using the Set-VMNetworkAdapter cmdlet. Note that although the AllowTeaming parameter expects a Boolean value, the valid options are On and Off, not $True or $False. For example:

```
Set-VMNetworkAdapter -VMName 743-01 -AllowTeaming On
```

Enable Remote Direct Memory Access on network adapters bound to a Hyper-V virtual switch using Switch Embedded Teaming

In previous versions of Windows Server and Hyper-V, you could not configure RDMA with network adapters that were part of a NIC team or a virtual switch. With Windows Server 2016, you can now enable RMDA on both network adapters that are part of a virtual switch, with or without Switch Embedded Teaming (SET). The first step in configuring RDMA with SET is to enable Data Center Bridging. Then, you can create a virtual switch with an RDMA vNIC and SET. For example:

```
New-VMSwitch -Name SETvSwitch -NetAdapterName "SLOT 2","SLOT 3" -EnableEmbeddedTeaming
$True
```

After creating the vswitch, you can add the network adapters to the VM, and enable RDMA. For example:

```
Add-VMNetworkAdapter -SwitchName SETswitch -Name SMB_1 -managementOS
```

```
Add-VMNetworkAdapter -SwitchName SETswitch -Name SMB_2 -managementOS
```

```
Enable-NetAdapterRDMA "vEthernet (SMB_1)","vEthernet (SMB_2)"
```

> **NEED MORE REVIEW?**   **RDMA WITH SET**
>
> For more information on RDMA with SET, visit *https://technet.microsoft.com/en-us/library/ mt403349.aspx*.

Chapter summary

- The requirements and how to install Hyper-V
- Upgrading from previous versions of Hyper-V
- Management tools and remote management for Hyper-V
- Configuration versions and generation types of individual virtual machines
- Using nested virtualization with Hyper-V
- How to manage memory for a virtual machine
- Configuring dynamic memory, NUMA, and smart paging
- Using resource metering and integration services
- Using Linux on Hyper-V
- Moving, converting, importing, and exporting VMs
- Creating and managing VHD and VHDX disk files
- Configuring differencing, fixed, and dynamically expanding disks
- Managing standard and production checkpoints
- Adding and managing virtual network adapters
- Optimizing network performance

Thought Experiment

A company is planning to create two servers that run Hyper-V in a workgroup. The servers must consume only the minimum resources that are required, and must be managed remotely. One of the Hyper-V servers must host a VM that must also use the Hyper-V role.

After deploying the hosts, the company plans to deploy both Windows and Linux guest operating systems. Both operating systems must include the drivers for hardware that is being passed to the VM.

The disks on the VMs must be thinly provisioned to maximize the capacity that is available on the hosts. Checkpoints that use VSS must be used to capture consistent snapshots.

Using this information, answer the following questions.

1. How should the company install Hyper-V?
2. How should the management roles be configured?
3. Name a Linux operating system that the company can use.
4. What type of disks must the VMs use?
5. What type of checkpoints must the VMs use?

Thought Experiment Answers

1. Based on this scenario, Hyper-V should be installed on a Nano Server. This consumes the absolute minimum amount of resources for the environment.
2. Because the hosts are in a workgroup, the WSMAN-trusted hosts must be configured for remote management.
3. Red Hat, CentOS, Ubuntu, or SUSE
4. The disks must be dynamically expanding to be thinly provisioned.
5. Only Production checkpoint types use VSS for consistent snapshots.

CHAPTER 4

Implement Windows Containers

In this chapter we cover how to use containers to host virtualized images on a server. Containers are supported on both Windows Server and Hyper-V, however, the way they act and respond are slightly different. Containers can be isolated to ensure they operate independently of any other container or host that they are running on. In the first section of this chapter, we cover the basic process to deploy containers and go through the basic management aspects for containers.

Skills in this chapter:

- Deploy Windows Containers
- Manage Windows Containers

Skill 4.1: Deploy Windows Containers

In this section we outline the basics for deploying containers on either Windows Server, Nano Server, or Hyper-V. We also detail how to change the Docker daemon configuration for startup, and detail specifics for images, such as tagging.

> **This section covers how to:**
>
> - Determine installation requirements and appropriate scenarios for Windows Containers
> - Install and configure Windows Server container host in physical or virtualized environments
> - Install and configure Windows Server container host to Windows Server Core or Nano Server in a physical or virtualized environment
> - Install Docker on Windows Server and Nano Server
> - Configure Docker daemon start-up options
> - Install a base operating system
> - Tag an image
> - Uninstall an operating system image
> - Create Windows Server containers
> - Create Hyper-V containers

Determine installation requirements and appropriate scenarios for Windows Containers

Windows Containers is a new feature that is only available on Windows Server 2016, Nano Server, and Windows 10 Professional and Enterprise Anniversary Update editions. If you plan on using Hyper-V containers, then the Hyper-V role must also be installed on the computer or server. To use Windows Containers, the operating system must be installed as the C drive. If you plan to only use Hyper-V containers, then the operating system can be installed on any drive.

From a physical aspect, Windows Containers with Hyper-V requires nested virtualization. Nested virtualization has the following requirements:

- At least 4 GB of RAM for the Hyper-V host
- A processes that uses Intel VT-x

Also, the container host VM must have at least two virtual processors and dynamic memory must be disabled. As of this writing, Windows Server 2016 offers two container images: Server Core and Nano Server. If the host operating system is a Nano Server, then only the Nano Server image is available.

Install and configure containers

For the purpose of preparing for the exam, we've combined two of the listed skills:

- Install and configure Windows Server container host in physical or virtualized environments
- Install and configure Windows Server container host to Windows Server Core or Nano Server in a physical or virtualized environment

For either host's operating system, whether it is physical or virtual, containers is listed as a Windows Feature. For servers with a GUI, it can be installed from the Add Roles and Features wizard. Containers can also be installed by using Windows PowerShell by using the Install-WindowsFeature cmdlet. For example:

Figure 4-1 shows installing the Containers feature by using the Install-WindowsFeature cmdlet.

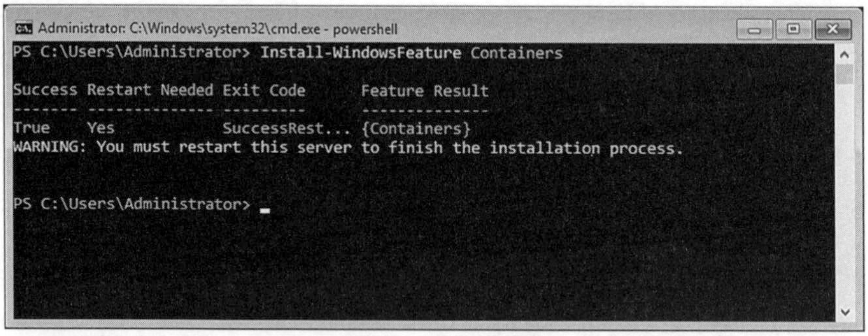

FIGURE 4-1 Install-WindowsFeature

```
Install-WindowsFeature Containers
```

If you're using Nano Server, you must first install the Nano Server Package, and then install the Container Feature. For example:

```
Install-PackageProvider NanoServerPacakage
```

```
Install-NanoServerPackage -Name Microsoft-NanoServer-Containers-Package
```

Install Docker on Windows Server and Nano Server

To manage containers on either Windows Server 2016 or Nano Server, you must also install the Docker service. Most all Docker installation and configuration options have both a PowerShell cmdlet or a Docker command line option. To install Docker on Windows Server 2016, it must be downloaded from the Docker website. You can do this manually, or by using PowerShell. For example:

Figure 4-2 shows downloading and configuring the environment for the docker service to run.

FIGURE 4-2 Obtaining docker

```
Invoke-WebRequest "https://aka.ms/tp5/b/dockerd" -OutFile "$env:TEMP\docker-1.12.0.zip"
-UseBasicParsing
```

```
Expand-Archive -Path "$env:TEMP\docker-1.12.0.zip" -DestinationPath $env:ProgramFiles
```

```
[Environment]::SetEnvironmentVariable("Path", $env:Path + ";C:\Program Files\Docker",
[EnvironmentVariableTarget]::Machine)
```

```
& $env:ProgramFiles\docker\dockerd.exe --register-service
```

```
Start-Service Docker
```

```
docker tag windowsservercore:10.0.14300.1000 windowsservercore:latest
```

> **NOTE**
>
> The **Invoke-WebRequest** command in this example specifically uses Technical Preview 5, which was available at the time of writing. Locate the latest version that is available by using the Docker website before using this command in a lab environment.

After the installation is complete, run the **docker info** command. A portion of the output is shown in Figure 4-3.

FIGURE 4-3 Docker info

The above example is broken down like this:

1. First, the Docker engine and client is downloaded from the Docker website.

2. Then, the code extracts the compressed folder into the Program Files directory.

3. The path is set as a system variable, and the service is created and started.

4. Finally, the Docker image must be tagged with the version "latest."

For installing Docker on Nano Server, the same overall process must be followed. However, Nano Server does not currently support the Invoke-WebRequest cmdlet. Therefore, you must manually download the Docker files and copy them to the Nano Server operating system. From there you can set the environment variable, create the service, and then start the service. For Nano Server, you must also enable the FPS-SMB-In-TCP firewall rule. For example:

```
Set-NetFirewallRule -Name FPS-SMB-In-TCP -Enabled True
```

Configure Docker daemon start-up options

Docker is configured by using a daemon.json file, which is located in the installation path of the directory. When using Docker on Windows Server 2016, only a subset of the configuration options is available. When creating the JSON file, only the necessary configuration changes need to be included in the file. For example, to configure the Docker Engine to accept connections on port 2375, add the following to the daemon.json file:

```
{

    "hosts": ["tcp://0.0.0.0:2375"]

}
```

You can also configure Docker by using the `sc config` command. When using `sc config`, you are modifying the Docker Engine configuration flags directly on the Docker service. For example:

Figure 4-4 shows running the sc command to modify the docker service.

FIGURE 4-4 Service configuration

```
sc config docker binpath= "\"C:\Program Files\docker\dockerd.exe\" --run-service -H
tcp://0.0.0.0:2375"
```

> **NEED MORE REVIEW?** **DOCKER DAEMON**
>
> For more information on configuring the Docker daemon, visit *https://msdn.microsoft.com/en-us/virtualization/windowscontainers/docker/configure_docker_daemon*.

Install a base operating system

Before you can deploy a container, you must download a base operating system image. The procedure is the same whether you plan to manage Server Core or Nano Server base images. Obtaining the image is accomplished by running two PowerShell cmdlets: Install-PackageProvider, and Install-ContainerImage. For example:

```
Install-PackageProvider ContainerImage -Force
```

```
Install ContainerImage -Name WindowsServerCore
```

This process might take a few minutes because it downloads the Server Core container image. After installing the image, you need to restart the Docker service. For example:

```
Restart-Service Docker
```

You can also use the docker command to download the base image. For example:

```
docker pull microsoft/windowsservercore
```

After downloading the images, you can also view the downloaded images with the docker command. For example:

```
docker images
```

Figure 4-5 shows the results of downloading the images and how they are displayed after being downloaded.

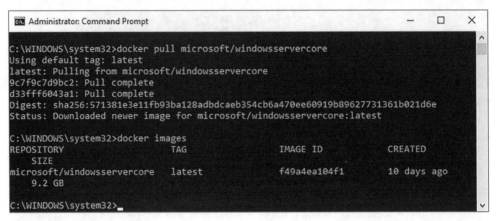

FIGURE 4-5 Obtaining images

Tag an image

When you download an image into the repository, you must also assign a tag to the image. Tagging an image enables you to set a version on the image, which is useful if you plan to have multiple versions. Microsoft suggests after downloading an image, to tag it at the "latest." For example:

```
docker tag windowsservercore:10.0.14300.1000 windowsservercore:latest
```

The Docker tag can contain upper and lowercase characters, digits, underscores, periods, and dashes. However, the tag cannot start with a period or dash, and can be up to 128 characters.

> **NEED MORE REVIEW?** **DOCKER TAG**
>
> For more information on using the Docker tag, visit *https://docs.docker.com/engine/reference/commandline/tag/*.

Uninstall an operating system image

As we have mentioned, most actions when using Docker can be completed by using PowerShell or the Docker daemon. To uninstall a container image from the repository, use the Uninstall-ContainerOSImage cmdlet. For example:

```
Uninstall-ContainerOSImage -FullName CN=Microsoft_NanoServer_10.0.14304.1003
```

Create Windows Server containers

You can deploy a container by using the Docker daemon. One of the first tasks you might need to do is view a list of the available container images. For example, the following command returns a list of available Microsoft images:

```
docker search Microsoft
```

A portion of the output is included for reference:

```
NAME                             DESCRIPTION
microsoft/aspnet                 ASP.NET is an open source server-side Web ...
microsoft/dotnet                 Official images for working with .NET Core...
mono                             Mono is an open source implementation of M...
microsoft/azure-cli             Docker image for Microsoft Azure Command L...
microsoft/iis                    Internet Information Services (IIS) instal...
```

Therefore, if you want to use the ASP.NET image, use the Docker daemon to pull the image:

```
docker pull microsoft/aspnet
```

Create Hyper-V containers

Windows Server containers and Hyper-V containers are created and managed, and are functionally identical. Both types of containers also use the same container images. The difference between a Windows Server container and a Hyper-V container is the level of isolation that is present to the host, or other containers on that host. The first difference is that when creating the container, specify the --isolation=hyperv parameter.

```
docker run -it --isolation=hyperv nanoserver cmd
```

To demonstrate the isolation of a Hyper-V container, assume that a Windows Server container has been deployed. You start a running ping on the container.

```
docker run -d windowsservercore ping localhost -t
```

If you use the docker daemon, you can view the task thread that is running the ping.

```
docker top windowservercore
```

```
4369 ping
```

In this example, the process ID within the container is 4369. Within the container, you can also view the thread.

```
get-process -Name ping
```

The following output is returned:

```
Handles  NPM(K)    PM(K)     WS(K) VM(M)    CPU(s)     Id  SI ProcessName

-------  ------    -----     ----- -----    ------     --  -- -----------

     67       5      820      3836 ...71      0.03    4369   3 PING
```

If you follow the same process when using a Hyper-V container, you receive a different end result. You can create and view the process from the host, using the Docker daemon.

```
docker run -d --isolation=hyperv nanoserver ping -t localhost

docker top nanoserver

2371 ping
```

However, the difference is when trying to view the process on the container host.

```
Get-process -Name ping

Get-Process : Cannot find a process with the name "ping". Verify the process name and
call the cmdlet again.

At line:1 char:1

+ Get-Process -Name ping

+ ~~~~~~~~~~~~~~~~~~~~~~

    + CategoryInfo          : ObjectNotFound: (ping:String) [Get-Process],
ProcessCommandException

    + FullyQualifiedErrorId : NoProcessFoundForGivenName,Microsoft.PowerShell.Commands.
GetProcessCommand
```

The difference is in the process name. By using a Hyper-V container, the process is run by the vmwp process. The vmwp process is the virtual machine process on the host, and is protecting the process from the host operating system.

```
Get-Process -Name vmwp

Handles  NPM(K)    PM(K)     WS(K) VM(M)    CPU(s)     Id  SI ProcessName

-------  ------    -----     ----- -----    ------     --  -- -----------

   1737      15    39452     19620 ...61      5.55    2376   0 vmwp
```

Skill 4.2: Manage Windows Containers

In this section, we outline how to manage containers after they have been deployed. This includes using the Docker daemon to manage images, as well as using Windows PowerShell. We also cover configuring port mapping and networking options for use with Windows Containers.

> **This section covers how to:**
> - Manage Windows or Linux containers using the Docker daemon
> - Manage Windows or Linux containers using Windows PowerShell
> - Manage container networking
> - Manage container data volumes
> - Manage Resource Control
> - Create new container images using Dockerfile
> - Manage container images using DockerHub repository for public and private scenarios
> - Manage container images using Microsoft Azure

Manage Windows or Linux containers using the Docker daemon

After you have downloaded the image type that you plan to use, you can use the daemon to identify the images that have been downloaded.

```
docker images
```

The following output is returned:

```
REPOSITORY          TAG          IMAGE ID          CREATED          SIZE

microsoft/aspnet    latest       accd044753c1      11 days ago      7.907 GB
```

You can also deploy a container by using the Docker daemon.

```
docker run -d -p 80:80 microsoft/iis ping -t localhost
```

Creating a new image can be performed by using the Docker daemon with the `commit` parameter.

```
docker commit 475059caef8f windowsservercoreiis
```

Removing an image is performed by using the Docker daemon with the `rmi` parameter. However, if any other container depends on the image that you are trying to remove, the command fails. The `rmi` parameter accepts either the image name or the ID of the image.

```
docker rmi windowsservercoreiis
```

To view the list of dependencies with Docker, use the `history` parameter.

```
docker history windowsservercoreiis
```

The following output is returned:

```
IMAGE            CREATED           CREATED BY      SIZE          COMMENT

2236b49aaaef     3 minutes ago     cmd             171.2 MB

6801d964fda5     2 weeks ago                       0 B
```

Manage Windows or Linux containers using Windows PowerShell

As of this writing, the PowerShell for Docker module is in development. The team writing the module has adopted the Microsoft Open Source Code of Conduct, and welcomes contributions to the project in the form of bugs, suggestions, proposals, and pull requests through the Github repository. The project is available on Github here: *https://github.com/Microsoft/Docker-PowerShell/.*

The PowerShell module for Docker is simply an alternative to the Docker daemon. You can use the module as a replacement for, or in conjunction with, the Docker daemon. The PowerShell module can target any operating system that is running the Docker engine on both Windows and Linux.

To compile the project, you need to obtain the .NET Core SDK, and the .NET SDKs for versions 4.5 and 4.6. The Docker endpoint that you are planning to connect to must support the API version 1.24.

The latest release version of Docker can also be downloaded from GitHub here: *https://github.com/Microsoft/Docker-PowerShell/releases*. Download and extract the compressed folder, and then use the Import-Module cmdlet, pointing to the extracted folder. This makes the Docker cmdlets available on the computer.

Manage container networking

Container networks are similar to virtual networks through Hyper-V. Each container has a virtual network adapter that is connected to a virtual switch. To force isolation between containers that are running on the same host, compartments are created for each container. A Windows Server host uses Host vNICs to attach to the virtual, while Hyper-V containers use a synthetic VM NIC to attach to the virtual switch.

Containers support four different networking modes:

- **Network Address Translation (NAT)**   Each container receives an IP address from a private address pool. Port forwarding or mapping can be configured to transmit data from the host to the container.

- **Transparent**   Each container endpoint has a direct connection to the physical network that the host is using. The IP address range that is being used on the physical network can be used on the container either as a static address or dynamically assigned.

- **L2 Bridge**   Each container endpoint is in the same subnet as the host that is running it. The container IP address is assigned statically from the same prefix as the host. All container endpoints on the host use the same MAC address.

- **L2 Tunnel**   This mode should only be used in a Microsoft Cloud Stack.

By default, the Docker engine creates an NAT network when the Docker service runs for the first time. The default network that is used is 172.16.0.0/12. You can customize the network prefix used by modifying the daemon.json configuration file. The endpoints in the container are attached to this network and assigned an IP address from the private network. Table 4-1 outlines connections for a single-host environment.

TABLE 4-1 Single host connection types

Single host	Container to container	Container to external
NAT	Connects using Hyper-V Virtual Switch	Routed through WinNAT with address translation
Transparent	Connects using Hyper-V Virtual Switch	Direct access to physical network
L2 Bridge	Connects through Hyper-V Virtual Switch	Access to physical network by using MAC address translation

Additionally, Table 4-2 outlines the connections for a multi-host environment.

TABLE 4-2 Multi-host connection types

Multi-host	container to Container	Container to external
NAT	References external container host IP and port, routed through WinNAT with translations	References external container host IP and port, routed through WinNAT with translations
Transparent	Directly references container IP endpoint	Direct access to physical network
L2 Bridge	Directly references container IP endpoint	Access to physical network by using MAC address translation

NAT networks

By default, when an endpoint is created, it connects to the NAT network. To specify the network that a container should attach to, use the --network parameter.

```
docker run -it --network=NatNetwork <image>
```

To access any applications that run within a container, you need to map the ports from the host to the endpoint.

```
docker run -it -p 80:80 <image>
```

```
docker run -it -p 8082:80 windowsservercore cmd
```

The first command creates a port map between TCP port 80 on the host to TCP port 80 of the container endpoint. The second command uses port 8082 on the host, and forwards it to port 80 of the endpoint.

EXAM TIP

Port mapping must either be configured when the endpoint is created, or when the endpoint is in a STOPPED state. You cannot modify container port mapping while the endpoint is running.

Transparent networks

To use a transparent network, you must first create the network.

```
docker network create -d transparent TransparentNetwork
```

If the container host is virtualized, and you need to use DHCP for the IP address assignment, then you must also use MAC address spoofing on the VM network adapter. Without MAC address spoofing, the Hyper-V host blocks the network traffic from the containers in the VM with identical MAC addresses.

```
Get-VMNetworkAdapter -VMName ContainerHost | Set-VMNetworkAdapter -MacAddressSpoofing On
```

L2 Bridge networks

To use a L2 Bridge network, you must create a container network that uses the driver named l2bridge. The subnet and gateway for the network must also be specified when creating the object.

```
docker network create -d l2bridge --subnet=10.10.0.0/16 --gateway=10.10.0.1
BridgeNetwork
```

EXAM TIP

When using an L2 Bridge network type, only static IP addresses are supported.

Options for all network types

You can use the Docker daemon to list the available networks.

```
docker network ls
```

The following output is returned:

NETWORK ID	NAME	DRIVER	SCOPE
0a297065f06a	nat	nat	local
d42516aa0250	none	null	local

To remove a network, use the network rm parameter.

```
docker network rm "nat"
```

Figure 4-6 displays the networks on a docker host.

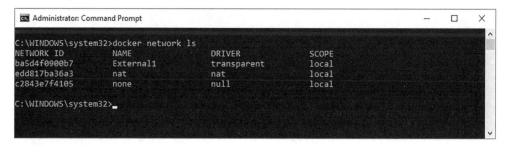

FIGURE 4-6 Listing networks

Manage container data volumes

Data volumes are storage locations that are visible to both the container host and the container endpoint. The data that is in the volume can be shared between the two systems, as well as with other containers on the same host. Creating a new volume is part of the run parameter with the Docker daemon.

```
docker run -it -v c:\volume1 windowsservercore cmd
```

By default, new data volumes are created in C:\ProgramData\Docker\Volumes on the container host. In the command, the C:\Volume1 indicates that the volume is be accessible within the container endpoint at that path.

After you have created a volume, to mount it to a different container, specify the source and destination paths using the same parameters:

```
docker run -it -v c:\source:c:\destination windowsservercore cmd
```

You can also pass-through a single file from the container host to the endpoint. The syntax is basically the same as specifying an existing volume.

```
docker run -it -v c:\container-share\config.ini windowsservercore cmd
```

Similarly, you can also mount a full drive from the container host to the endpoint. Note that when mounting a full drive, a backslash is not included with the drive letter.

```
docker run -it -v d: windowsservercore cmd
```

Finally, data volumes can be inherited from other endpoints using the --volumes-from switch in the run parameter. This is useful if the applications in multiple containers are sharing the same data.

```
docker run -it --volumes-from Volume1 windowsservercore cmd
```

Manage resource control

Docker includes the ability to manage the CPU, disk IO, network, and memory consumption that an endpoint consumes. This ensures that you are able to manage the container host resources efficiently, as well as ensuring that you maximize the performance of all services running on a host.

By default, the CPU is divided equally among all endpoints running on a container host. To change the share that an endpoint has, use the --cpu-shares switch with the run parameter. The --cpushares parameter accepts a value between 1 and 10000. The default weight of all endpoints is 5,000.

```
docker run -it --cpu-shares 2 --name dockerdemo windowsservercore cmd
```

Create new container images using Dockerfile

You can use Docker to automatically build images by reading the instructions that are placed in a Dockerfile. A Dockerfile is a text document that lists the commands that you would use in the CLI to create an image manually. After creating the Dockerfile, use the `build` parameter with the Docker daemon to automatically create the image.

```
docker build -f C:\Dockerfile .
```

The Docker daemon commits each line of the file one by one before outputting the image ID of for the endpoint that you have created.

Manage container images using Docker Hub repository for public and private scenarios

The Docker Hub is a repository that contains pre-built images. These images can be downloaded onto a host and used in a development or production environment. These images can also be used as a base for Windows container applications. To retrieve a list of the available images in the Docker Hub, use the search parameter with the Docker daemon:

```
docker search *
```

The following output is returned:

```
NAME                     DESCRIPTION                           STARS
OFFICIAL    AUTOMATED

microsoft/sample-django  Django installed in a Windows Server Core ...   1
[OK]

microsoft/dotnet35       .NET 3.5 Runtime installed in a Windows Se...   1        [OK]
[OK]

microsoft/sample-golang  Go Programming

...
```

Downloading an image from the Docker Hub is the same as retrieving a base image. Use the `pull` parameter with the Docker daemon:

```
docker pull microsoft/aspnet
```

The following output is returned:

```
Using default tag: latest

latest: Pulling from microsoft/aspnet

f9e8a4cc8f6c: Pull complete


b71a5b8be5a2: Download complete
```

After downloading the image, it is available when viewing the images through the Docker daemon.

```
docker images
```

The following output is returned:

REPOSITORY	TAG	IMAGE ID	CREATED	VIRTUAL SIZE
microsoft/aspnet	latest	b3842ee505e5	5 hours ago	101.7 MB

To upload an image to the Docker Hub, use the push parameter with the Docker daemon. First, you must login with your Docker ID to access the Hub.

```
docker login
```

The following output is returned:

```
Login with your Docker ID to push and pull images from Docker Hub. If you don't have a
Docker ID, head over to https://hub.docker.com to create one.

Username: username

Password:
```

```
Login Succeeded

docker push username/containername


The push refers to a repository [docker.io/username/containername]

4341be770beb: Pushed

fed398573696: Pushed

latest: digest: sha256:ae3a2971628c04d5df32c3bbbfc87c477bb814d5e73e2787900da13228676c4f
size: 2410
```

Manage container images using Microsoft Azure

You can use Docker on Microsoft Azure a few different ways:

- Deploy container hosts using the Docker Machine Azure driver
- Use the Docker VM Extension on Azure VMs
- Use the Docker VM Extension with Docker Compose
- Deploy a Docker Swarm cluster on Azure Container Services

The Azure Docker VM Extension installs and configures the Docker daemon, client, and Docker Compose on a Linux VM in Azure. This enables you to define and deploy container applications using Docker Compose and Docker Machine.

Combine the extension with the Azure Resource Manager, and you can create and deploy templates for almost all aspects of your Azure environment.

> *NEED MORE REVIEW?* **DOCKER VM EXTENSION**
>
> For more information on the Docker VM Extension, visit *https://azure.microsoft.com/en-us/documentation/articles/virtual-machines-linux-dockerextension/*.

Chapter summary

- The basics of using containers to run virtualized images.

- How to install Docker on Windows Server and Nano Server

- How to configure the start-up options for the Docker daemon

- Performing a base operating system install

- Tagging an image for use with containers

- Creating containers for both Windows Server and Hyper-V

- Managing containers using the Docker daemon and Windows PowerShell

- Creating NAT, Transparent, and L2 Bridge networks for containers

- Creating and managing data volumes for use by multiple container endpoints

- Managing container host resources using Resource Control

- Automating the build process for an image using Dockerfile

- Using the Azure VM Extension with Docker

Thought Experiment

A company is testing containers and images in their development environment. They have installed the Docker engine on a Windows Server host, and deployed a base image connected to the default network. The company would like the images to connect directly to the physical network. They also plan to automate the creation of future images and store them in the Docker Hub.

Using this information, answer the following questions:

1. What should be modified to configure the Docker daemon startup options?

2. Which network is the image that has been deployed connected to?

3. What type of network must the company create to achieve the goal?

4. What type of file does the Dockerfile need to be?

5. Which Docker daemon command is used to store images in the Docker Hub repository?

Thought Experiment Answers

1. The JSON configuration file should be created or modified to change the startup options of the Docker daemon.

2. By default, images connect to a default NAT network.

3. A transparent network must be created to enable the images to connect directly to the physical network.

4. The Dockerfile script is a plain-text file that contains the actions to create an image.

5. The `docker push` command uploads the specified image to the Docker Hub after logging into the service.

Implement high availability

This chapter covers a major component of the upgrade exam. In addition to several skills being covered, there are many new features that have been introduced or enhanced that we discuss in this chapter. These features include:

- Cluster Operating System Rolling Upgrade
- Storage Replica
- Cloud witness
- Virtual machine resiliency
- Site-aware clusters
- Workgroup and multi-domain clusters
- Virtual machine node fairness
- Virtual machine start order

In addition to these topics, we also cover other details of high availability using Hyper-V, failover clustering, and Storage Spaces Direct.

Skills in this chapter:

- Implement high availability and disaster recovery options in Hyper-V
- Implement failover clustering
- Implement Storage Spaces Direct
- Manage failover clustering
- Manage VM movement in clustered nodes

Skill 5.1: Implement high availability and disaster recovery options in Hyper-V

This section explains the basic high availability and disaster recovery options that are available in Hyper-V. These options do not require any additional management components or failover clusters. Hyper-V has built-in redundancy and failover options.

> **This section covers how to:**
> - Implement Hyper-V replica
> - Implement Live Migration
> - Implement shared-nothing Live Migration
> - Configure CredSSP or Kerberos authentication protocol for Live Migration
> - Implement storage migration

Implement Hyper-V replica

A Hyper-V replica enables you to replicate virtual machines on one Hyper-V host to another host, either in the same physical location or a different location. The replication data can also be encrypted by using certificates. The certificate that is used can be local, self-signed, or supplied by a Certification Authority (CA).

Windows Server 2012 R2 introduced extended replication which enables you to replicate a virtual machine to multiple sites. For example, you can replicate the VM to a secondary failover as well as an extended third site. There are a few additional considerations to be aware of when using an extended replica:

- You cannot use application-consistent replication.
- You can failover to the third site if necessary.
- You can run a test failover to either site without disruption.

A failover with Hyper-V replica is not an automatic process. There are three different types of failover that you can perform:

- **Test failover**   You can test whether the replicated VM can start in the second or third site. This process creates a duplicate VM during the testing process that is started. The VM in the production environment is not affected. When you complete the failover process, the duplicate VM is deleted.
- **Planned failover**   This method enables you to failover during a planned maintenance or downtime for specific sites. To perform a planned failover, the source VM must first be powered off. The failover process replication still occurs, but from the secondary

site to the original primary. This ensures that both sites still maintain synchronized data.

- **Unplanned failover** When an unexpected outage occurs you can perform an unplanned failover. This type of failover should only be used if the source VM fails and must be started in a secondary site. If recovery history is used, you can also recover to a previous snapshot.

Configuring a Hyper-V replica is a multi-step process that requires planning from networking, storage, and server management aspects. The general steps to successfully implementing a Hyper-V replica include:

1. **Set up the Hyper-V servers** This includes the primary source server and at least one replication destination. Additional components that could need to be configured include networking and storage.

2. **Set up the replication** Enable both Hyper-V servers to be members of the replica. This ensures that replication can occur both from the primary to the secondary, and from the secondary to the primary in the event of a failover.

3. **Test the deployment** Conduct a test failover after all VM settings have been configured. This ensures that the communication and replication is ready for production. As part of the test, ensure that the duplicate VM is created on the replica.

4. **Run a planned failover** Run a planned failover to complete the process of moving the active VM from the primary to the secondary replica. This might be necessary during planned maintenance or downtime events. A planned failover can also be performed to ensure that an unplanned failover is successful.

5. **Respond to an unplanned failover** Unplanned failovers do not automatically transfer a VM if the primary VM is unavailable. You must manually failover the VM to the secondary replica.

6. **Set up extended replication** Configuring an extended replica provides another level of failover by using a third replica site. You can use the third site simply as another replica location, or move workloads to specific servers in the event of a planned or unplanned failover.

NEED MORE REVIEW?

For details and instructions for each step of the process of deploying a Hyper-V replica, visit *https://technet.microsoft.com/library/jj134207.aspx*.

Implement Live Migration

Live Migration is the ability to move VMs or VM storage without a failover cluster. Moving a VM or its storage can be performed from the Hyper-V Manager or from Windows PowerShell.

To perform a live migration, first enable it from the settings of the Hyper-V host. To enable live migrations, the machine must be a domain member. Live migration is not available in a Hyper-V workgroup. Figure 5-1 shows the settings from the Hyper-V Manager.

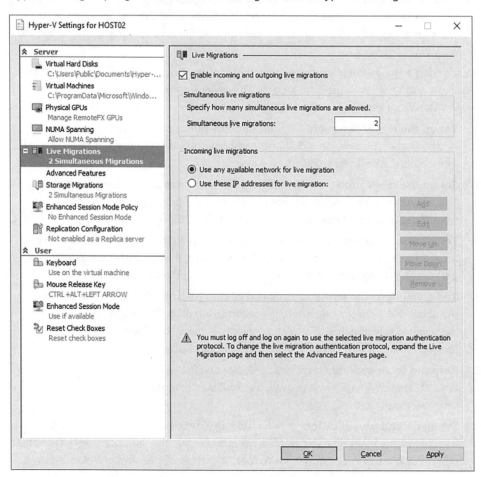

FIGURE 5-1 Live Migration settings

The first step to perform the migration using Hyper-V Manager is to right-click the VM you plan to migrate, and click Move. The Move Wizard is displayed, as shown in Figure 5-2. The first option is whether to move the virtual machine, or move the storage of the virtual machine. In this section, we move the virtual machine.

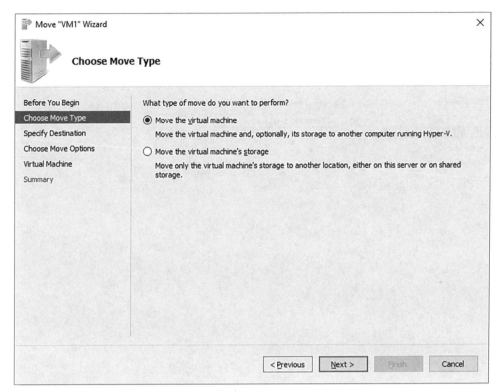

FIGURE 5-2 Move Wizard choose move type

You are then prompted to specify the destination for the move. This can be any other Hyper-V host that you have permission to administer. Figure 5-3 shows specifying the destination host.

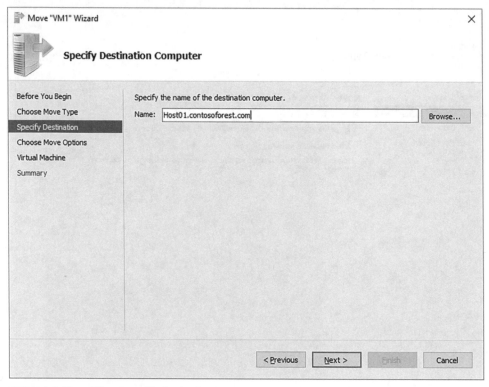

FIGURE 5-3 Move Wizard specify destination

You are then prompted for additional details of the migration type. The available options during a VM migration are shown in Figure 5-4:

- **Move The Virtual Machine's Data To A Single Location** This option moves all VM files, including disks, snapshots, and configuration information to a single specified location.

- **Move The Virtual Machine's Data By Selecting Where To Move The Items** This option presents additional options for moving the storage of the VM, which we discuss in a later section.

- **Move Only The Virtual Machine** This option moves only the running configuration of the VM, but not the storage. The storage of the VM must be shared between the source and destination Hyper-V hosts.

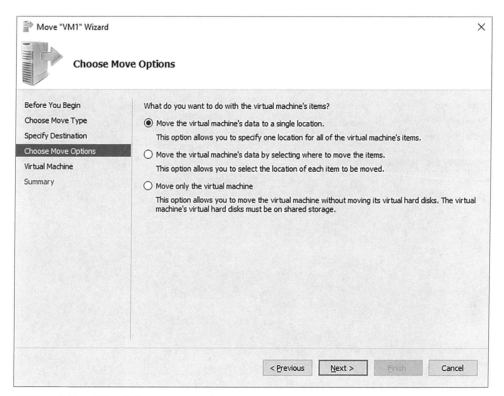

FIGURE 5-4 Move Wizard choose move options

If you select to move only the virtual machine, then no additional options are displayed and you complete the wizard. If you plan to move all of the VM files to a single location, one additional screen is displayed, prompting you for the destination directory to store the VM and its files. Figure 5-5 shows specifying the destination directory.

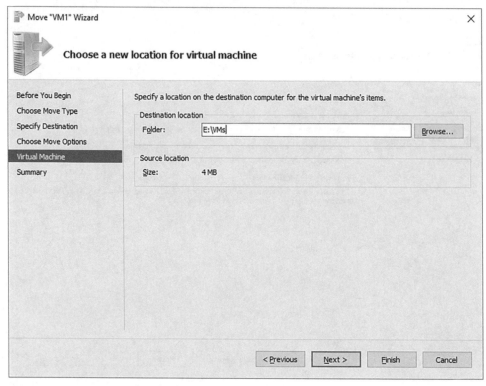

FIGURE 5-5 Move Wizard virtual machine

You can also move a VM by using Windows PowerShell and using the Move-VM cmdlet. For example, to move a VM named VM1 to a Hyper-V server named Host2, run the following command:

```
Move-VM "VM1" Host2
```

You must also configure a network to be used by the live migration service, which is accomplished by using the Set-VMHost cmdlet. For example:

```
Set-VMHost –UseAnyNetworkForMigration $true
```

Implement shared nothing Live Migration

A "shared nothing" migration is simply the ability to migrate a VM across hosts that do not share common features, and are not in a failover cluster. By default, a migration using the Move wizard as discussed completes, even if the Hyper-V hosts do not share the same storage.

One additional component to migrating VMs is processor compatibility. If you need to migrate a VM between Hyper-V hosts that do not share the same physical features, you can limit some VM features to ensure that a migration can occur. For example, if you need to move from an Intel-based Hyper-V server to an AMD-based host, you should enable processor compatibility before completing the migration. These settings are per-VM within the Processor tree, as shown in Figure 5-6.

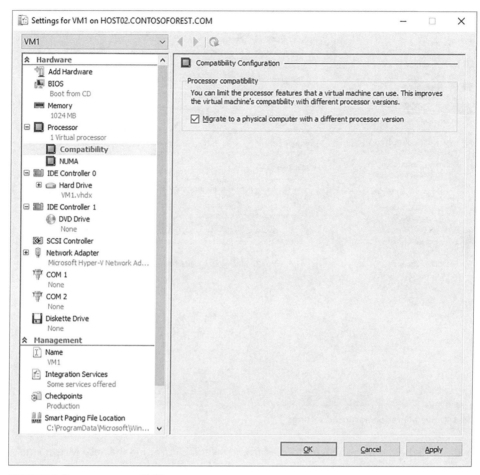

FIGURE 5-6 Processor compatibility

Configure CredSSP or Kerberos authentication protocol for Live Migration

With Windows Server 2016, the Hyper-V Manager communicates with the hosts by using the WS-MAN protocol. This enables using Credential Security Support Provider (CredSSP), Kerberos, or HTML authentication. CredSSP is now the default method of authentication for live migrations, and does not require constrained delegation to be enabled in Active Directory. Figure 5-7 shows the advanced features of configuring Live Migration, including CredSSP.

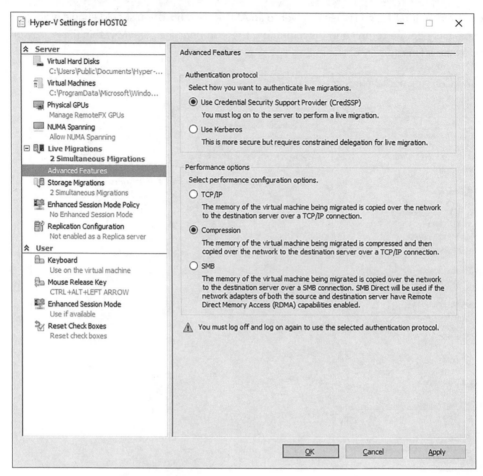

FIGURE 5-7 Live Migration advanced settings

Enabling Kerberos can also be performed from PowerShell by using the Set-VMHost cmd-let. For example:

```
Set-VMHost -VirtualMachineMigrationAuthenticationType Kerberos
```

You can also enhance the performance of a live migration by configuring additional options. These include:

- **TCP/IP** With this option, the memory of the VM is transferred during the migration by using the available network over a typical TCP/IP connection.

- **Compression** With this option, the memory of the VM is first compressed before being sent to the destination by using a TCP/IP connection.

- **SMB** With this option, the memory of the VM is copied to the destination by using a SMB connection. If both the source and destination network adapters use Remote Direct Memory Access (RDMA), then SMB Direct is used for the copy.

If you plan to use Kerberos as the authentication protocol, then you must also configure constrained delegation within Active Directory for each Hyper-V host. Constrained delegation is enabled by modifying the computer object properties for the host in Active Directory. For each host in the environment, add two services that refer to the other Hyper-V hosts in the environment: *cifs* and *Microsoft Virtual System Migration Service*.

For example, if you had four Hyper-V hosts named Host1 – Host4, then the delegation settings on Host1 must contain each service for Host2, Host3, and Host4. Figure 5-8 shows adding these two services on the Host02 computer object, specifying Host01 for each service.

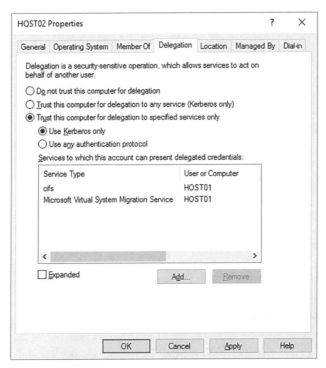

FIGURE 5-8 Host02 Delegation properties

Implement storage migration

Performing a migration from Hyper-V manager is as simple as right-clicking a VM, and then selecting Move. The Move Wizard is displayed, walking you through the available options to move the VM or VM storage, based on what is available. Figure 5-9 shows the second screen of the Move Wizard.

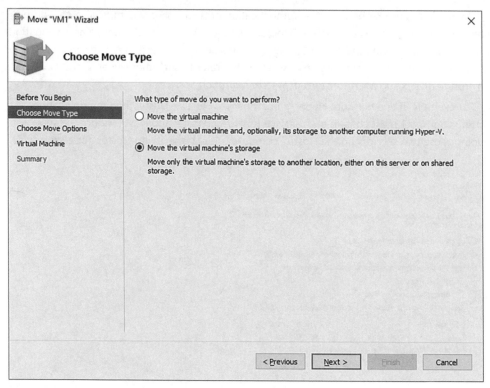

FIGURE 5-9 Move Wizard move type selection

When moving the storage of a virtual machine, there are a few different options in the wizard, as shown in Figure 5-10.

- **Move All Of The Virtual Machine's Data To A Single Location**   This option moves all VM data, regardless of its current location, to a single destination.

- **Move the Virtual Machine's Data to Different Locations**   This option enables you to first select which items you plan to move, and then specify the destination for each item. Items include the VHD files, configuration files, checkpoints, and smart paging files.

- **Move Only the Virtual Machine's Virtual Hard Disks**   This option enables you to move only the VHDs that are being used with the VM.

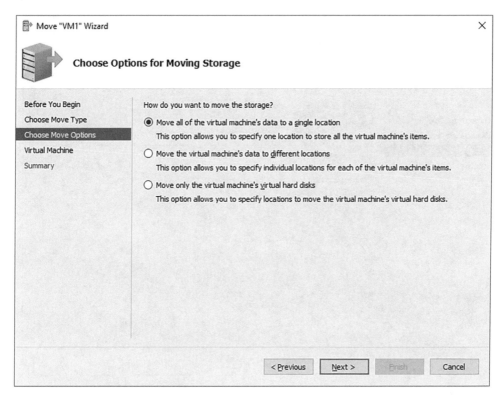

FIGURE 5-10 Move Wizard choose move options

Depending on the option you select, the wizard is automatically prompt for additional information. For example, choosing Move the virtual machine's data to different locations adds a new page in the wizard for each configuration item. Figure 5-5 shows an example of specifying the destination for the VM.

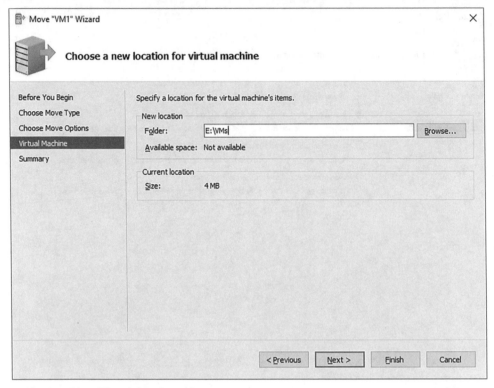

FIGURE 5-11 Move Wizard virtual machine

Moving a VM's storage can also be accomplished by using the Move-VM cmdlet. For example, to move a VM named VM1 to Host02 in the E:\VMs directory run the following command.

```
Move-VM "VM1" Host02 -IncludeStorage -DestinationStoragePath E:\VMs
```

Skill 5.2: Implement failover clustering

In this section, we discuss several skills that are involved or need to be considered when creating a failover cluster. This includes the type of cluster to implement, cluster details such as quorum, networking, or storage. We also cover cluster management features including cluster-aware updating and cluster operating system rolling upgrade. Finally, we discuss features that can be used to augment failover clusters, such as CSVs, Storage Replica, and virtualized clusters.

This section covers how to:

- Implement Workgroup, Single, and Multi-Domain clusters
- Configure quorum and Implement Cloud Witness
- Configure cluster networking
- Restore single node or cluster configuration
- Configure cluster storage
- Implement Cluster-Aware Updating
- Implement Cluster Operating System Rolling Upgrade
- Configure and optimize Clustered Shared Volumes
- Configure clusters without network names
- Implement Scale-Out File Server
- Determine different scenarios for the use of SoFS versus the Clustered File Server
- Determine usage scenarios for implementing guest clustering
- Implement a Clustered Storage Spaces solution using Shared SAS storage enclosures
- Implement Storage Replica
- Implement VM resiliency
- Implement shared VHDX as a storage solution for guest clusters

Implement workgroup, single, and multi-domain clusters

In previous versions of Windows Server, the nodes within a cluster had to be in the same domain. With Windows Server 2016, cluster nodes can span different domains, or be members of a workgroup. The traditional method of having all clusters nodes in the same domain is a single-domain cluster. For the purposes of this section, we focus primarily on workgroup and multi-domain clusters.

There are a few prerequisites for implementing workgroup or multi-domain clusters:

- A local user account must be created on all nodes.
- The user account must have the same name and password on each node.
- The user account must be a member of the local Administrators group.
- The LocalAccountTokenFilterPolicy registry key at HKLM\SOFTWARE\Microsoft\Windows\CurrentVersion\Policies\System must be created and set to 1.
- When the cluster is created, it must be created as an Active Directory-Detached Cluster.
- The administrative access point must be set to DNS.

The first step to creating a failover cluster of any type is to install the Failover Cluster feature. This can be accomplished from Server Manager using the Add Roles and Features Wizard, or by using the Install-WindowsFeature cmdlet.

After you have installed the Failover Cluster feature, you can create a cluster from PowerShell or by using the Failover Cluster Manager. The first step is to select the servers that you are including in the cluster. The Failover Cluster Manager ensures that the server has the Failover Cluster feature installed, and verify the settings on the server. Adding a server is shown in Figure 5-12.

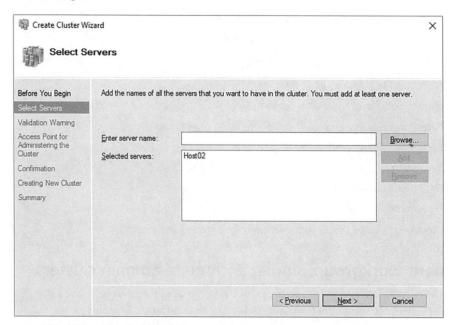

FIGURE 5-12 Create Cluster Wizard select servers

The next step, performing validation, is optional. Validation ensures that the servers you are configuring as part of a failover cluster meet the supported requirements. If you select Yes, then a separate wizard launches above the Create Cluster Wizard and must be completed before returning. The validation warning is shown in Figure 5-13.

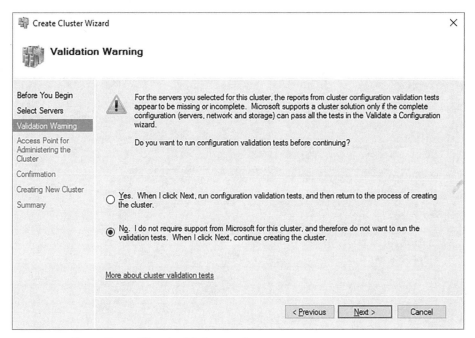

FIGURE 5-13 Create Cluster Wizard validation warning

Next, set a name for the cluster that is less than 15 characters. This is the name that is used when administering the cluster, as shown in Figure 5-14.

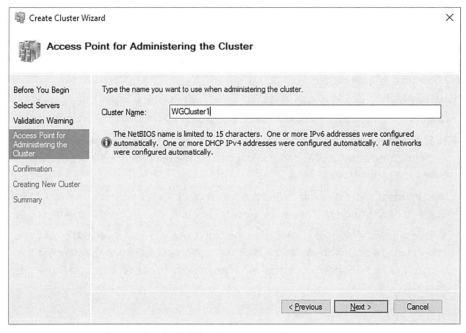

FIGURE 5-14 Create Cluster Wizard administration access point

Finally, the confirmation screen details the settings for the cluster. Notice in Figure 5-15 that the cluster registration is set to DNS only. This indicates that the cluster is not a member of Active Directory domain, and is a workgroup cluster.

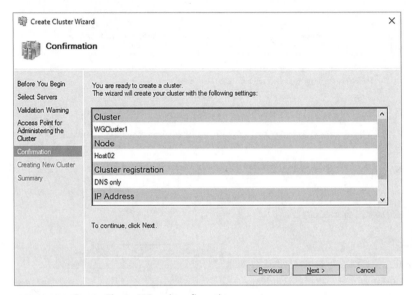

FIGURE 5-15 Create Cluster Wizard confirmation

Configure quorum and configure cloud witness

The latest recommendation from Microsoft is to always configure a quorum witness, regardless of how many nodes in the cluster exist. By using Dynamic Quorum, the cluster automatically manages the vote that the quorum witnesses. There are three types of quorum available when configuring a failover cluster:

- **Disk Witness** This was previously known as Node and Disk Majority. Disk witness monitors a storage volume to use to decide quorum.
- **File Share Witness** This was previously known as Node and File Share Majority. File share witness monitors a UNC path file share to decide quorum. The file share must not be used by the cluster.
- **Cloud Witness** This is new for Windows Server 2016. Cloud witness uses Azure blob storage to decide quorum. This section focuses primarily on using a cloud witness.

With a cloud witness, a blob file is created in the blob storage. There is very little cost associated with using a cloud witness, as the blob file is only updated when the state of the cluster changes. Figure 5-16 shows a diagram of a common multi-site failover cluster that uses a cloud witness.

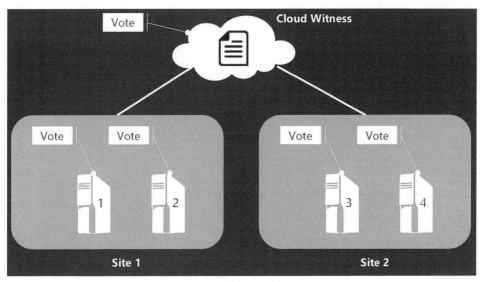

FIGURE 5-16 Multi-site failover cluster with cloud witness

The four general steps to using a cloud witness for quorum are:

1. **Create an Azure storage account using locally-redundant replication**   It is important to select locally redundant, so that there is consistency for the cluster management.

2. **Copy the storage access keys associated with the storage account**   By default, each storage account generates two access keys that can be used to access the storage account. The key is necessary to connect to Azure from the on-premises cluster.

3. **Copy the blob URL**   There are three URLs associated with the storage account: blobs, tables, and queues. A cloud witness uses blob storage, so this is the URL that is used to connect to. Note that the URL can vary by country or region, so be sure to document the URL for any storage account that you create.

4. **Complete the quorum configuration on the cluster by using the wizard, or PowerShell**   The Configure Cluster Quorum Wizard walks you through the steps to creating a cloud witness. You can also configure the cluster quorum by using the Set-ClusterQuorum cmdlet.

The Configure Cluster Quorum Wizard can be launched from the More Actions menu of the Failover Cluster Manager. To add a quorum witness, choose the Select the Quorum Witness option in the wizard, as shown in Figure 5-17.

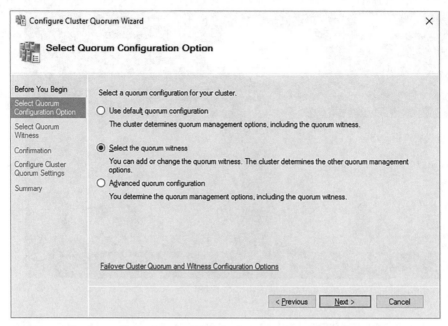

FIGURE 5-17 Configure Cluster Quorum Wizard select quorum configuration option

Next, you are able to select the type of quorum witness to configure, as shown in Figure 5-18. Again, focus on creating a cloud witness.

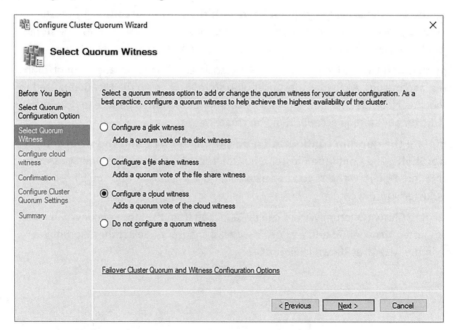

FIGURE 5-18 Configure Cluster Quorum Wizard select quorum witness

The wizard prompts you for the name of the storage account that the blob container was created in, one of the access keys for the storage account, and the endpoint URL for the container. The configured details are shown in Figure 5-19.

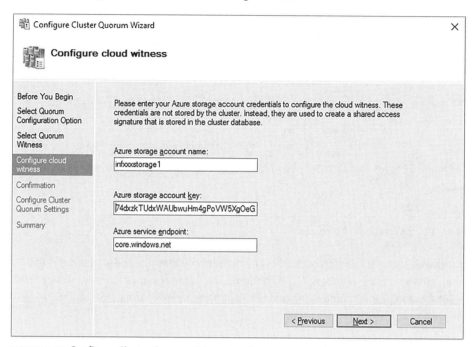

FIGURE 5-19 Configure Cluster Quorum Wizard configure quorum witness

The configuration details that are needed are all to be found in the Azure portal where the storage account is configured. Figure 5-20 displays a portion of the Azure portal that contains the storage account name and access key for the container. The service endpoint is populated by default, and does not need to be changed.

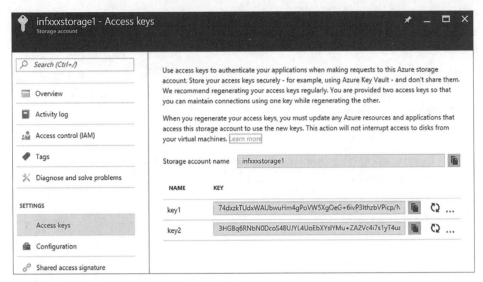

FIGURE 5-20 Storage account in Azure portal

In the above example, the storage account name is infxxxstorage1. The access key is the string that begins with the numbers 74. To configure the quorum witness by using PowerShell, use the Set-ClusterQuorum cmdlet. For example, using the same information, run the following command.

```
Set-ClusterQuorum –CloudWitness –AccountName infxxxstorage1 –AccessKey 74dxzkTUdxWAUbwuH
m4gPoVW5XgOeG+6ivP3lthzbVPicp/NEK6ivjGdA1J0oVcUuNRfLtaeYQ6WHZSwzq3/9Q==
```

Figure 5-21 shows the successful result of running the command.

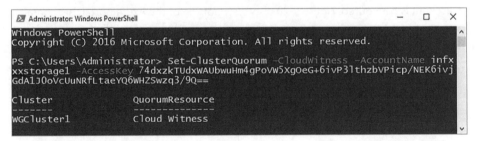

FIGURE 5-21 Set-ClusterQuorum command

Configure cluster networking

After configuring the cluster and adding the nodes, the Failover Cluster Manager automatically detects the networks that are available on the nodes. Figure 5-22 shows the default configuration after adding two hosts to the cluster, with each host having access to the same two networks.

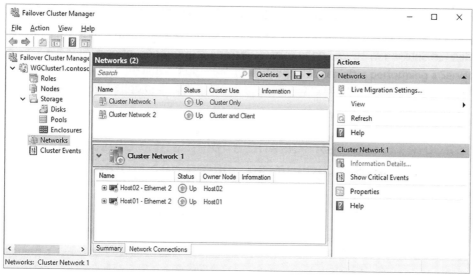

FIGURE 5-22 Failover Cluster Manager Networks

Each network can be configured to either allow or prevent cluster network communications. This communication is for cluster operations, and does not include any client traffic. For client connectivity, a network must specifically be granted as client use. Figure 5-23 shows the properties of a cluster network, with both options enabled.

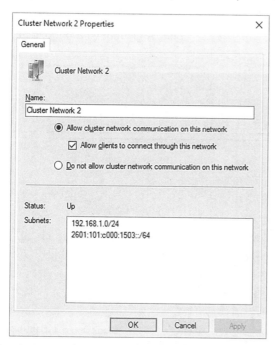

FIGURE 5-23 Cluster Network Properties

Restore single node or cluster configuration

Performing a restore on a single node in a cluster, or entire cluster configuration, is no different than performing a backup and restore of any service or component on a Windows Server. Combining a failover cluster and Windows Backup scenario for an item on the exam seems unlikely; but you can prepare by understanding the default backup options within Windows Server 2016.

Configure cluster storage and implement a Clustered Storage Spaces solution using Shared SAS storage enclosures

There are three different types of storage that can be configured with failover clustering:

- **Disks** Disks that are shared between nodes can be added to a Cluster Shared Volume or assigned to a specific failover cluster role.

- **Pools** Groups of disks that are combined logically to create a single volume. Clustered pools use the underlying Storage Spaces technology to create a virtual disk using the group of physical disks on the node.

- **Enclosures** Direct-attached disk chassis that contain multiple physical disks.

You should validate the configuration of the cluster before attempting to configure storage. This ensures that the cluster is configured and can support clustered storage across all nodes. As an example, we create a storage pool for the cluster. From the Failover Cluster Manager on the Pools screen, click the New Storage Pool. Figure 5-24 shows the New Storage Pool Wizard.

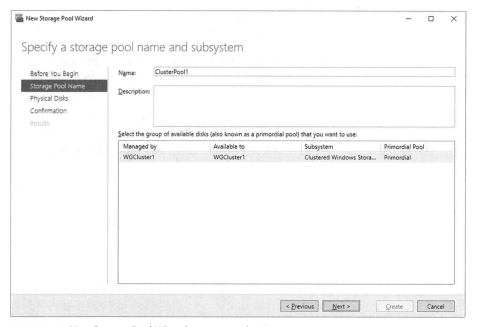

FIGURE 5-24 New Storage Pool Wizard storage pool name

Then, you are prompted to select the disks to use for the storage pool. You need at least three disks to create a storage pool for use with failover clustering. Figure 5-25 shows the available disks for the storage pool.

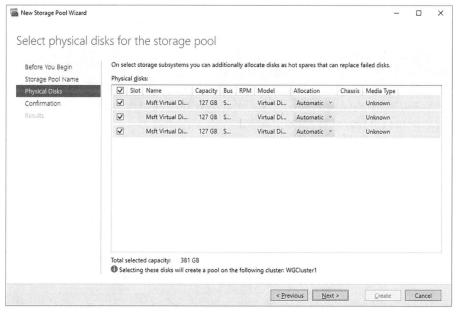

FIGURE 5-25 New Storage Pool Wizard physical disks

Implement Cluster-Aware Updating

Cluster-Aware Updating (CAU) was introduced in Windows Server 2012 to reduce the effort and difficulty of performing software updates on cluster nodes. CAU has not been updated significantly for Windows Server 2016. To use CAU, the cluster must be joined to an Active Directory domain. CAU is not available on workgroup clusters.

Performing Windows Updates typically requires a system reboot after performing the update. CAU helps to automate the process of performing the updates for all nodes that are in a cluster. Figure 5-26 shows the CAU tool for a cluster named WGCluster1. Neither node in the cluster has been updated.

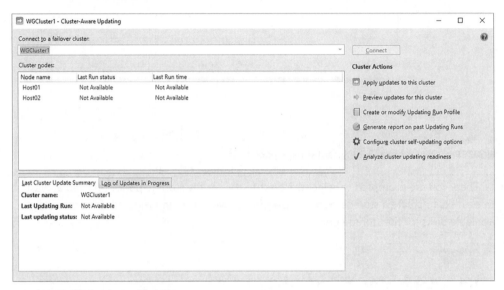

FIGURE 5-26 Cluster-Aware Updating

You cannot apply updates without enabling the CAU self-updating role. To enable the role, configure the self-updating options from the CAU screen. Figure 5-27 shows the first configuration screen of the self-updating options wizard.

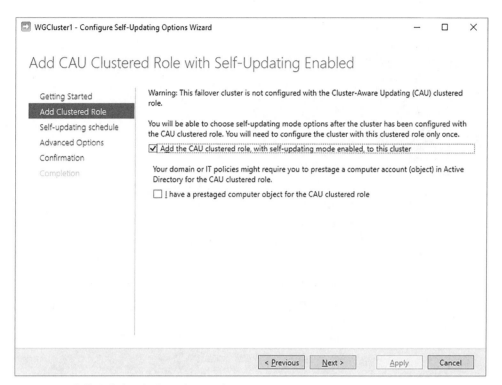

FIGURE 5-27 Self-Updating Options cluster role

After selecting the option to enable the role, you can configure the schedule to perform the self-updating process. Then you can configure advanced options for the cluster. The advanced options enable you to configure time boundaries, retry limits, and pre and post update scripts that must also be run when updating. Figure 5-28 shows a portion of the advanced options that are available.

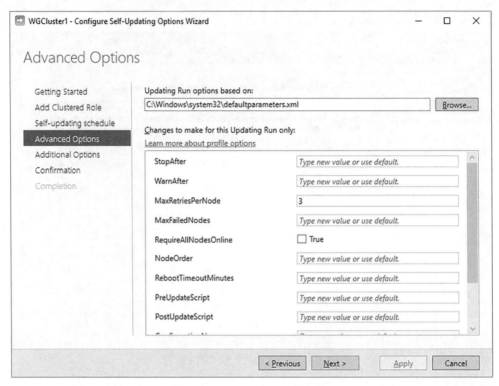

FIGURE 5-28 Self-Updating Options advanced options

By default, only important updates are installed based on the CAU tool. An additional option is to also include the recommended updates on the cluster. After applying the self-updating options, the cluster can be updated by using CAU.

Implement Cluster Operating System Rolling Upgrade

Cluster Operating System Rolling Upgrade is a new feature in failover clustering for Windows Server 2016. If a Windows Server 2012 R2 failover cluster is running the Hyper-V or Scale-Out File Server roles, you can add Windows Server 2016 nodes without taking the failover cluster offline.

For each node in the cluster, follow the process to upgrade the operating system in the correct phase. This ensures that the cluster does not require downtime to complete the upgrade. The overall steps to perform the upgrade include:

1. Pause the node and drain all virtual machines, if necessary.

2. Ensure that all virtual machines are migrated to another node in the cluster.

3. Suspend and evict the node from the cluster.

4. Install Windows Server 2016 on the node and add it to the cluster.

5. Repeat steps 1-4 for each node in the cluster.

6. After all nodes have been upgraded, run the Update-ClusterFunctionalLevel cmdlet.

Until the Update-ClusterFunctionalLevel cmdlet is run, the process can be suspended or reversed. You can also add Windows Server 2012 R2 hosts until the functional level has been updated. To retrieve the current functional level, run the Get-Cluster cmdlet.

```
Get-Cluster | Select ClusterFunctionalLevel
```

If the ClusterFunctionalLevel value is set to 8, then the cluster is at Windows Server 2012 R2. If the value is 9, then the cluster is at Windows Server 2016. It is also recommended that you disable Cluster-Aware Updating before attempting to perform za Rolling Operating System Upgrade. While the name implies upgrading the operating system, a best practice is to perform a clean installation of the operating system. An in-place upgrade is not recommended for cluster nodes.

Configure and optimize clustered shared volumes (CSVs)

CSVs were introduced in Windows Server 2008 R2 and have become a widely used featured of failover clusters. CSVs can be clustered VHDs for Hyper-V VMs, or scale-out file shares using the Scale-Out File Server (SoFS) clustered role. NTFS and Resilient File System (ReFS) can be used for VMs, however, ReFS is not supported with SoFS.

CSVs can be created from a cluster-available disks in the nodes of the cluster. You can either use the wizard in the Failover Cluster Manager, or by using Windows PowerShell. To retrieve a list of disks that can be used in a cluster, run the Get-ClusterAvailableDisk cmdlet. To add the disks, run the Add-ClusterDisk cmdlet. You can combine these two into a single command:

```
Get-ClusterAvailableDisk | Add-ClusterDisk
```

After you have added the available disks, create a CSV by using the Add-ClusterSharedVolume cmdlet.

```
Add-ClusterSharedVolume -Name "CSV1"
```

Configure clusters without network names

A failover cluster without a network name is simply an Active Directory-detached cluster. However, this is different than a workgroup cluster, where the nodes are not joined to a domain. For an Active Directory-detached cluster, the nodes must be joined to a domain. As with a workgroup cluster, the administrative access point is also DNS. Without Active Directory, the failover cluster uses NTLM as the authentication method, and not Kerberos.

You can create an Active Directory-detached cluster by using the New-Cluster Windows cmdlet, not the Failover Cluster Manager. For example:

```
New-Cluster Cluster1 -Node Server1,Server2 -StaticAddress 10.0.0.10 -NoStorage
-AdministrativeAccessPoint Dns
```

Implement Scale-Out File Server (SoFS)

SoFS is a subset of the File Server role when configuring a failover cluster. SoFS requires that CSVs be configured for storage. SoFS is useful for high-performance applications that need access to data across any node. Figure 5-29 shows adding the SoFS role to a failover cluster.

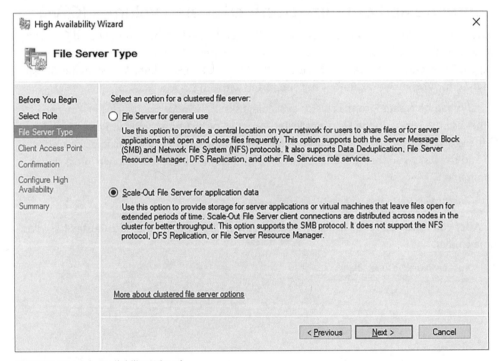

FIGURE 5-29 High Availability Wizard

Determine different scenarios for the use of SoFS vs. clustered File Server

SoFS is not designed for use in a general purpose file share environment. SoFS is designed for applications that keep files open for long periods of time, and require additional resources to process and change those files. SoFS distributes client connections across all nodes in the cluster to enhance performance, and can increase complexity and trouble-shooting for general file shares. Additionally, SoFS only use CSVs as storage, and cannot use individual disks. SoFS is not compatible with other file share technologies, including deduplication, DFS, and BranchCache.

Determine usage scenarios for implementing guest clustering

With advances in pass-through technologies in Hyper-V, guest clustering isn't as complex with Windows Server 2016. A guest cluster is a failover cluster that is created using VMs instead of physical hosts. However, Hyper-V offers virtual SAN connectivity, so clustering storage and networking using VMs can be performed the same as if using physical hosts.

Implement Storage Replica

As discussed in Chapter 2, Storage Replica can be used for block-level replication between servers or clusters for disaster recovery. You can also use Storage Replica to stretch a failover cluster between sites. You can use synchronous replication to enable crash-consistent volumes, or use asynchronous replication for longer distance or lower latency connections.

With failover clusters, Storage Replica can be used to replicate data from one cluster to another, or stretch a cluster across different sites. With cluster to cluster replication, you grant Storage Replica access on the cluster name instead of individual nodes. For example:

```
Grant-SRAccess -ComputerName SR-SRV01 -Cluster SR-SRVCLUSB
```

```
Figure 5-30 shows a cluster to cluster Storage Replica.
```

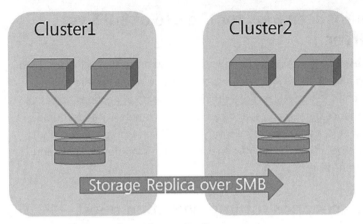

FIGURE 5-30 Cluster to cluster Storage Replica

NEED MORE REVIEW?

For details and instructions for using cluster to cluster Storage Replica, visit *https://technet. microsoft.com/en-us/windows-server-docs/storage/storage-replica/cluster-to-cluster-storage-replication*.

You can also use Storage Replica in a stretch cluster. A stretch cluster is a single failover cluster that is spanned across multiple sites. However, with Storage Replica, the sites use different physical storage for each site. Storage Replica ensures that the data is mirrored between sites.

NEED MORE REVIEW?

For details and instructions for using a stretch cluster with Storage Replica, visit *https:// technet.microsoft.com/en-us/windows-server-docs/storage/storage-replica/stretch-cluster-replication-using-shared-storage*.

Figure 5-31 shows a stretch cluster used with Storage Replica.

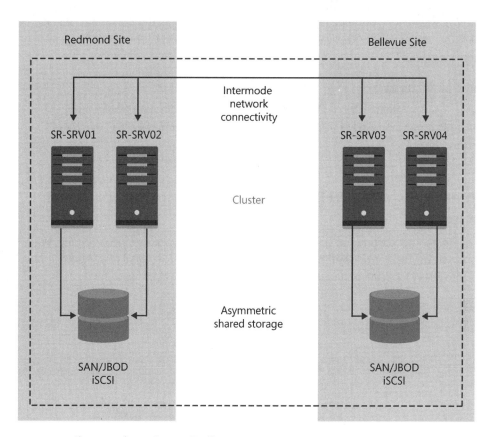

FIGURE 5-31 Cluster to cluster Storage Replica

Implement VM resiliency

Windows Server 2016 includes increased resiliency with Hyper-V failover clusters. There are two primary resiliency enhancements:

- **Compute resiliency** There are additional options that can be configured for Hyper-V VMs that help to reduce intra-cluster communication.
- **Storage resiliency** VMs are more resilient to transient storage failures.

New options for compute resiliency include:

- **Resiliency level** Defines how failures are handled.
- **Resiliency period** Defines how long VMs can run when they are isolated.

You can also configure quarantines for nodes that are deemed unhealthy. These nodes cannot join a cluster, and prevents nodes from affecting other nodes in the cluster.

If a VM experiences a storage failure to the underlying storage, the VM pauses. When paused, the VM retains the application context for any existing I/O. When the storage recovers and is presented again to the VM, the VM recovers and returns to a running state.

> **NEED MORE REVIEW?**
>
> For more information on VM resiliency with failover clusters, visit *https://blogs.msdn. microsoft.com/clustering/2015/06/03/virtual-machine-compute-resiliency-in-windows-server-2016/.*

Implement shared VHDX as a storage solution for guest clusters

Another method of configuring storage for virtualized clusters is to use VHDX sharing. Windows Server 2012 R2 introduced the ability to enable sharing on a virtual disk. Figure 5-32 shows the ability to create a shared drive from the settings of a VM.

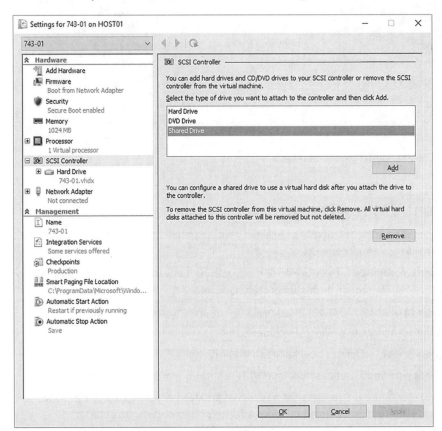

FIGURE 5-32 Creating a shared drive

In Windows Server 2012, sharing was an advanced option of a VHDX file. In Windows Server 2016, a shared drive uses a VHDS file format, and can be shared among virtual machines. VHDS file can only be fixed or dynamically expanding, and cannot be a differencing disk. Figure 5-33 shows creating a VHD Set by using the New Virtual Hard Disk Wizard.

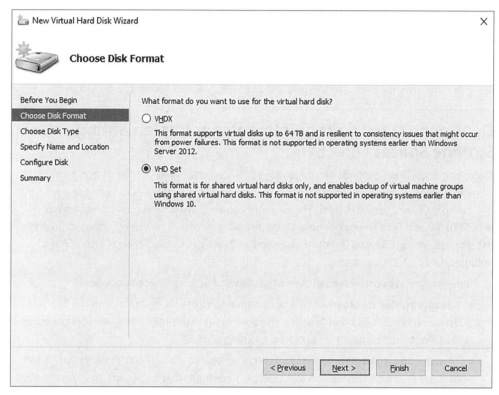

FIGURE 5-33 Creating a shared drive

The shared storage can be added to multiple virtual machines, enabling you to create a virtualized cluster without exposing any underlying storage.

Skill 5.3: Implement Storage Spaces Direct

This section covers how to:

- Determine scenario requirements for implementing Storage Spaces Direct
- Enable Storage Spaces direct using Windows PowerShell
- Implement a disaggregated Storage Spaces Direct scenario in a cluster
- Implement a hyper-converged Storage Spaces Direct scenario in a cluster

Determine scenario requirements for implementing Storage Spaces Direct

Storage Spaces Direct expands on the existing Storage Spaces technology of using local storage for high availability and scalability. Storage Spaces Direct does not require any shared SAS or Fibre Channel environment. The network connectivity between the servers are used with SMB 3.0 and SMB Direct (Remote Direct Memory Access) to efficiently connect to and use storage. Storage Spaces Direct can be used with Scale-Out File Server, Cluster Shared Volumes, and Failover Clustering.

There are two supported scenarios in which Storage Spaces Direct can be used:

- **Disaggregated deployment**   The commuting cluster is separate from the Storage Spaces Direct servers that host the storage. Virtual Machines storage is configured on a Scale-out File Server, and is accessed by using SMB 3.0.
- **Hyper-converged deployment**   The compute and storage components are stored and use the same cluster. The VM storage is configured as local storage using the Cluster Shared Volumes, and a Scale-Out File Server is not necessary.

Enable Storage Spaces Direct using Windows PowerShell

The disks that you plan to use with Storage Spaces Direct must not have any partitions or data already existing on them. If any partitions or data already exist, the data is not included with Storage Spaces Direct. Enabling Storage Spaces Direct is accomplished by running a single command:

```
Enable-ClusterStorageSpacesDirect -CimSession Cluster1
```

By running the command, Storage Spaces Direct automatically performs a few tasks:

1. Create a storage pool using the available disks.

2. Configure a cache, if necessary. This is only used if there is more than one media type available.

3. Create two tiers. The first tier is named Capacity. The second tier is named Performance. The tiers are configured with a mix of device types and resiliency.

Other PowerShell cmdlets that can be used with Storage Spaces Direct include:

- **Test-Cluster**   This tests the suitability of a configuration.

- **Enable-ClusterS2D**   Configures a cluster for the Storage Spaces Direct using local SATA or NVMe devices.

- **Optimize-StoragePool**   Rebalances the storage optimization if the underlying storage changes.

- **Debug-StorageSubsystem**   Displays any faults that can affect the storage.

Implement a disaggregated Storage Spaces Direct scenario in a cluster

As discussed in the earlier section, "Determine scenario requirements for implementing Storage Spaces Direct," a disaggregated scenario is simply a separation of the storage environment from the computing environment. In this scenario, you would configure the Hyper-V Failover Cluster as usual. Then configure the Storage Spaces environment on a separate cluster of servers. Figure 5-34 illustrates this separation of roles.

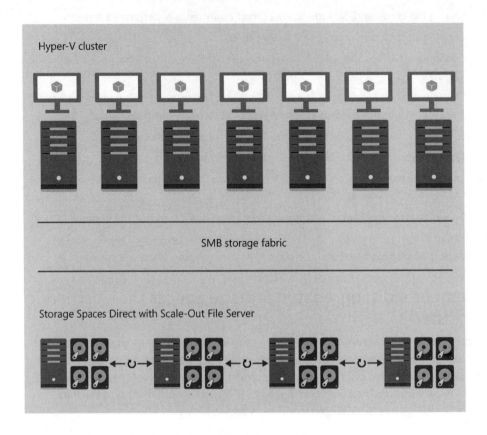

FIGURE 5-34 Disaggregated Storage Spaces Direct deployment

Implement a hyper-converged Storage Spaces Direct scenario in a cluster

As discussed in the earlier section, "Determine scenario requirements for implementing Storage Spaces Direct," a hyper-converged scenario is the combination of the computing and storage environment into the same cluster of servers. This deployment type eliminates the need for a Scale-Out File Server. Figure 5-35 shows a hyper-converged deployment scenario.

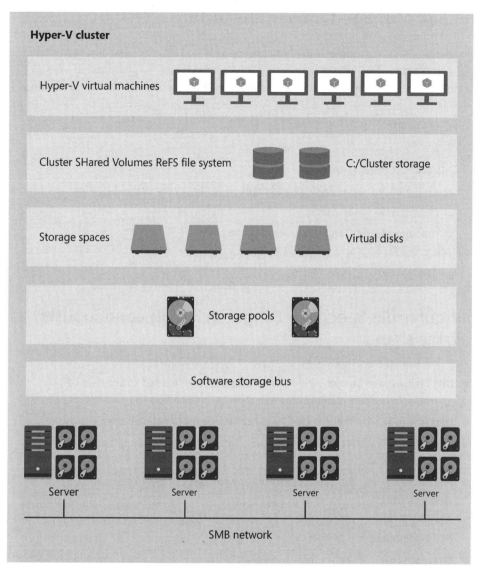

FIGURE 5-35 Hyper-converged Storage Spaces Direct deployment

NEED MORE REVIEW?

For a step-by-step of using a hyper-converged deployment of Storage Spaces Direct, visit *https://technet.microsoft.com/en-us/windows-server-docs/storage/storage-spaces/hyper-converged-solution-using-storage-spaces-direct.*

Skill 5.4: Manage failover clustering

In this section, we discuss some of the basics to monitor and manage a failover cluster after it has been created. This includes configuring roles on the cluster and monitoring VMs that run in the cluster. Then, we cover how to configure failover, preference, and startup settings for services and roles in the cluster. Finally, we discuss site-aware failover clusters, and how to configure preferred clusters and groups for clusters.

> **This section covers how to:**
> - Configure role-specific settings, including continuously available shares
> - Configure VM monitoring
> - Configure failover and preference settings
> - Implement stretch and site-aware failover clusters
> - Enable and configure node fairness

Configure role-specific settings, including continuously available shares

There are several roles that can be configured by using Failover Cluster:

- **DFS Namespace Server**   Provides an alias that can be used to access a DFS namespace. The DFS Namespaces role must be installed on the nodes in the cluster.
- **DHCP Server**   Enables the DHCP service to failover between nodes in a cluster.
- **Distributed Transaction Coordinator**   Supports distribution of applications that perform transactions.
- **File Server**   Provides a central location where files can be accessed through the failover cluster.
- **Generic application**   Provides high availability for applications that are not typically designed to run in a cluster.
- **Generic script**   Provides high availability for a script that runs in the Windows Script Host.
- **Generic service**   Provides high availability for a service that is not typically designed to run in a cluster.
- **Hyper-V Replica Broker**   Enables the failover cluster to participate in replication with Hyper-V.

- **iSCSI Target Server**   Provides SCSI storage over TCP/IP in the failover cluster.
- **iSNS Server**   An Internet Storage Name Service server that provides discovery of iSCSI Targets.
- **Message Queuing**   Enables distributed applications running at different times to communicate across networks.
- **Other server**   Provides a client access point and storage only.
- **Virtual Machine**   Enables VMs that are running on a physical host.
- **WINS server**   Enables users to access resources by using NetBIOS names.

You can combine file servers running in a failover cluster with the SMB 3 protocol to provide continuously available file shares to an environment. SMB 3 provides several benefits, including:

- **SMB Transparent Failover**   Enables a file share to be continuously available with SMB 3 clients. When a failover occurs, the SMB 3 client refreshes the connection to another node in the cluster.
- **SMB Scale-out**   Enables additional bandwidth to be used by multiple cluster nodes.
- **SMB Multichannel**   Uses multiple network interfaces to increase the performance of the SMB connection.

Configure VM monitoring

VMs that are configured in a failover cluster can have the VM itself as well as applications in the VM monitored by the Hyper-V host. The guest VM and the Hyper-V host must either belong to the same domain, or have a trust relationship configured between domains. The pre-defined Virtual Machine Monitoring rules must also be enabled on the VM. Figure 5-36 shows the rules that must be enabled. These rules include:

- Virtual Machine Monitoring (DCOM-In)
- Virtual Machine Monitoring (Echo Request – ICMPv4-In)
- Virtual Machine Monitoring (Echo Request – ICMPv6-In)
- Virtual Machine Monitoring (NB-Session-In)
- Virtual Machine Monitoring (RPC)

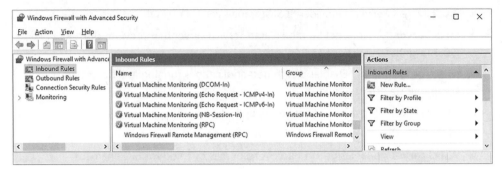

FIGURE 5-36 Windows Firewall Inbound Rules

After you have modified the firewall, you can configure monitoring for the VM from the Failover Cluster Manager. Right-click a VM, and in the More Actions menu, click Configure Monitoring. You are prompted with a list of services that exist on the VM.

After selecting the service to monitor, you can also configure recovery settings for the service. By default, the first two times a service fails, the failover cluster attempts to restart the service. If the service fails to start, then a failover would be performed. Therefore, if you need to immediately failover (rather than try to wait for the service to restart), you need to change the first recovery action to *Take No Action*. This ensures that the VM failovers, as the monitored service is considered down.

Configure failover and preference settings

You can modify the properties of a role to assign settings for a role, as shown in Figure 5-37.

- **Preferred owners** The ordered list of nodes that attempt to handle client requests or moves.

- **Start-up priority** In the event of a failure, you can assign Low, Medium, High, or No Auto Start for a role. If No Auto Start is configured, the role is failed over after all other roles, but is not automatically started. By default, all roles have a Medium priority.

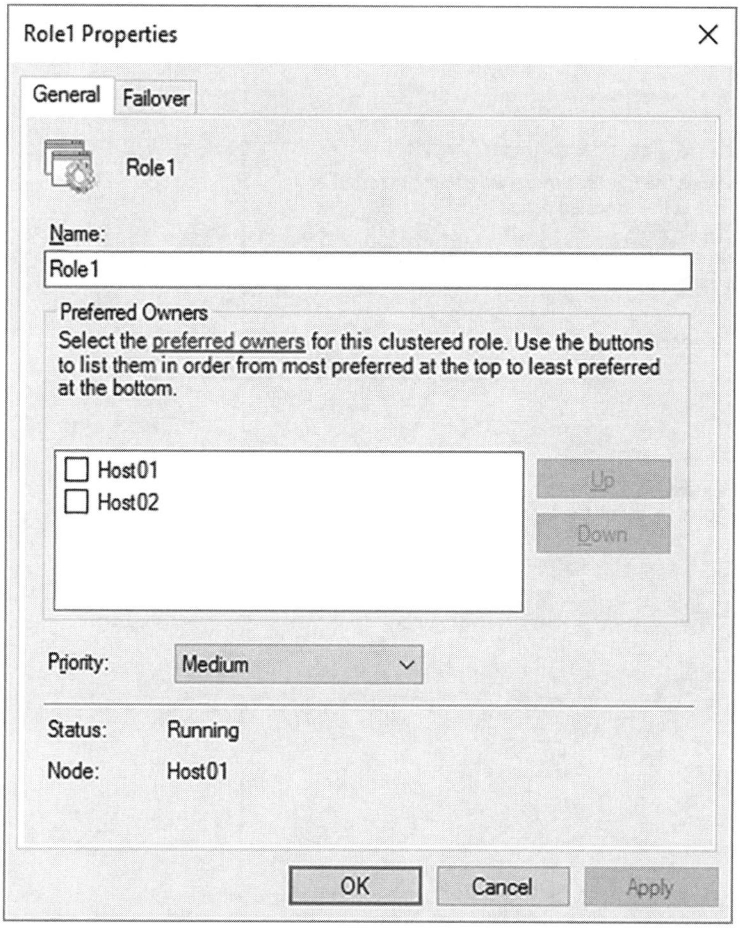

FIGURE 5-37 Role general properties

You can also control the number of times that the failover cluster service tries to restart or failover a role. These settings can be configured from the Failover tab, as shown in Figure 5-38.

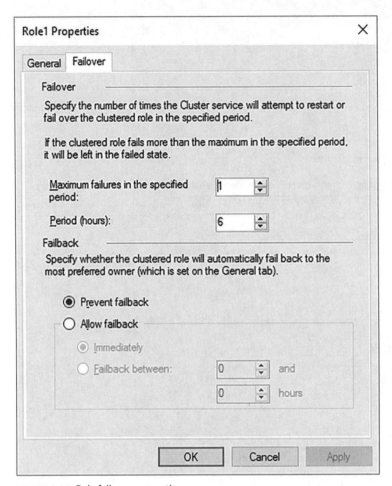

FIGURE 5-38 Role failover properties

Windows Server 2016 also introduces the ability to control the start order of VMs. VMs can be grouped into tiers, which can be used to define dependencies for starting order. This ensures that more important virtual machines are started before others. For example, you can configure all domain controllers to start first.

Implement stretch and site-aware failover clusters

We discussed using a stretch cluster earlier in the "Storage Replica" section. However, using a site-aware failover is new to Windows Server 2016. A site-aware failover cluster builds on a stretch cluster, where nodes in the same cluster are not in the same physical site. Site-awareness gives the cluster the ability to better control failovers, placement, heartbeats between nodes, and quorum.

A new configuration option is to control the cross-site heartbeat. These thresholds can be configured by modifying new cluster properties:

- **CrossSiteDelay** This property is set to 1,000 by default, and defines the amount of time in milliseconds that a heartbeat is sent to nodes across sites.
- **CrossSiteThreshold** This property is set to 20 by default, and defines the number of heartbeats that can be missed before the interface is considered to be down.
- **PreferredSite** The site that is assigned to a role for placement. The nodes of the site must first be assigned to the site before it can be set to preferred. During a cold start, VMs are also placed in the preferred site. The preferred site is also elected to be the active site in the event of a split quorum. The `LowerQuorumPriorityNodeID` property is deprecated with Windows Server 2016.

Preferred sites can also be configured more granularly by using cluster groups. This enables you to control site placement on a group basis, in addition to the cluster. Groups in a cluster are placed based on the following priority order:

1. Storage affinity site
2. Group preferred site
3. Cluster preferred site

Enable and configure node fairness

VM node fairness is another new feature in Windows Server 2016. Node fairness enables load balancing between nodes in a cluster. Nodes that are overcommitted are identified based on virtual machine memory and processor use in the node. VMs are then automatically migrated to nodes that are not as heavily used, if available. The threshold of the load balancing can be configured and tuned to ensure the best cluster performance. By default, node fairness is enabled in a Windows Server 2016 failover cluster; but is disabled when System Center Virtual Machine Manager Dynamic Optimization is enabled.

Skill 5.5: Manage VM movement in clustered nodes

This section covers the basic operations that are used when managing a failover cluster. This includes performing a live, quick, or storage migration of a virtual machine. It also includes importing, exporting, and copying these VMs. Finally, VM health protection and draining a node on shutdown are also discussed. These topics are covered briefly, as they do not introduce anything new in Windows Server 2016.

> **This section covers how to:**
> - Perform live migration
> - Perform quick migration
> - Perform storage migration
> - Import, export, and copy VMs
> - Configure VM network health protection
> - Configure drain on shutdown

Perform live migration

Performing a live migration is similar to performing a move through the Hyper-V Manager. In the context of a failover cluster, a live migration copies the running memory of a VM to the destination node before committing the migration. When using CSVs, the migration is almost instant, as no transfer of disk ownership is necessary. A live migration can be used in a planned maintenance or transfer, but not as an unplanned failover. To perform a live migration, you must enable the feature from the Hyper-V settings, as discussed earlier in this chapter.

Perform quick migration

As with a live migration, a quick migration copies the running memory of a VM. However, that memory is saved to disk rather than being transferred to the destination node. This still provides for a fast migration, but again cannot be used for an unplanned failover.

Perform storage migration

A storage migration copies the physical data from the node that currently owns the data to the destination node. The time that it takes to complete the migration depends on the size of the VM, and the storage connectivity method for the nodes.

Import, export, and copy VMs

Importing, exporting, and copying VMs are methods of manually transferring a VM from one node to another. Exporting a VM consolidates the VM into the files that are specified during the export process. They can then be copied and imported to a different node.

Configure VM network health protection

Windows Server 2012 R2 introduced a new option named Protected Network in the advanced settings of VM network adapters. Configuring a protected network is useful to protect a highly available VM from a failed network connection. With the protected network option enabled, the physical node monitors the network for disruptions. If the network connection goes down, then the VM is migrated to another physical node that has a working network connection.

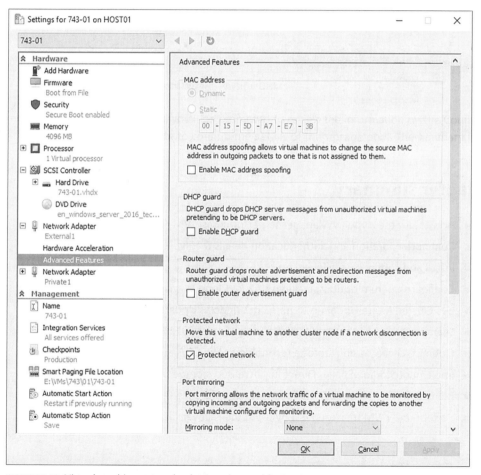

FIGURE 5-39 Virtual machine network adapter advanced features

Configure drain on shutdown

Drain on shutdown is a necessary process to efficiently suspend a node. When a node is active, there can be several connections to the roles that operate on the node. By setting a node to drain, a node does not respond to any future requests in the cluster. Therefore, as existing connections complete or drop, the node is essentially removed from a cluster without affecting any existing, or future, connections.

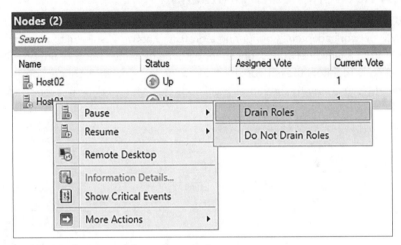

FIGURE 5-40 Draining a failover cluster node

Chapter summary

- How to use the Hyper-V Manager to perform basic VM management
- Configure migration and authentication details for Hyper-V servers
- Install and configure a failover cluster
- Configure quorum options, including Azure Cloud Witness
- Use Cluster-Aware Updating to perform Windows Updates
- Seamlessly upgrade clusters from Windows Server 2012 R2 to Windows Server 2016
- Optimize clusters using storage technologies like CSVs and Storage Replica
- Implement Storage Spaces Direct for increased storage performance
- Manage failover clusters using failover and preference settings
- Perform basic VM management by using the Failover Cluster Manager.

Thought Experiment

A company currently has a single site with two standalone Hyper-V hosts. Each Hyper-V host is connected to an external iSCSI enclosure. The storage enclosure stores the data for all virtual machines that the hosts run.

The company plans to open an additional office in the same city. As part of the plan, the secondary office should be used with active connections, and serve as a backup if the primary office experiences a failure. Both offices should use a third site to determine which site is primary in the event of a failure. If the third site is unavailable from both offices, the original primary should accept the active client requests.

Using the above scenario, answer the following questions.

1. What should be deployed in the primary office to accomplish the goal?
2. What should be deployed in the secondary office to accomplish the goal?
3. What technology should be used to ensure the secondary office maintains the latest available data?
4. What technology should be used to ensure only one site is active in the event of a failure?
5. What should be configured to ensure that the primary site is used in the event of a third-site failure?

Thought Experiment Answers

1. The two Hyper-V servers should be placed in a failover cluster.
2. Two Hyper-V servers should be deployed as part of the same failover cluster, to service active requests when online.
3. Storage Replica should be used to synchronously transfer data from the primary office to the secondary, and back again if necessary.
4. A cloud witness should be configured to ensure a site is always active in the event of a failure.
5. The primary site should be configured as the preferred site to ensure it is active in the event the cloud witness is unavailable.

CHAPTER 6

Implement DNS

This chapter covers one skill that is represented on the exam, implementing and configuring DNS servers. There are a few new technologies introduced in Windows Server 2016 for DNS servers:

- **DNS Policies** Policies can be created to specify how DNS servers respond to client requests.

- **Response Rate Limiting** Mitigates denial of service attacks on DNS.

- **DNS-based Authentication of Named Entities** Uses Transport Layer Security Authentication to inform clients to expect a certificate from a Certification Authority for the DNS zone.

- **Unknown record support** Add records that are not explicitly supported by Windows Server DNS.

- **IPv6 root hints** Native IPv6 root hints have been added to DNS.

We discuss these new technologies and review key technologies that already exist for DNS in this chapter.

Skills in this chapter:

- Implement and configure DNS servers

Implement and configure DNS servers

This section explains how DNS is used in a Windows Server environment. DNS has several components that include forwarders, root hints, policies, logging, and more. Each of these components are discussed, including how to configure the options for a typical enterprise environment.

This section covers how to:

- Determine DNS installation requirements
- Determine supported DNS deployment scenarios on Nano Server
- Install DNS
- Configure forwarders
- Configure Root Hints
- Configure delegation
- Implement DNS policies
- Configure Domain Name System Security Extensions
- Configure DNS Socket Pool
- Configure cache locking
- Enable Response Rate Limiting
- Configure DNS-based Authentication of Named Entities
- Configure DNS logging
- Configure delegated administration
- Configure recursion settings
- Implement DNS performance tuning
- Configure global settings using Windows PowerShell

Determine DNS installation requirements

The DNS server role can be installed on any edition or version of Windows Server, including Nano Server. There are two primary use cases for running DNS on a Windows Server:

- **Active Directory integration**   Active Directory Domain Services requires a DNS server for the directory to function properly. Once integrated, the DNS zones that are configured on the server can be stored in Active Directory for increased security.
- **DNS and DHCP integration**   You can enable DNS records to be updated automatically when devices join the network for the first time, or if a device changes on the network. This works independently of Active Directory.

Determine supported DNS deployment scenarios on Nano Server

DNS can be installed on Nano Server, and offers the same features, security, and functionality as installing it on Server Core or graphical versions of Windows Server. The only difference in using Nano Server is the management of the server role after it has been deployed.

After deploying DNS on a Nano Server, you can manage it by using Windows PowerShell remoting. Create a new session with the Nano Server by running the Enter-PSSession cmdlet.

```
Enter-PSSession -ComputerName "Nano1"
```

After connecting remotely to the Nano Server, you can import the PowerShell module for DNS by running the Import-Module cmdlet.

```
Import-Module DNSServer
```

You can then run any DNS PowerShell cmdlet on the Nano Server. Alternatively, you can run the DNS Manager from a separate management computer, and connect to the DNS service that is running on the Nano Server. This gives you the ability to manage the DNS service through the DNS Manager console as if it was installed on a server with a graphical interface.

Install DNS

DNS can be installed by using the Add Roles and Features Wizard through Server Manager, or by using Windows PowerShell with the Install-WindowsFeature cmdlet.

```
Install-WindowsFeature DNS
```

If adding the package to Nano Server, the package would be installed by using the Install-NanoServerPackage cmdlet.

```
Install-NanoServerPackage -Package Microsoft-NanoServer-DNS-Package
```

Configure forwarders

When a DNS server receives a request to translate a domain name that it does not know, a forwarder is used to transfer the request to another DNS server. DNS forwarders use recursive queries as the list of forwarders are processed. A recursive query either accepts a record that is provided, or displays an error if the record cannot be found. Forwarders do not accept referrals to other DNS servers. The next DNS server could be a different DNS server within a corporate network, the ISP, or a public DNS server. Figure 6-1 shows the Forwarders configured for a DNS server, using Verisign and OpenDNS public servers, respectively.

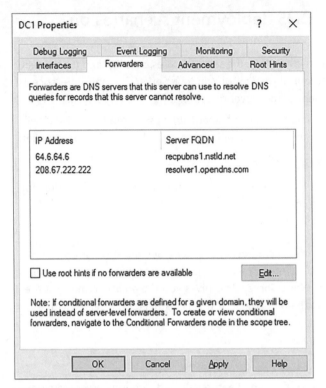

FIGURE 6-1 DNS Forwarders

An option shown in Figure 6-1 for forwarders is the Use Root Hints If No Forwarders Are Available. This uses any configured root hints if the forwarders that have been configured are not available. By default, this option is disabled. From the GUI, forwarders are managed by modifying the properties of the DNS server. However, using Windows PowerShell, forwarders have separate cmdlets. To configure a forwarder with PowerShell, use the Add-DnsServerForwarder cmdlet.

```
Add-DnsServerForwarder 8.8.8.8
```

To configure whether root hints are used if a forwarder is unavailable, run the Set-DnsServerForwarer cmdlet.

```
Set-DnsServerForwarder -UseRootHint $False
```

Conditional forwarders

Another type of forwarder is a conditional forwarder. Conditional forwarders are useful for partner organizations or other DNS domains that an organization might have access to. For example, if your organization has partnered with adatum.com, then you can configure a conditional forwarder. Rather than use the global forwarders or root hints to identify unknown resources in the domain, a conditional forwarder routes DNS requests for adatum.com to the specified server. Figure 6-2 shows creating a conditional forwarder from DNS Manager.

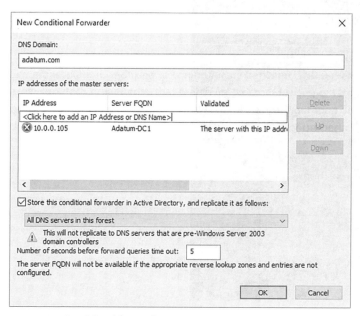

FIGURE 6-2 Conditional forwarder

After forwarders have been configured, you can verify DNS is working properly by using nslookup. The nslookup tool is a command-line utility that enables you to query specific record types using DNS. Figure 6-3 shows performing successful queries for: Microsoft.com, the local domain contosoforest.com, and the partner domain adatum.com.

If you plan to use PowerShell to create a conditional forwarder, use the Add-DnsServerConditionalForwarderZone cmdlet.

```
Add-DnsServerConditionalForwarderZone –Name adatum.com –MasterServers 10.0.0.105
```

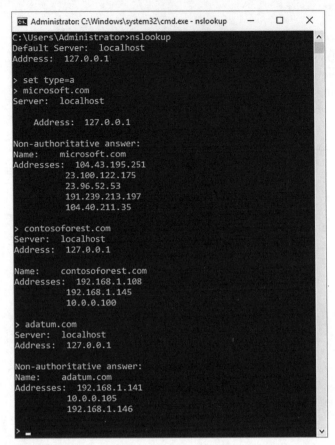

FIGURE 6-3 nslookup results

Configure root hints

Unlike forwarders which perform recursive queries, root hints perform iterative queries. If a DNS server cannot find the record for a query in the local configuration, it can query a DNS server on the internet. A root server responds with a referral to the DNS server that hosts the authoritative zone for the top-level domain (.com, .net, etc). The local server then queries the referred server for the record, which responds with another referral to the authoritative server for the DNS domain (contoso.com). The query and referral process continues until the record is successfully located, or the authoritative server says that the record does not exist.

Windows Server 2016 introduces default root hints for IPv6 queries, so that IPv6 records can be located using iterative queries just as IPv4 addresses can be. These root hints have been pushed by Internet Assigned Numbers Authority (IANA), and can be used for IPv6 queries. Figure 6-4 shows the default root hints that have been added to Windows Server 2016.

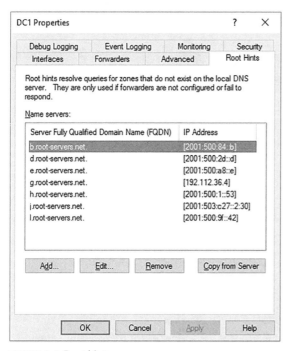

FIGURE 6-4 Root hints

Root Hints can also be retrieved or configured by using PowerShell. To retrieve the same list that the GUI displays, run the Get-DnsServerRootHint cmdlet. To add additional root hints, use the Add-DnsServerRootHint cmdlet.

```
Add-DnsServerRootHint -NameServer a.root-servers.net -IPAddress 2001:503:ba3e::2:30
```

Configure delegation

Zone delegation enables you to divide a DNS namespace into multiple zones. These additional zones can be stored and replicated to other DNS servers. This is useful if you need to delegate management for a portion of a namespace, or want to improve network distribution by dividing larger zones.

Creating a new delegation zone can be performed from DNS Manager by right-clicking the forward lookup zone that you plan to split, then click New Delegation. The New Delegation Wizard appears. The first configuration screen prompts for the domain that is delegated. For example, we specify the fully qualified domain name (FQDN) emea.contosoforest.com to be delegated as a separate domain. Figure 6-5 shows the New Delegation Wizard.

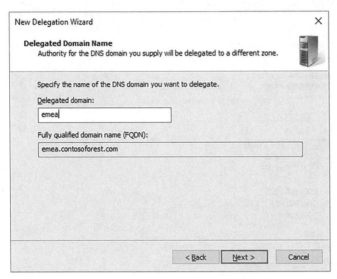

FIGURE 6-5 New Delegation Wizard

You are then prompted to enter the FQDN of the DNS server that is authoritative for the zone. You must also resolve the FQDN to the available IP addresses for that specific server. Figure 6-6 displays configuring the FQDN and associated IP addresses for delegation.

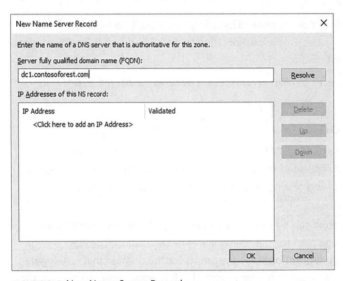

FIGURE 6-6 New Name Server Record

After you complete the wizard, the delegation zone is created in the forward lookup zone. You can also create the zone by using the Add-DnsServerZoneDelegation cmdlet.

```
Add-DnsServerZoneDelegation -Name contosoforest.com -ChildZoneName emea.contosoforest.
com -IPAddress 10.0.0.100 -NameServer DC1
```

Implement DNS policies

Windows Server 2016 introduces DNS policies to manage queries based on configurable parameters. There are a few scenarios in which DNS policies can be useful:

- **Application high availability** DNS queries are forwarded to the healthiest endpoint for an application.
- **Traffic management** Use the closest available DNS server for client queries.
- **Split-brain DNS** If DNS records are split for internal and external addresses, clients receive the appropriate response depending on their location.
- **Filtering** Manage an IP blocking list to prevent malicious queries.
- **Forensics** DNS clients that are suspected to be malicious can be redirected.
- **Time-based redirects** Provide different responses to DNS queries based on the time of day.

There are three new objects in DNS that are used to manage DNS policies:

- **Client subnet** Represents an IPv4 or IPv6 subnet where queries originate from.
- **Recursion scope** Groups of settings that control recursion for a DNS server.
- **Zone scope** Sets of DNS records for zones on the DNS server.

There are two policies that can be configured at either the zone or server level, and a single server-only level policy.

- **Query Resolution Policy** Can be applied to either a DNS server or a specific DNS zone. Query resolution policies are used to control incoming client queries and define how the DNS server handles the requests.
- **Zone Transfer Policy** Can be applied to either a DNS server or a specific DNS zone. Zone transfer policies control whether zone transfers are configured to either Deny or Ignore zone changes for a DNS topology.
- **Recursion policy** Recursion policies are only applied to the server level and control whether queries are denied or ignore recursion for the queries. You can also choose to configure a set of forwarders that are used for the queries.

The overall process to creating a policy includes first creating the objects, and then creating the policies. For example:

1. Create the subnet objects that DNS clients are connecting from.
2. Create the zone scopes and resource records for each network as needed.
3. Create a policy to manage the queries from the defined subnets.

As of this writing, policies are only configured by using PowerShell. To view the available cmdlets that can be used with policies, run the Get-Command cmdlet.

```
Get-Command -Module DNSServer *policy* | Select Name
```

The command returns a list similar to the following, which lists the cmdlets that are built-in to the DNS PowerShell module:

```
Name
----
Add-DnsServerQueryResolutionPolicy
Add-DnsServerZoneTransferPolicy
Disable-DnsServerPolicy
Enable-DnsServerPolicy
Get-DnsServerQueryResolutionPolicy
Get-DnsServerZoneTransferPolicy
Remove-DnsServerQueryResolutionPolicy
Remove-DnsServerZoneTransferPolicy
Set-DnsServerQueryResolutionPolicy
Set-DnsServerZoneTransferPolicy
```

> **NEED MORE REVIEW? CONFIGURING DNS POLICY**
>
> For details and instructions for configuring a DNS policy, visit *https://technet.microsoft.com/en-us/windows-server-docs/networking/dns/deploy/dns-policies-overview.*

Configure Domain Name System Security Extensions

The process of using DNSSEC has not changed significantly from Windows Server 2012 or Windows Server 2012 R2 to Windows Server 2016. If a zone is supported by an authoritative DNS server, you can secure the zone by using zone signing. By signing the zone with DNS-SEC, you are validating the zone without changing any of the queries or responses of DNS. To validate a DNS response, the response must include a digital signature. The signatures are contained in a DNSSEC resource record that are created during zone signing. Figure 6-7 illustrates transforming regular DNS records to using DNSSEC.

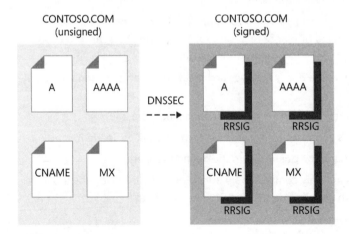

FIGURE 6-7 DNSSEC Illustration

The overall checklist to deploying DNSSEC includes:

1. Selecting a deployment method
2. Signing a DNS zone
3. Deploying trust anchors
4. Deploying DNS client policies
5. Deploy IPsec policies to protect zone transfers
6. Review and manage name resolution

Configure DNS socket pool

The DNS socket pool randomizes the source port that is used with DNS queries. In Windows Server 2008, the DNS service used a predictable source port number. When using a socket pool, the DNS server randomly selects a port number to mitigate attacks on the server. Beginning with Windows Server 2012 R2, the DNS socket pool has 2,500 random ports enabled by default and does not typically require additional configuration. To modify the number of ports, use the dnscmd utility.

```
dnscmd /Config /SocketPoolSize 3000
```

Configure cache locking

With cache locking, when a DNS server receives a query and then provides a response, the response is cached locally so that it can respond quicker to future requests. The timeout value for the cache is determined by the Time To Live (TTL) value of the DNS record that was obtained. Cache locking prevents the record from being overwritten if an update is received, until the TTL has expired. Cache locking was introduced in Windows Server 2008 R2 and has not changed significantly through to Windows Server 2016. By default, the cache locking percentage is set to 100. To modify the percentage, use dnscmd.

```
dnscmd /Config /CacheLockingPercent 90
```

Enable Response Rate Limiting (RRL)

Response Rate Limiting (RRL) is a new feature that is introduced with Windows Server 2016. RRL enables you to avoid Denial of Service (DoS) attacks on clients using the DNS server. RRL provides configuration settings to control how to respond to requests when receiving numerous requests. This mitigates a DoS attack using the DNS servers. The following settings can be configured with RRL:

- **Responses per second** The maximum number of responses a single client receives in one second.
- **Errors per second** The maximum number of errors that are sent to a single client in one second.

- **Window** The number of seconds that responses are suspended if a server blocks a client.

- **Leak rate** Determines the frequency that a DNS server responds to queries when requests are suspended. By default, if a server suspends a client for 10 seconds, the leak rate is 5. The DNS server responds to one of every five requests sent to the server.

- **TC rate** Informs the client that DNS requests have been suspended. By default, if the TC rate is 3, the server issues a request for a TCP connection for every 3 queries that are received. The TC rate should be configured lower than the leak rate to ensure that the client can connect using TCP before leaking responses.

- **Maximum responses** The maximum number of response that the server issues to clients while in a suspended state.

- **White list domains** The list of domains that are excluded from RRL settings.

- **White list subnets** The list of subnets that are excluded from RRL settings.

- **White list server interfaces** The DNS server interfaces that are excluded from RRL settings.

By default, RRL is disabled. You can either set RRL to log only the effects a configuration would have, or to enable the configuration. To enable or modify the RRL settings, use the Set-DnsServerResponseRateLimiting cmdlet. You can also use the Set-DnsServerRRL alias to reference the cmdlet.

```
Set-DnsServerRRL -Mode LogOnly
```

To create any of the white list objects, use the Add-DnsServerResponseRateLimitingExceptionList cmdlet.

```
Add-DnsServerResponseRateLimitingExceptionlist -Name "Whitelist1" -Fqdn "EQ,*.contoso.com"
```

Configure DNS-based Authentication of Named Entities

DANE is another new feature that is introduced with Windows Server 2016. DANE uses Transport Layer Security Authentication to communicate to DNS clients to expect a certificate from a Certification Authority for the DNS zone. This ensures that a man-in-the-middle attack from presenting a different certificate to successfully corrupt DNS.

For example, if the website www.contoso.com uses a certificate from a CA named TrustedCA, the DNS server would identify and save that the certificate is issued from that server. Then, if a malicious redirect occurs sending users to a different web server that presents a certificate signed from ExternalCA, the connection would be aborted. This is because by using DANE, the client is aware that the certificate that appears valid, is not actually from the CA that is trusted and registered with DNS.

Configure DNS logging

Windows Server 2016 provides enhanced DNS logging and diagnostics compared to Windows Server 2012 R2. However, when additional logging is enabled, the performance of the server can be affected. There are two primary types of logging:

- **Diagnostic logging** Provides detailed data from the DNS server for requests that are sent and received. Logs can be gathered by using packet capture tools. Recommended only for temporary use when detailed information is necessary,

- **Audit and analytic event logging** DNS Audit events are logged by default, and DNS Analytic events are not logged.

By default in Windows Server 2016, additional logging is enabled and can be viewed by using Event Viewer.

> **NEED MORE REVIEW? DNS LOGGING**
>
> For more information on DNS logging, visit *https://technet.microsoft.com/en-us/library/dn800669(v=ws.11).aspx.*

Configure delegated administration

There are three primary methods of delegating access to DNS:

- **The DnsAdmins Active Directory security group** The security group grants permission to the members of the group to manage any DNS server in an Active Directory domain.

- **Modifying the DNS server properties** If the DNS server is in a workgroup, or you plan to grant read-only permissions to some administrators, you can modify the properties of the DNS server.

- **Modifying the zone properties** Individual zones inherits the permissions from the DNS server. However, you can disable the inheritance or modify the permissions, similar to managing files and directories.

Figure 6-8 shows the default settings for the DnsAdmins security group on a DNS server.

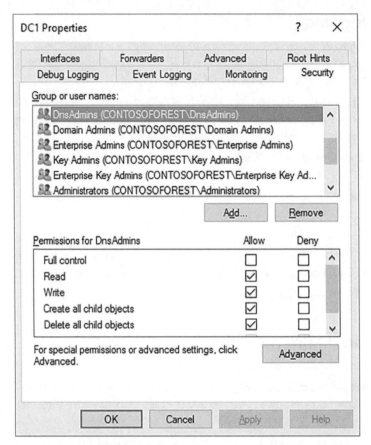

FIGURE 6-8 Server level permissions

If you need to provide junior administrators the ability to view the DNS contents of the zones, create a new security group and assign the Read permission. You could also have a separate group that can create and update DNS objects, but not delete them.

Modifying the properties of a zone is a similar process. The zone inherits the permissions that have been assigned at the server level. You can also add additional security groups that can manage the zone. Figure 6-9 shows the default properties of a forward lookup zone.

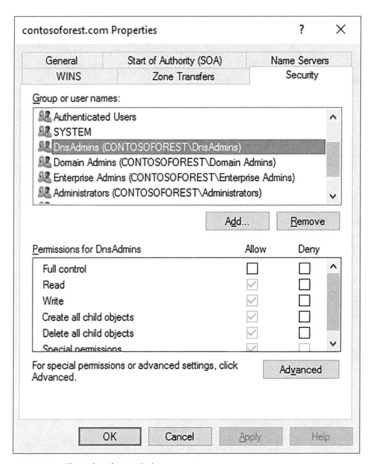

FIGURE 6-9 Zone level permissions

Configure recursion settings

As discussed in the earlier section "Configured Root Hints," recursive DNS queries use forwarders and references to identify a DNS record. By using a forwarder in DNS, the DNS server
uses recursive queries by default. This enables the server to forward the DNS request for
unknown domains to the next DNS server configured. The next server refers the request to a
different DNS server if it, too, does not have information about the record. This process could
continue a few times before locating a non-authoritative response for the request. You can
enable or disable recursion at the server level by using the Set-DnsServerRecursion cmdlet,
or by using DNS Manager. Disabling recursion should be used in limited environments, as it
can prohibit access to the Internet if not configured properly. Figure 6-10 shows the available
options on the Advanced tab, including recursion.

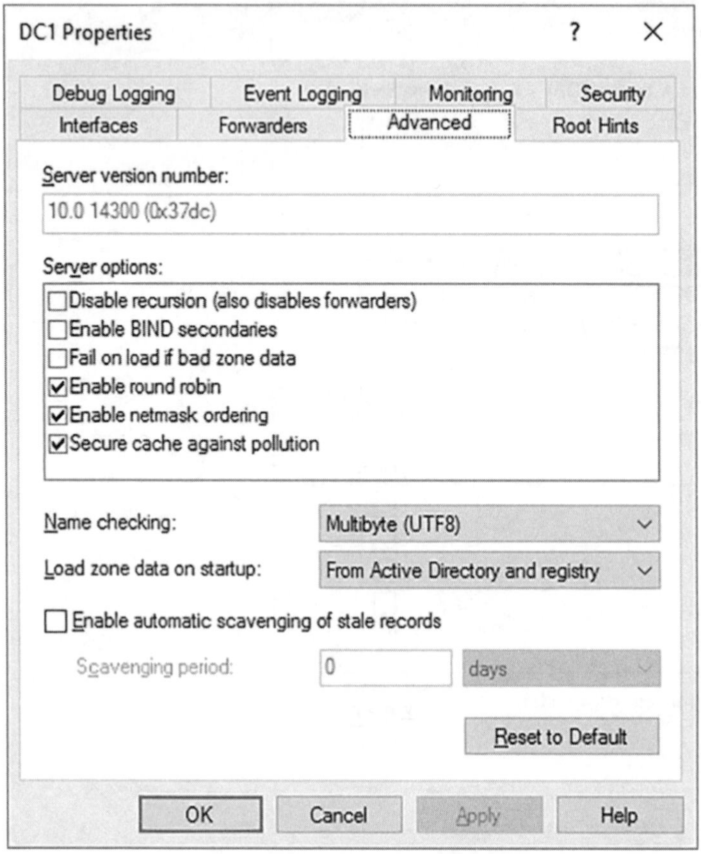

FIGURE 6-10 Advanced DNS settings

In addition to enabling or disabling recursion, the PowerShell cmdlet also lets you configure specific recursion settings. For example, the `RetryInterval` setting specifies the amount of time in seconds before a DNS server uses recursion. By default, the `RetryInterval` is set to three seconds, but can be configured with a value from 1 to 15. Another configurable parameter is the `AdditionalTimeout` setting. This specifies the number of seconds before a DNS server waits after using a recursive request to receive a response from the next DNS server. By default, this setting is set to four seconds, but accepts a value from 0 to 15.

```
Set-DnsServerRecursion -RetryInterval 2
```

Recursion can also be enabled or disabled for specified forwarders by using a recursion scope. A scope specifies a specific forwarder or forwarders to enable or disable recursion with. The Set-DnsServerRecursionScope cmdlet provides this option.

```
Set-DnsServerRecursionScope -Name "DisabledScope" -Forwarder 192.168.0.1
-EnableRecursion $False
```

Implement DNS performance tuning

Performance tuning is a relative topic, and depends on the size of the domain, the physical specifications of a server, network performance, number of requests, and more. It would be very challenging to create a question on the exam for performance that only had one correct answer, without obviously stating the problem and thus providing a clear and simple resolution. Some simple methods of increasing DNS performance could include:

- **Modifying firewall properties** Ensure that UDP port 53 is allowed on each DNS server and has local only mapping enabled.

- **Increase the number of logical cores** The DNS service creates threads based on the total number of logical cores that are on the server. For a virtual machine, provide the maximum number of logical cores.

- **Set the UDP receive thread count to 8** Modify the UdpRecvThreadCount DWORD parameter that is located at HKEY_LOCAL_MACHINE\SYSTEM\CurrentControlSet\Services\DNS\Parameters to ensure that all logical threads are used.

- **Maximize network adapter buffers** Set the receive buffers to "Maximum" by using the Set-NetAdapterAdvancedProperty cmdlet.

> *NEED MORE REVIEW?* **SOME DNS PERFORMANCE**
>
> The Windows Server Networking team tested performance of DNS on Windows Server 2012 R2. To review the results, visit *https://blogs.technet.microsoft.com/networking/2015/08/13/name-resolution-performance-of-authoritative-windows-dns-server-2012-r2/.*

Configure global settings using Windows PowerShell

The DNS module for Windows PowerShell has a total of 130 cmdlets that can be used to view or configure various components of a DNS server. Two of the cmdlets that have been added in Windows Server 2016 that we did not discuss in the previous sections include:

- **Add-DnsServerZoneTransferPolicy** Creates a new policy for zone transfers, and includes whether to deny or ignore a zone transfer. Associated cmdlets include Get, Set, and Remove-DnsServerZoneTransferPolicy.

- **Add-DnsServerResourceRecord** Updated to support unknown record types. Associated cmdlets include Get, Set, and Remove-DnsServerResourceRecord.

Chapter summary

- Preparing for and installing the DNS Server role
- Configuring forwarders and conditional forwarders for lookup zones
- Using Root Hints to identify authoritative DNS servers
- Configuring delegation for DNS
- Implementing policies to be used by DNS servers and clients
- Using security extensions to secure DNS
- Explaining the Socket Pool and cache locking to mitigate DNS attacks
- Enabling Response Rate Limiting to mitigate DNS attacks
- Delegating administration to manage or view DNS for other administrators
- Enabling, disabling, and configuring recursive DNS queries
- Using Windows PowerShell to manage DNS servers and settings

Thought Experiment

A company has a production environment and a test environment. The production environment is in an Active Directory domain with DNS integrated into the domain. The test environment is in a workgroup with a separate DNS server. The company needs to prohibit the test environment from resolving any names in the production environment, but must use the production server as a name server for the Internet. The production servers must be configured to suspend responses to queries in the event of a DNS request flood. The test environment must also wait 10 seconds before using non-authoritative DNS servers. You must also enable a junior administrator to be able to view all objects and settings on the DNS server without enabling them to make changes.

Given the above scenario, answer these questions.

1. What should be used to prohibit resolution between networks?
2. What should be used to suspend queries when flooded?
3. How should the junior administrator be granted permissions?
4. What must be configured in the test environment to wait 10 seconds for non-authoritative responses?

Thought Experiment Answers

1. You can disable recursion to prevent the test DNS server from using the forwarder. Use a scope to specify recursion for the specific forwarder.

2. Response Rate Limiting should be configured to suspend queries when the DNS server is flooded with requests.

3. The junior administrator can be delegated permissions based on a custom security group that only has the Read permission to the DNS server.

4. The test environment must have the timeout period recursion setting modified to wait 10 seconds before using non-authoritative responses.

Implement IP Address Management

In this chapter, we will discuss how to install, configure, and use the built-in IP Address Management functionality. In past exams, IPAM was a major component of the exam skills that are tested. You should anticipate and be prepared to understand how to install and configure IPAM on Windows Server 2016.

- Windows Server 2016 introduces new features to IPAM, including:
- Enhanced DNS service management
- Multiple Active Directory Domain Services forest support
- Purge Utilization Data
- Windows PowerShell cmdlets for Role-Based Access Control

IPAM in Windows Server 2016 also improves on the existing IP address management and integrated DNS and DHCP management from the IPAM console.

Skills in this chapter:

- Install and configure IPAM
- Manage DNS and DHCP using IPAM

Skill 7.1: Install and configure IPAM

In this section, we explain how to install and configure the basic IPAM configuration. This includes the default database to use, provisioning the server and Group Policy settings, configuring server discovery, and setting IP addresses. We also explain how to back up and restore an IPAM database, which enables you to migrate that database from a previous version of Windows Server to Windows Server 2016. We also cover how to use a Microsoft SQL Server as the database engine, and how to integrate IPAM with System Center.

This section covers how to:

- Provision IPAM manually or by using Group Policy
- Configure server discovery
- Create and manage IP blocks and ranges
- Monitor utilization of IP address space
- Migrate existing workloads to IPAM
- Configure IPAM database storage using SQL Server
- Determine scenarios for using IPAM with System Center Virtual Machine Manager for physical and virtual IP address space management

Provision IPAM manually or by using Group Policy

IPAM is a feature that can be added by using the Add Roles And Features wizard, or by using the Install-WindowsFeature cmdlet. After installing the feature, one of the first tasks that you must complete is to provision the IPAM server. Figure 7-1 shows the first configuration option when provisioning IPAM, which is to specify the database that is being used.

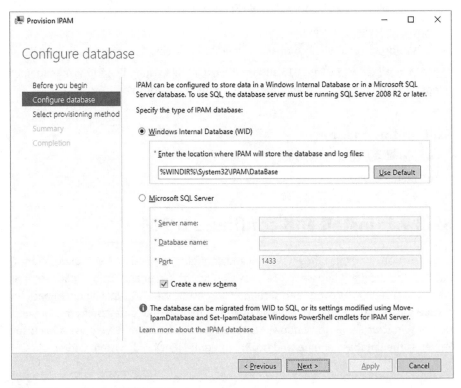

FIGURE 7-1 Configuring IPAM database

By default, IPAM uses a Windows Internal Database. We explain how to use a Microsoft SQL Server database later in this section. After configuring the database, you are prompted to select the provisioning type. There are two provisioning options:

- **Manual**   This requires that the network shares, security groups, and firewall rules are created and managed individually on each server.

- **Group-Policy-based**   This uses Group Policy Objects (GPOs) that are created in each domain that you plan to manage with IPAM. IPAM configures the GPOs as necessary, and the GPOs are applied to the servers in the domain. When using GPOs, the wizard asks for the prefix to name all GPOs with. For example, if you specify IPAM as the prefix, a GPO is named IPAM_DHCP for managed DHCP servers. Figure 7-2 shows selecting the provision method.

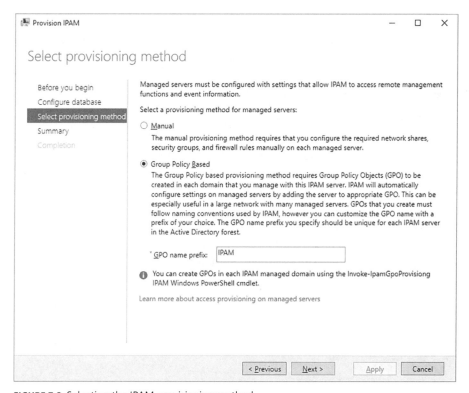

FIGURE 7-2 Selecting the IPAM provisioning method

EXAM TIP

If you select a GPO-based deployment, you cannot revert to a manual deployment. However, a manual deployment can be changed to GPO-based by using the Set-IpamConfiguration cmdlet.

You can provision the server by using the Invoke-IpamServerProvisioning cmdlet, then provision the GPOs by using the Invoke-IpamGpoProvisioning cmdlet.

```
Invoke-IpamServerProvisioning -ProvisioningMethod Automatic -GpoPrefix "IPAM-"
Invoke-IpamGpoProvisioning -Domain contosoforest.com -GpoPrefixName IPAM -IpamServerFqdn
ipam.contosoforest.com
```

Choosing the manual deployment method requires you to manually create or configure different options on each managed server, including:

- Network shares
- Security groups
- Firewall rules

DHCP servers

A managed DHCP server requires that all three options be configured on the servers. Table 7-1 summarizes the rules that must be configured on a managed DHCP server.

Table 7-1 DHCP server firewall changes

Firewall direction	Setting name	Description
Inbound	DHCP Server Management	Access DHCP server configuration data
Inbound	Remote Service Management	Access DHCP server configuration data
Inbound	File and Printer Sharing	Access DHCP server utilization data
Inbound	Remote Event Log Management	Access DHCP server logs

A universal security group must also be created in the domain with the name IPAMUG. The members of the security group must include the computer account objects for each DHCP server. Figure 7-3 shows the correct settings for the group.

FIGURE 7-3 IPAMUG Properties

Once created, the IPAMUG universal security group must be added to the DHCP Users and Event Log Readers security groups on each managed server. Figure 7-4 shows adding the user group to the local groups on the DHCP server. If the server is also a domain controller, then the Event Log Readers group in the Builtin container should be used.

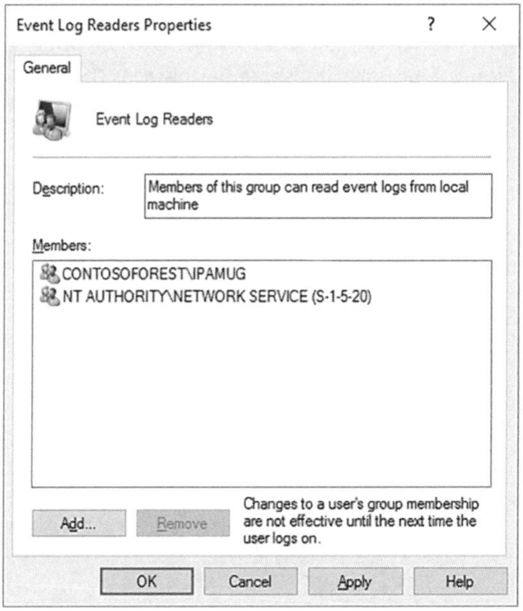

FIGURE 7-4 Event Log Readers Properties

The third configuration that must be made on a managed DHCP server is to create a network share of the %windir%\system32\dhcp directory, named dhcpaudit. Figure 7-5 shows the properties of the DHCP directory that has been shared.

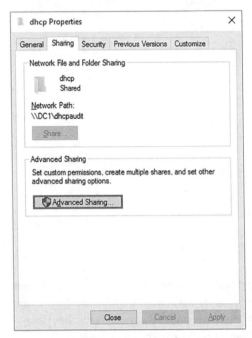

FIGURE 7-5 DHCP directory properties

The permissions of the share must be modified to enable the IPAMUG universal security group to read the contents of the directory. Figure 7-6 shows the share permissions that are applied to the directory.

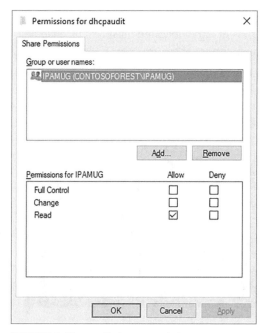

FIGURE 7-6 Dhcpaudit share permissions

After making the required group membership changes, you must restart the DHCP service. This ensures that the new permission levels are activated.

DNS Servers

Similar to DHCP servers, DNS servers must have several configuration changes when deploying IPAM manually. These changes include:

- Inbound firewall rules
- Security group changes
- Delegated DNS access

Table 7-2 summarizes the DNS server firewall changes.

TABLE 7-2 DNS server firewall changes

Firewall direction	Setting name	Description
Inbound	DNS Service	Discover managed DNS servers
Inbound	Remote Service Management	Manage DNS servers
Inbound	Remote Event Log Management	Monitor DNS zones and services

Just as with a DHCP server, a DNS server must have the IPAMUG universal security group added to the Event Log Readers security group. Event log monitoring must also be enabled on a managed DNS server. To enable event log monitoring, perform these steps.

1. Open a PowerShell session, and run the following command.

```
Get-ADComputer <IPAM Server Name>
```

2. Copy the SID value for the IPAM server to the clipboard, as shown in Figure 7-7.

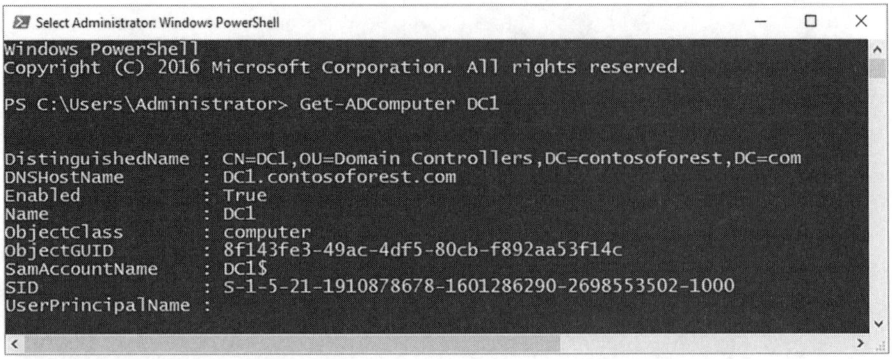

FIGURE 7-7 Get-ADComputer cmdlet

3. On the DNS server, open the registry editor.

4. Navigate to the HKLM\System\CurrentControlSet\Services\EventLog\DNS Server hive.

5. Double-click the CustomSD key.

6. At the end of the value field, append the following to the string, replacing the SID value for the server. Figure 7-8 shows adding the value to the key.

```
(A;;0x1;;; S-1-5-21-1910878678-1601286290-2698553502-1000)
```

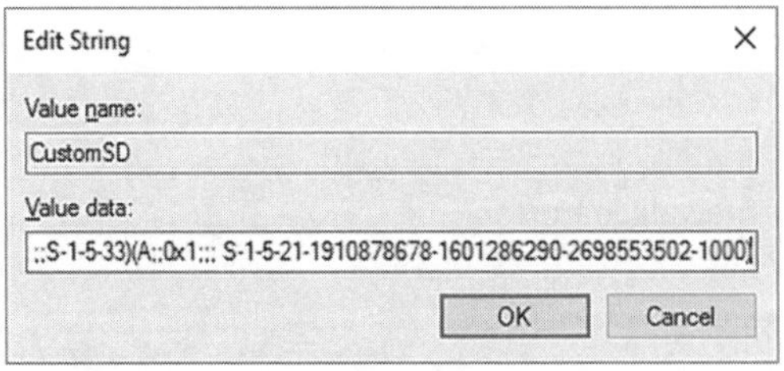

FIGURE 7-8 CustomSD registry key

7. Click OK and then close the registry editor.

The third configuration for managed DNS servers is to add the IPAM server to the DnsAdmins security group. This ensures that the IPAM server can perform administrative tasks on the DNS server. Figure 7-9 shows that the IPAMUG, which contains the computer object for the IPAM servers, has been delegated rights to the DNS server.

FIGURE 7-9 DnsAdmins security group

Domain controller or NPS servers

For managed DCs or Network Policy Servers (NPS), there are similar configuration changes that must be made. These servers must have the inbound Remote Event Log Management firewall rule enabled. The IPAMUG universal security group must be added to the Event Log Readers security group on both DCs and NPS servers.

Configure server discovery

After provisioning the IPAM server, the next in the deployment process is to configure and start server discovery. Figure 7-10 shows the discovery set for the forest and root domain. To include the domain in discovery, click Add.

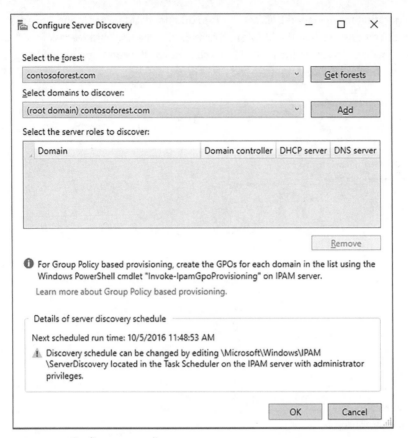

FIGURE 7-10 Configure server discovery

With Windows Server 2016, you can also manage other Active Directory forests if a two-way forest trust has been configured. After you click add for the domain, you can configure whether to discover the domain controllers, DHCP servers, and DNS servers for the domain. You can also add the domain to be discovered by using the Add-IpamDiscoveryDomain cmdlet.

```
Add-IpamDiscoveryDomain -Name "contosoforest.com"
```

By default, after discovering the servers in the environment the manageability status is set to unspecified. To configure a server as being managed, edit the server in the discovery list. Set the Manageability Status to Managed, as shown in Figure 7-11.

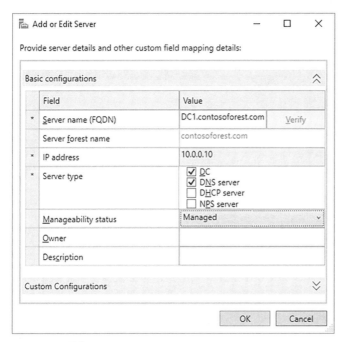

FIGURE 7-11 Edit server

Create and manage IP blocks and ranges

IPAM address blocks define the IPv4 or IPv6 addresses that are be managed. IPAM automatically labels the IPv4 blocks as either public or private blocks based on Internet Assigned Numbers Authority (IANA) ranges. IP address blocks are typically divided into smaller chunks, named ranges. IP address ranges can be used as a DHCP scope or pool of static addresses that can be used on hosts. Ranges are comprised of individual IP addresses. Figure 7-12 shows creating an IPv4 address block.

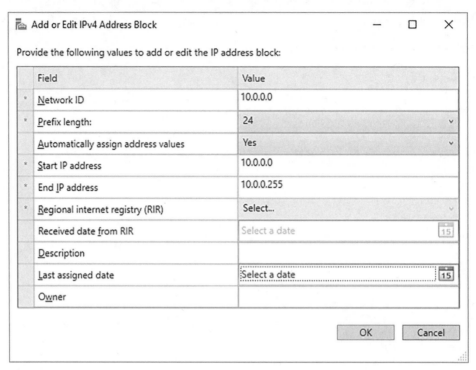

FIGURE 7-12 IPv4 address block

Adding a block of IP addresses can also be completed from PowerShell using the Add-IpamBlock cmdlet.

```
Add-IpamBlock -NetworkId "10.0.0.0/8"
```

Adding a range of IP addresses is like creating a block. The range expects the network ID and either the subnet prefix or subnet mask. Figure 7-13 shows creating an IPv4 address range.

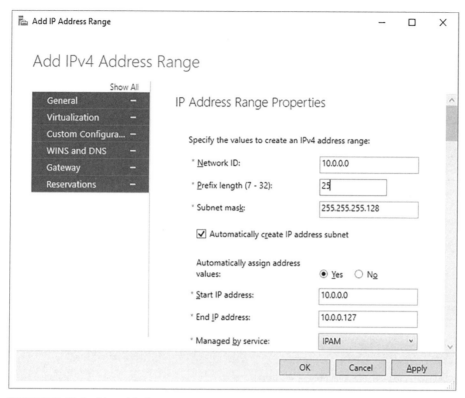

FIGURE 7-13 IPv4 address block

Like creating a block of IP addresses, a range can be created by using the Add-IpamRange cmdlet.

```
Add-IpamRange -NetworkId "192.168.0.0/24"
```

Monitor utilization of IP address space

After you have added the blocks and ranges to the IPAM configuration, you can find available addresses a few different ways. From the IPAM interface in server manager, right-click a range and then click Find and Allocate Available IP Address. The tool searches the IP address range for the next available IP address based on the search criteria, as shown in Figure 7-14.

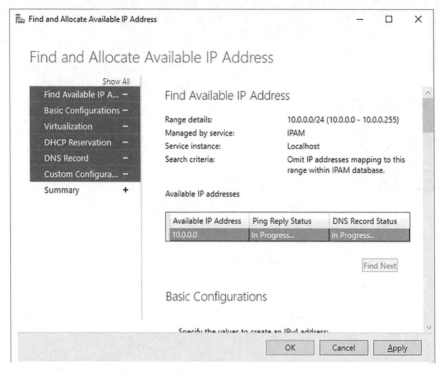

FIGURE 7-14 Find and Allocate Available IP Address

After locating an available IP address, you can use the same tool to then allocate that IP address as a DHCP reservation, create a DNS record, or provide any other custom configuration with the IP address.

The IP Address Blocks and IP Address Range Groups pages in the IPAM interface also displays the utilization rate for each block or range. The three states that a block or range can be in are:

- **Under** If the IP address allocation is less than 20 percent, then the block or range is considered under-utilized.

- **Optimal** If the IP address allocation is between 20 and 80 percent, then the block or range is considered optimal.

- **Over** If the IP address allocation is over 80 percent, then the block or range is considered over-utilized.

Figure 7-15 shows a portion of the IPAM interface that displays the utilization rate.

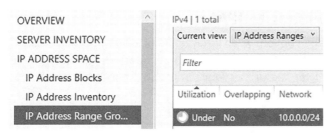

FIGURE 7-15 IP address range utilization

The under and over utilization rates can also be configured by modifying the utilization threshold for the IPAM configuration. From Server Manager, click Manage, and then click IPAM Settings. On the IPAM Settings screen, click Configure Utilization Threshold. Figure 7-16 shows the configuration screen for the threshold settings.

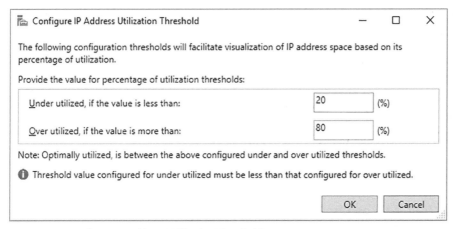

FIGURE 7-16 Configure IP Address Utilization Threshold

There are also three PowerShell cmdlets that can be used to identify available IP addresses.

- **Find-IpamFreeAddress**   This cmdlet finds one or more available IP addresses that are in a range of addresses defined on the IPAM server.
- **Find-IpamFreeRange**   This cmdlet finds free IP ranges that are available on the IPAM server.
- **Find-IpamFreeSubnet**   This cmdlet finds free IP subnets that are available on the IPAM server.

Migrate existing workloads to IPAM

If you selected the default installation options when installing IPAM, the Windows Internal Database (WID) files are located in the %WINDIR%\System32\ipam\Database directory. There are two files listed: *ipam.mdf* and *ipam_log.ldf*. To migrate from an existing installation, follow these general steps:

1. Stop the WID service on the existing server

2. Backup the IPAM database files on the existing server

3. Install the IPAM feature on the new server, specifying the WID database type

4. Stop the WID service on the new server

5. Restore the database files from the backup

6. Start the WID service on the new server

After migrating the workload to a new server, or performing an in-place upgrade, use the Update-IpamServer cmdlet to update the IPAM schema based on the new operating system.

If you are using a Microsoft SQL Server to host the database on the existing server, you can simply specify the server during the IPAM installation on the new server. If you need to migrate the SQL database, use the Move-IpamDatabase cmdlet as explained in the next section.

Configure IPAM database storage using SQL Server

As mentioned in the earlier section named "Provision IPAM manually or by using Group Policy," a Microsoft SQL Server can also be used to store the IPAM database. The SQL server instance and database must be created to be used with IPAM. IPAM uses the NT AUTHORITY\ Network Service user account for all operations, for either a WID or SQL server database. To use a SQL server, the network service account must be granted the following SQL roles:

- db_datareader
- db_datawriter
- db_ddladmin

Additionally, the user account must also be granted the Alter and View database state permission levels for *dbo*. After the instance and database have been created, and you have assigned the appropriate permissions to the network service account, you can migrate the database to the SQL server by using the Move-IpamDatabase cmdlet.

```
Move-IpamDatabase -DatabaseServer SQL1 -DatabaseName IPAMDB -DatabasePort 1433
-DatabaseAuthType Windows
```

Determine scenarios for using IPAM with System Center Virtual Machine Manager for physical and virtual IP address space management

IPAM can be integrated with System Center Virtual Machine Manager (VMM) to manage the logical networks and virtual machine networks in VMM. To configure VMM to integrate with IPAM, a dedicated user account must be created. The user account, or a group that contains the user account, must be granted the IPAM ASM Administrator role to enable VMM to manage IPAM. We explain the different role-based access control levels later in this chapter.

After the user account is created, specify the account as a Run As account in VMM. Create a network service, specifying the Run As account, for the Microsoft IP Address Management Provider. VMM then connects to the IPAM server using the credentials that you specified. Table 7-1 compares the VMM names to the names of objects used in IPAM.

TABLE 7-1 Comparing VMM and IPAM object names

VMM object name	IPAM object name
Logical network	Virtualized IP address space
Network site	Virtualized IP address space
IP address subnet	IP address subnet
IP address pool	IP address range
VM network	Virtualized IP address space

Skill 7.2: Manage DNS and DHCP using IPAM

In this section, we discuss how to use IPAM to manage various aspects of DHCP and DNS. This includes the server properties, scopes, policies, and failover configuration to be used on the DHCP servers in the environment. The DNS options include server properties, zones, and individual records. We will also explain the new support for multiple AD DS forests, and how to delegate administration with RBAC.

> **This section covers how to:**
> - Manage DHCP server properties using IPAM
> - Configure DHCP scopes and options
> - Configure DHCP policies and failover
> - Manage DNS server properties using IPAM
> - Manage DNS zones and records
> - Manage DNS and DHCP servers in multiple Active Directory forests
> - Delegate administration for DNS and DHCP using role-based access control

Manage DHCP server properties using IPAM

After configuring the IPAM environment and successfully managing the discovered servers, you can begin managing the individual services on these servers. Figure 7-17 shows the DNS and DHCP services that are on a discovered server.

FIGURE 7-17 Managed DHCP and DNS services

Right-clicking a service offers multiple options, including managing the DHCP server properties from IPAM. Figure 7-18 displays the Edit DHCP Server properties configuration screen from the IPAM interface.

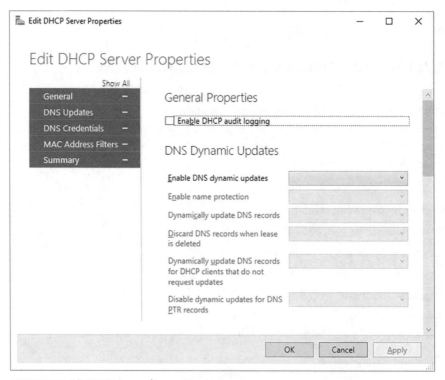

FIGURE 7-18 Edit DHCP Server Properties

The DHCP properties that can be modified include:

- **General**   The only option from IPAM is to enable DHCP audit logging.
- **DNS Dynamic Updates**   This enables dynamic updates on the server, and allows for additional configuration for name protection and lease options.
- **DNS Dynamic Update Credentials**   The credentials that are used to register names with dynamic updates.
- **MAC Address Filters**   Whether an allow or deny list is used for the DHCP server.

> **NEED MORE REVIEW? MORE ON DNS AND IPAM**
>
> For more information on managing DNS with IPAM, watch this presentation at *https://channel9.msdn.com/Blogs/windowsserver/Windows-Server-2016-DNS-management-in-IPAM*.

Configure DHCP scopes and options

When you right-click the DHCP service from the IPAM interface, you are presented several options that involve configuring the scopes and options on the DHCP server. Figure 7-19 shows a portion of the IPAM interface that displays the available options.

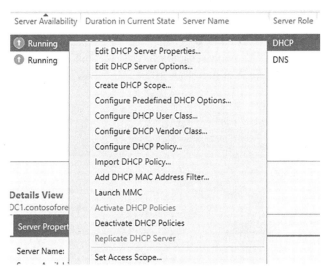

FIGURE 7-19 DHCP options in IPAM

The available options that can be configured from IPAM include:

- **Edit DHCP Server Options**   These are the options that can be configured for the DHCP server.
- **Create DHCP Scope**   This create a new IPv4 DHCP scope on the DHCP server, including DNS updates and advanced options.

- **Configure Predefined DHCP Options** This enables you to create DHCP Standard Options for the server.

- **Configure DHCP User Class** This enables you to create user classes on the DHCP server.

- **Configure DHCP Vendor class** This enables you to create vendor classes on the DHCP server.

Configure DHCP policies and failover

Configuring DHCP policies and failover is also performed by right-clicking the DHCP service from the IPAM console. Figure 7-12 also shows that you can manage DHCP policies from IPAM:

- **Configure DHCP Policy** Enables you to create a DHCP policy that contains criteria, conditions, and options for the specified policy.

- **Import DHCP Policy** Enables you to import an existing policy at either the server or scope level to the IPAM database.

- **Deactivate DHCP Policies** This deactivates the policies that are applied to the selected DHCP server.

Manage DNS server properties using IPAM

Managing DNS from the IPAM interface is performed the same way as DHCP, but with fewer options when you right-click the service. Figure 7-20 shows a portion of the IPAM interface with the available DNS options.

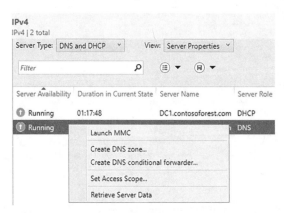

FIGURE 7-20 DNS options in IPAM

The available options include:

- **Launch MMC** This launches the DNS Manager MMC snap-in from the IPAM interface.

- **Create DNS zone**   This enables you to create a forward or reverse lookup zone with advanced options directly from IPAM.
- **Create DNS Conditional Forwarder**   This enables you to create a conditional forwarder with advanced options directly from IPAM.
- **Set Access Scope**   Configure the access scope for the DNS server.
- **Retrieve Server Data**   Obtain the latest data from the DNS server.

Manage DNS zones and records

Individual zones and records can be managed from the DNS Zones tab of the IPAM interface. Figure 7-21 shows a portion of the IPAM interface that displays the available DNS zone options.

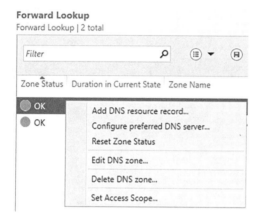

FIGURE 7-21 DNS zone options in IPAM

The available DNS zone options that can be configured from the IPAM interface include:

- **Add DNS Resource Record**   This creates a record type, such as an A record, in the DNS zone.
- **Configure Preferred DNS Server**   Select the authoritative DNS server for the DNS zone that is used by IPAM.
- **Reset Zone Status**   Reset the status of the DNS zone in the IPAM database. Use the Retrieve Server Data option to collect the latest data from the DNS server.
- **Edit DNS Zone**   Enables you to modify the name servers, scavenging, updates, and zone transfer settings for the zone.
- **Delete DNS Zone**   Remove the zone from the DNS server.
- **Set Access Scope**   Set the access scope on the IPAM server.

Manage DNS and DHCP servers in multiple Active Directory forests

In Windows Server 2012 R2, IPAM had to be in the same forest as the DNS and DHCP servers that were to be managed. With Windows Server 2016, IPAM can discover DNS and DHCP servers across forests, provided there is a two-way forest trust established. After the forest trust has been established, simply select the additional forests in the Configure Server Discover dialog box to add domains from remote forests. Figure 7-22 shows the Configure Server Discovery screen. To identify additional forests, click the Get Forests button.

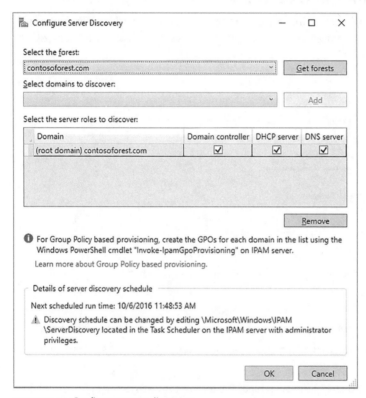

FIGURE 7-22 Configure server discovery

After the additional domains have been added to the IPAM database, the management process is the same regardless of which forest the server is in.

Delegate administration for DNS and DHCP using Role-Based Access Control (RBAC)

While the day-to-day tasks of managing and configuring IPAM are simple enough, the more complex aspect is understanding the different role-based security groups that are used with IPAM. Table 7-3 summarizes the available groups and their associated permission level.

TABLE 7-3 IPAM role-based access control

Task	IPAM administrators	IPAM ASM administrators	IPAM IP audit administrators	IPAM MSM administrators	IPAM users
Server Inventory	Manage	Manage	Manage	Manage	View
IP Address Space	Manage	Manage	View	View	View
Monitor and Manage	Manage	View	View	Manage	View
Event Catalog	View	View	View	View	View
IP Address Tracking	View	Denied	View	Denied	Denied
Common management tasks	Manage	Manage	Manage	Manage	Manage

The Access Control tab of the IPAM interface lists the available roles that are used with IPAM.

EXAM TIP

You should be familiar with each of these roles and the permissions that are granted as part of that role. A common question when permissions and roles are used is to ask the least privileged role that achieves a goal, to ensure that you do not over-assign permissions.

The IPAM roles include that are listed on the Access Control tab include:

- **DNS Record Administrator Role**   This enables management of the DNS resource records.

- **IP Address Record Administrator Role**   This enables management of IP addresses, including locating unallocated addresses, as well as creating and deleting IP addresses.

- **IPAM Administrator Role**   This provides all permissions to manage IPAM.

- **IPAM ASM Administrator Role**   This provides permissions to manage the IP address spaces, blocks, subnets, ranges, and individual addresses.

- **IPAM DHCP Administrator Role**   This provides the permission to manage a DHCP server and its associated scopes and options.

- **IPAM DHCP Reservations Administrator Role**   This provides the permission that are needed to manage DHCP reservations.

- **IPAM DHCP Scope Administrator Role**   This provides the permissions to manage DHCP scopes.

- **IPAM DNS Administrator Role**   This role provides the permission to manage a DNS server, zones, and records.

- **IPAM MSM Administrator Role**   This role provides permissions to manage DHCP and DNS servers as well as the scopes and options for each service.

Chapter summary

- How to deploy and provision IPAM and the required GPOs
- Configuring server discovery to locate servers to be managed by IPAM
- Creating and managing IP address blocks and ranges
- Locating available IP addresses by using the interface and PowerShell
- Moving and migrating a WID database to a new server
- Moving the WID database to a Microsoft SQL Server database
- Configuring IPAM with System Center VMM
- Managing DHCP servers and scopes by using IPAM
- Managing DNS servers and zones by using IPAM
- Using IPAM to manage multiple forests
- Role-based permissions that are used by IPAM

Thought Experiment

A company has a single Active Directory forest with multiple child domains. The company has partnered with another organization, and a two-way Active Directory forest trust has been established. The company plans to use IPAM with a Windows Internal Database, but needs to ensure that the database is part of the backup strategy. The following users must be configured to manage the IPAM environment. Each user must not have more permissions than are necessary.

- User1 must be configured to manage IP address blocks.
- User2 must be configured to manage DNS and DHCP servers.
- User3 must be configured to manage IP address allocation in IPAM.

Using the above information, answer the following questions.

1. How many IPAM servers must be deployed to manage both forests?
2. How should the IPAM database be included in the backup strategy?
3. Which role should User1 be added to?
4. Which role should User2 be added to?
5. Which role should User3 be added to?

Thought Experiment Answers

1. One. With Windows Server 2016, IPAM can manage multiple Active Directory forests if a two-way trust has been established.

2. The MDF and LDF files should be included in backup, that are typically located in the %WINDIR%\System32\IPAM\Database directory.

3. User1 should be a member of the IPAM ASM Administrator Role. This enables the user to manage IP address blocks and ranges, but not other aspects of the IPAM configuration.

4. User2 should be a member of the IPAM MSM Administrator Role. This enables the user to manage DNS and DHCP without managing other aspects of IPAM.

5. User3 should be a member of the IPAM IP Address Record Administrator Role. This enables the user to manage IP address allocation within IPAM.

CHAPTER 8

Implement network connectivity and remote access solutions

This chapter covers one skill that is represented on the exam, which is implementing Virtual Private Networks (VPNs) and DirectAccess. This is a small portion of the exam, and has not changed significantly since Windows Server 2012 R2. The same protocols, authentication options, and DirectAccess requirements that exist in Windows Server 2012 R2 still apply to Windows Server 2016.

Skills in this chapter:

- Implement Virtual Private Network and DirectAccess solutions

Implement Virtual Private Network and DirectAccess solutions

In this section, we discuss how to implement a VPN and DirectAccess solution. We explain the various VPN protocols and authentication options that can be used with the protocols. DirectAccess is also explained, including how to install and configure it using the available wizard.

This section covers how to:

- Implement remote access and site-to-site VPN solutions using remote access gateway
- Configure different VPN protocol options
- Configure authentication options
- Configure VPN reconnect
- Create and configure connection profiles
- Determine when to use remote access VPN and site-to-site VPN and configure appropriate protocols
- Install and configure DirectAccess
- Implement server requirements
- Implement client configuration
- Troubleshoot DirectAccess

Implement remote access and site-to-site VPN solutions using Remote Access Gateway

A remote access gateway, or RAS Gateway, is installed with the Remote Access server role. When installing the server role, there are three role services that can be included:

- **DirectAccess and VPN (RAS)**   This installs the DirectAccess service to provide a method of seamless Connectivity for client computers connecting to a corporate network. The VPN services enable encrypted tunnels to connect remote clients to corporate offices.
- **Routing**   This enables support for NAT, BGP, RIP, and other multicast networks.
- **Web Application Proxy**   This publishes web-based applications from the corporate network to remote devices. Web application proxies are commonly used with Active Directory Federation Services (AD FS) to authenticate users before granting access to applications. AD FS is explained in Chapter 11.

EXAM TIP

While the Web Application Proxy is commonly used with AD FS, the role service requires the Remote Access server role to be installed.

When configuring a RAS Gateway, there are a few different VPN options:

- **Site-to-site VPN**   This connects two networks together, such as a branch office to a corporate office.

- **Point to site VPN**   This enables individual remote connections from client computers to a corporate office.

- **Dynamic routing with Border Gateway Protocol (BGP)**   BGP provides automatic route reconfiguration based on the routes that are connected from site-to-site VPNs.

- **Network Address Translation (NAT)**   NAT enables you to share a single IP address to connect multiple devices to a network.

- **DirectAccess server**   DirectAccess provides a method of seamless VPN services for client computers that are connecting to a corporate network.

The Remote Access server role can be installed by using the Add Roles and Features wizard, or by using the Install-WindowsFeature cmdlet. After installing the role, use the Routing and Remote Access MMC snap-in to manage the server role. The initial setup requires completing the Routing and Remote Access Server Setup Wizard. Figure 8-1 shows the default configuration of the RAS snap-in. Note that the server icon is showing as down because no configuration has been defined.

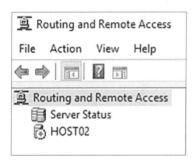

FIGURE 8-1 RAS snap-in

To perform the initial configuration on the RAS server, right-click the server and then select Configure And Enable Routing And Remote Access. Figure 8-2 shows the available options to configure the RAS server.

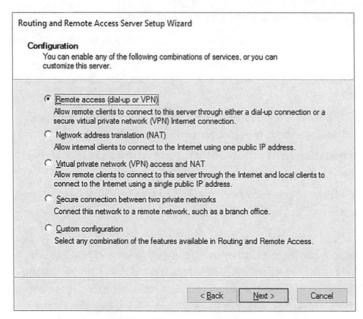

FIGURE 8-2 RAS Setup Wizard Configuration

To enable remote access and VPN access for remote clients, use the Remote Access option. The next configuration screen in the wizard prompts to configure the server for the type of connect: VPN or Dial-up. Figure 8-3 shows selecting VPN as the connection type.

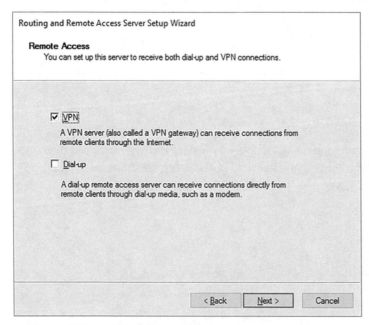

FIGURE 8-3 RAS Setup Wizard Remote Access

The next configuration option in the wizard is to bind the services to a specific network adapter. The available network adapters on the server are be displayed. By default, when a network adapter is selected, the necessary firewall rules are enabled for the adapter to allow inbound traffic on the adapter. Figure 8-4 shows the network adapter selection screen of the wizard.

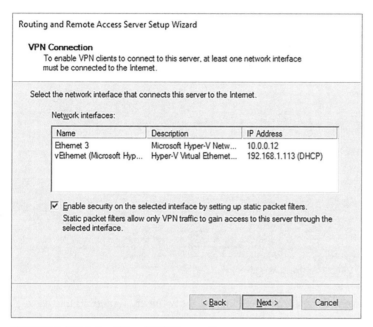

FIGURE 8-4 RAS Setup Wizard VPN Connection

For clients to connect to the network, they must have an IP address that is either on the network, or is routable for the network. The RAS server provides the option to assign IP addresses to clients automatically, from either a DHCP server on the network, or act as a DHCP server itself. You can also define a certain range of IP addresses for the RAS server to use specifically for remote clients. Figure 8-5 shows the IP Address Assignment screen of the wizard.

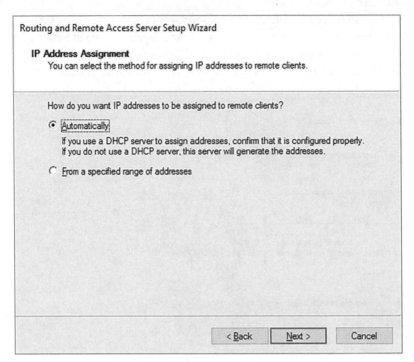

FIGURE 8-5 RAS Setup Wizard VPN IP Address Assignment

Finally, the last option in the wizard is to configure the authentication method for the remote clients. By default, the RAS server authenticates the clients using Windows Authentication through Extensible Authentication Protocol (EAP) or Microsoft encrypted authentication version 2 (MS-CHAP v2). Optionally, you can configure a RADIUS server to authenticate the clients, or configure the RAS server to act as a RADIUS server. Figure 8-6 shows the authentication configuration during the wizard.

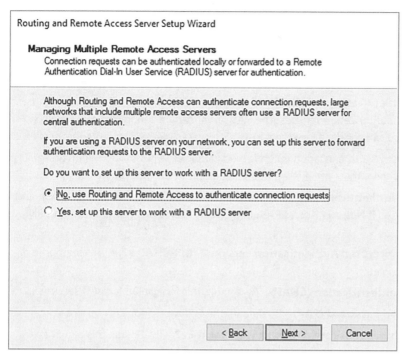

FIGURE 8-6 RAS Setup Wizard authentication options

You can also configure the RAS role by using the Install-RemoteAccess cmdlet.

```
Install-RemoteAccess -VpnType Vpn
```

Configure different VPN protocol options

A RAS server supports a few different VPN protocols for connectivity. These protocols include:

- **Point-to-Point Tunneling Protocol (PPTP)**   PPTP enables traffic to be encrypted and encapsulated before it is sent across the network. PPTP can be used for remote access and site-to-site VPNs. PPTP uses Microsoft Point-to-Point Encryption (MPPE) with encryption keys generated from MS-CHAP v2 or EAP-TLS authentication.

- **Layer Two Tunneling Protocol (L2TP)**   L2TP encrypts traffic over any point-to-point network, including IP and Asynchronous Transfer Mode (ATM) connections. L2TP uses IPsec Transport Mode for encryption services instead of MPPE.

- **Secure Socket Tunneling Protocol (SSTP)**   SSTP is the newest of the protocols and uses HTTPS to secure VPN traffic. This reduces firewall footprint by enabling an existing firewall port (443) to be used for VPN traffic. SSTP encapsulates the network traffic over SSL to provide transport-level security.

Configure authentication options

There are two primary authentication options that are used with a RAS server:

- **Windows authentication** This method is used by default for VPN connections, and queries Active Directory or local accounts as part of the authentication process.
- **RADIUS authentication.** RADIUS authentication uses an external source for authentication and authorization services. The RAS server can be configured as a RADIUS server, or you can specify an external RADIUS server from the RAS server properties.

By default, Windows authentication is configured with RAS VPN services. When using Windows authentication, there are a few authentication methods that can be used:

- **Extensible Authentication Protocol (EAP)** This method is enabled by default, and should be used if Network Access Protection (NAP) is also being used with the VPN service.
- **Microsoft Encrypted Authentication version 2 (MS-CHAP v2)** This method is also enabled by default.
- **Encrypted authentication (CHAP)** By default, this is disabled for VPN services.
- **Unencrypted password (PAP)** By default, this is disabled for VPN services.
- **Allow machine certificate authentication for IKEv2** By default, this certificate-based authentication is disabled for VPN services.
- **Unauthenticated access** By default, this is disabled for VPN services.

Figure 8-7 shows the Authentication Methods dialog box with the default options selected.

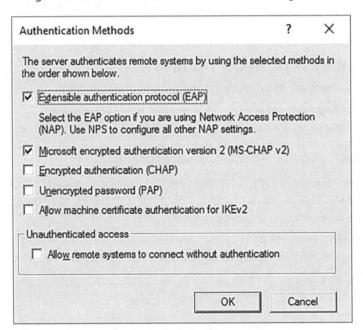

FIGURE 8-7 Windows Authentication Methods

Configure VPN reconnect

VPN Reconnect was introduced with Windows Server 2008. However, DirectAccess can replace a VPN as the recommended remote access method for client computers.

VPN reconnect is used with the IKEv2 tunneling protocol to provide seamless reconnects for mobile clients. This scenario can be whether a laptop is roaming between wireless access points, or a mobile phone that has been configured with a VPN connection. With other protocols, when a connection is interrupted, the device is typically disconnected. The connection would then have to be reestablished manually to access resources on the network. With VPN reconnect, the connection attempts to reconnect automatically from any interruption. VPN reconnect also uses multiple network adapters to attempt to establish a connection, if available.

Create and configure connection profiles

Remote connection profiles are used with System Center Configuration Manager and Microsoft Intune to enable users to access corporate resources, even if they are not on a domain-joined computer. These devices include:

- Windows-based personal computer
- Android devices
- iOS devices

With Intune, connection profiles enable you to deploy Remote Desktop Connection settings through a company portal. The portal is used to establish a remote desktop connect to either a Remote Desktop Services (RDS) server, or to their individual work computer on the network. Connection profiles can be used without Intune, but then requires a VPN connection for the remote desktop connection.

> *NEED MORE REVIEW?* **THE SYSTEM CENTER CONFIGURATION MANAGER**
>
> For more information on connection profiles with System Center Configuration Manager, visit *https://technet.microsoft.com/en-us/library/dn261225.aspx.*

Determine when to use remote access VPN and site-to-site VPN and configure appropriate protocols

The recommended deployment scenarios for a RAS gateway include:

- **Single tenant edge**   Connect an edge device in the network with a single tenant, either a corporate or branch office network, with another network over the Internet. This can be combined with BGP to provide dynamic routing based on the available connections. Combined with DirectAccess, remote client computers can connect to any resource anywhere on the network, regardless of physical location.

- **Multitenant edge**   A RAS gateway for multitenant environments enables a cloud provider to offer all the same features of a single tenant, including BGP, DirectAccess, and NAT. The primary difference is that the device filters or reroutes traffic based on the tenant that is being accessed.

Single tenant mode

Most corporate environments use the single tenant mode. In single tenant mode, a RAS gateway can be deployed as an edge device for a VPN server, DirectAccess server, or both. The RAS gateway can enable remote client computers with multiple options for connecting back to the corporate network.

Multitenant mode

If there are multiple tenants hosted in the datacenter that are accessed, then the multitenant mode should be used. Multitenancy enables a datacenter to provide a cloud infrastructure to support virtual machine workloads, virtual networks, and storage.

Virtual networks can be created by using Hyper-V Network Virtualization. A RAS gateway can be integrated with the Hyper-V Network Virtualization stack to route network traffic efficiently depending on the tenant that is being accessed.

With Windows Server 2016, a RAS gateway can route traffic to any resource within a private or hybrid cloud network. The RAS gateway can route traffic between physical and virtual networks at any location.

Install and configure DirectAccess

DirectAccess is a component of the Remote Access server role that provides seamless connectivity for remote clients to a corporate network. After configuring the RAS role on a server, DirectAccess can be enabled from either the Routing and Remote Access MMC snap-in, from the Remote Access Management Console, or by using Windows PowerShell. Figure 8-8 shows the Remote Access Management Console, where DirectAccess can be enabled from the Tasks panel.

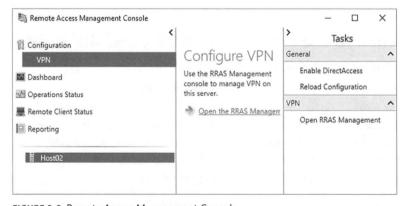

FIGURE 8-8 Remote Access Management Console

Enabling DirectAccess launches the Enable DirectAccess Wizard. One of the first steps of the wizard is to perform a prerequisite check on the server that you are enabling DirectAccess on. If successful, the wizard enables you to continue with the configuration. The first configuration item in the wizard is to select the security groups that contain the computer objects foe which DirectAccess is enabled. You can also determine whether to only enable DirectAccess for mobile computers, or to force tunneling so that all Internet traffic from the computer uses the corporate network. Figure 8-9 shows the configuration options for DirectAccess groups.

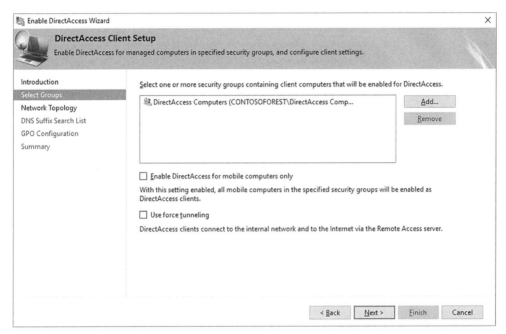

FIGURE 8-9 Selecting DirectAccess computer groups

Next, you identify the topology of the DirectAccess implementation. The RAS server can be in one of three configurations:

- **Edge**   The RAS server is directly connected to the Internet with no physical firewall or NAT device in place.
- **Behind An Edge Device (With Two Network Adapters)**   The RAS server is behind a network firewall or other device and has two network adapters. One network adapter is on the network with the firewall. The second network adapter is on the corporate internal network.
- **Behind An Edge Device (With A Single Network Adapter)**   The RAS server is behind a network firewall or edge device. The network adapter on the RAS server is connected to both the firewall and the internal corporate network.

For any configuration, the external FQDN or IP address that clients uses to connect must be specified. Figure 8-10 shows the network topology configuration in the wizard.

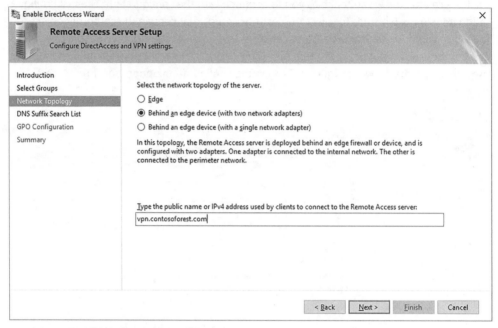

FIGURE 8-10 Specifying the network topology

After selecting the network topology, you can configure the DNS Suffix list that is used by DirectAccess clients. This is similar to setting a suffix list from DHCP. Anytime a DirectAccess client uses a single-label name, such as Server1, the server appends a list of DNS suffixes until a response is found for a FQDN. The order that the list is in is also important. If a match is found, then the remaining domains are skipped. If there are two Server1 objects in different lookup zones (or FQDNs), then the first in the list is returned to the DirectAccess client. Figure 8-11 shows configuring DirectAccess with the domain name and an additional domain.

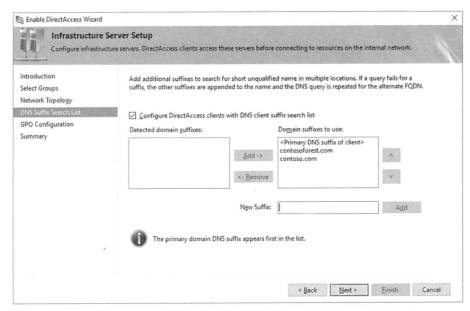

FIGURE 8-11 Specifying the network topology

The final step is to configure the Group Policy Objects (GPOs) that are used to apply the DirectAccess policies. Two GPOs are created and linked to the domain:

- **DirectAccess client GPO** This contains the client settings for the DirectAccess clients.
- **DirectAccess server GPO** This contains the RAS server settings for the DirectAccess server.

Figure 8-12 shows the confirmation to create the two new GPOs in the domain.

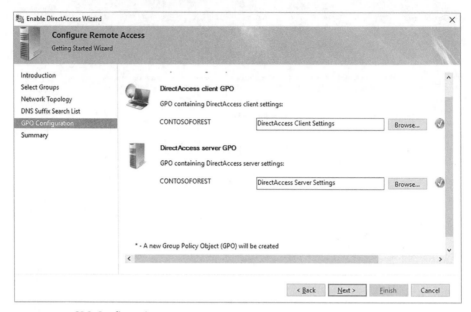

FIGURE 8-12 GPO Configuration

Implement server requirements

In studying for the exam, this topic can be slightly vague as to which requirements. For this book, we assume that you are familiar with the the DirectAccess prerequisites. These include:

- Windows Firewall enabled for all network adapter profiles.
- All versions of Windows Server beginning with 2008 R2 are supported.
- All Windows Enterprise clients beginning with Windows 7 are supported.
- Force tunnel with a single server, or using KerbProxy authentication is not supported.
- Changing policies by using another method than the DirectAccess Management Console or Windows PowerShell is not supported. Do not make changes directly to GPOs.

> *NEED MORE REVIEW?* **DEPLOYING DIRECTACCESS**
>
> For more information on the prerequisites for deploying DirectAccess, visit *https://technet. microsoft.com/en-us/windows-server-docs/networking/remote-access/directaccess/prereq- uisites-for-deploying-directaccess.*

Implement client configuration

Similar to the previous section, "Implement server requirements", implementing the client configuration is also vague. In a best practice configuration, the GPOs that are configured configure all of the necessary client components to enable the client to connect to the DirectAccess server.

It is possible to perform a configuration manually for a computer that has not been joined to the domain to receive the GPO settings. In that case, the client must be configured with a few different settings:

- The Teredo client must be set to the first IPv4 address of the DirectAccess server.
- The 6to4 relay must be set to the first IPv4 address of the DirectAccess server.
- The IP-HTTPS client must be enabled and configured.

Additionally, the Name Resolution Policy Table (NRPT) must be configured with the FQDN of the corporate intranet.

> **NEED MORE REVIEW? DIRECTACCESS CLIENT CONFIGURATION**
>
> For details on performing a manual DirectAccess client configuration, visit *https://technet. microsoft.com/en-us/library/ee649267(WS.10).aspx.*

Troubleshoot DirectAccess

Troubleshooting DirectAccess can be performed from either the Remote Access Management Console, or by using PowerShell. You can also use the Remote Access Best Practices Analyzer to identify any warnings or errors, then follow the provided steps to fix the issue. Some DirectAccess fixes involve modifying the registry, which should not be memorized for the exam. Overall, you should be able to:

- Restore a DirectAccess configuration using PowerShell
- Refresh a DirectAccess configuration using PowerShell
- Troubleshoot client connection issues
- Configure a proxy for an NRPT rule

> **NEED MORE REVIEW? TROUBLESHOOT DIRECTACCESS WITH WINDOWS SERVER 2016**
>
> For details on troubleshooting DirectAccess with Windows Server 2016, visit *https://tech-net.microsoft.com/en-us/windows-server-docs/networking/remote-access/directaccess/ troubleshooting-directaccess.*

Chapter summary

- Implementing the remote access server role
- Configuring VPN options by using the RAS server role
- Configuring authentication options through Windows or RADIUS authentication
- Using VPN reconnect to automatically reconnect mobile clients
- Setting connection profiles by using Intune or System Center
- Understanding scenarios for single tenant and multitenant deployments
- Installing and configuring the DirectAccess service
- Implementing prerequisites for DirectAccess
- Using GPOs to manage client configuration
- Understanding basic troubleshooting methods for DirectAccess

Thought Experiment

A company has a corporate office and three branch offices. The corporate office has approximately 10,000 client computers. Each branch office has approximately 1,000 client computers. Each branch office must have connectivity to the corporate office. The company also employs 1,000 sales and field staff that must connect remotely to the corporate network. All mobile clients run Windows 8.1 or Windows 10 Enterprise editions. Executive-level staff must have the ability to connect to the corporate network using their home computers that are not domain joined. IT staff must have the ability to VPN into the corporate networking using SSL.

Using the above scenario, answer the following questions.

1. How should the sales and field staff connect to the corporate office?
2. How should executive-level staff connect to the corporate network?
3. How should the branch offices connect to the corporate office?
4. Which VPN protocol should the IT staff use for the VPN connection?

Thought Experiment Answers

1. Sales and field staff should connect using DirectAccess for the most seamless experience.

2. Executive-level staff should use a company portal to access corporate resources from computers that are not domain joined.

3. The branch offices should be configured with a site-to-site VPN to connect to the corporate office.

4. IT staff should use the SSTP protocol, as it is the only protocol that connects using SSL.

CHAPTER 9

Implement an advanced network infrastructure

In this chapter, we will review the new features and skills that can be used with a network infrastructure in Windows Server 2016. From a networking perspective, the primary change to Windows Server 2016 is in the Software Defined Networking (SDN) components. These updating include the ability to:

- Mirror and route traffic to new or existing appliances
- Dynamically segment workloads similar to Microsoft Azure
- Use a distributed firewall and network security groups
- Deploy and manage the SDN with System Center Virtual Machine Manager
- Combine SDN with Docker for container networking

Windows Server 2016 also includes enhancements to the TCP stack, however, these changes are not called out on the exam skills. These improvements include:

- Increasing the Initial Congestion Window from 4 to 10
- TCP Fast Open (TFO) has been enabled to reduce the time to establish a TCP connection
- TCP Tail Loss Probe (TLP) has been implemented to assist in recovering from packet loss.
- Recent Acknowledgement (RACK) has been implemented to reduce the time required to transmit a packet

Skills in this chapter:

- Implement high performance network solutions
- Determine scenarios and requirements for implementing Software Defined Networking

Skill 9.1: Implement high performance network solutions

In this section, we discuss and outline the various high performance networking solutions that can be used with Windows Server 2016. This includes teaming network adapters with virtual switches and making individual network adapter configuration changes to enhance performance.

> **This section covers how to:**
>
> - Implement NIC Teaming or the Switch Embedded Teaming solution and identify when to use each.
> - Enable and configure Receive Side Scaling and enable and configure virtual Receive Side Scaling on a Virtual Machine Queue capable network adapter.
> - Enable and configure network Quality of Service with Data Center Bridging.
> - Enable and configure SMB Direct on Remote Direct Memory Access enabled network adapters.
> - Enable and configure SMB Multichannel.
> - Enable and configure Virtual Machine Multi-Queue.
> - Enable and configure Single-Root I/O Virtualization on a supported network adapter.

Implement NIC Teaming or the Switch Embedded Teaming solution and identify when to use each

NIC Teaming was introduced as a method of load balancing and failover for individual server hosts. NIC Teaming enables you to use two or more network adapters to provide bandwidth aggregation, or failover between adapters or external switches. With Windows Server 2016, Switch Embedded Teaming (SET) can be used with Hyper-V virtual switches to team up to eight network adapters into a single virtual network adapter.

Using SET provides similar benefits to traditional teaming, in that the virtual switch increases performance and redundancy using several underlying network adapters. Configuring SET is as simple as creating a NIC Team on the host machine, and then providing the team to the virtual switch. Figure 9-1 shows creating a NIC team. Note that the figure was taken from a virtual machine that does not enable all possible options that would be available on a physical host.

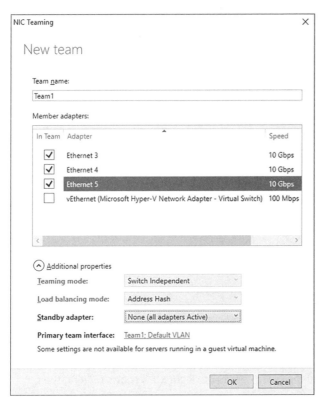

FIGURE 9-1 NIC Teaming

Enable and configure Receive Side Scaling and enable and configure virtual Receive Side Scaling on a Virtual Machine Queue capable network adapter

Receive Side Scaling (RSS) can be used for a virtual machine path to enable the VM to support additional network traffic loads. RSS distributes the traffic loads across multiple processor cores on the Hyper-V host and the VM. A VM can only use RSS if the processor on the host supports the feature, and if the VM is configured to use multiple processor cores.

RSS can be enabled from the Advanced tab of the network adapter properties. Figure 9-2 displays the Advanced tab with RSS enabled.

FIGURE 9-2 Network Adapter Properties

You can also enable RSS by using the netsh command. Figure 9-3 shows running the full netsh command.

```
netsh interface tcp set global rss=enabled
```

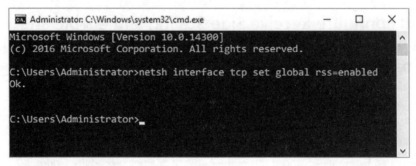

FIGURE 9-3 netsh RSS command

If you plan to use RSS in a virtual environment, then the Hyper-V host processor and network adapter must support RSS. Simply configure RSS by using the same methods within the virtual machine.

Enable and configure network Quality of Service with Data Center Bridging

Data Center Bridging (DCB) is based on an Institute of Electrical and Electronics Engineers (IEEE) standard for networking. DCB enables multiple types of network traffic to be sent across the same physical Ethernet media. DCB allocates bandwidth and Quality of Service (QoS) at the hardware level, rather than from the operating system. DCB is a feature that can be installed on server that runs Windows Server 2012 and later. Nano Server also supports using DCB by specifying the Microsoft-NanoServer-DCB-Package option.

Using DCB requires that each component of the network topology supports the capabilities. From a Windows Server perspective, DCB can only be configured by using the following PowerShell modules:

- netqos
- dcbqos
- netadapter

Some important cmdlets in the dcbqos module to be aware of include:

- **Enable-NetQoSFlowControl**   Enables priority-based flow control with DCB.
- **New-NetQoSTrafficClass**   Creates a new traffic class to be used with DCB.
- **Switch-NetQoSDcbxSetting**   Sets the policy for globally or for specific network adapters on the server.

Enable and configure SMB Direct on Remote Direct Memory Access enabled network adapters

As discussed in Chapter 3, "Implement Hyper-V," Remote Direct Memory Access (RDMA) provides direct memory access between computers without the need for the operating system. RDMA enables high performance with low latency for storage environments. RDMA is currently supported on three types of network adapters:

- Infiniband
- Internet Wide Area RDMA Protocol (iWARP)
- RDMA over Converged Ethernet (RoCE)

Windows Server 2016 introduces new RDMA support, including:

- Converged RMDA. RDMA adapters can be teamed for multiple types of network traffic.
- Switch Embedded Teaming (SET). Up to eight network adapters can be teamed and used with virtual switches and provide the same benefits as discussed earlier in this chapter.

NEED MORE REVIEW? USING RDMA WITH SET

For more information on using RDMA with SET, visit *https://technet.microsoft.com/en-us/library/mt403349.aspx*.

To obtain a list of network adapters on a server that can be used with RDMA, run the Get-NetAdapterRdma cmdlet. To enable SMB Direct on a specific network adapter, run the Enable-NetAdapterRdma cmdlet. To enable SMB Direct for all network adapters, run the Set-NetOffloadGlobalSetting cmdlet.

Enable and configure SMB Multichannel

SMB Multichannel provides a method of aggregating available bandwidth and redundancy if multiple paths are available between an SMB 3.0 client and server connection. SMB multichannel can be combined with Cluster Shared Volumes (CSV) to stream traffic across RDMA network adapters and increase performance. When combined with Hyper-V, SMB Multichannel provides increased performance for virtual machine migrations with low CPU utilization.

SMB Multichannel can be configured by using the Set-SmbServerConfiguration cmdlet. Figure 9-4 shows running the full command to enable SMB multichannel.

```
Set-SmbServerConfiguration -EnableMultiChannel $True
```

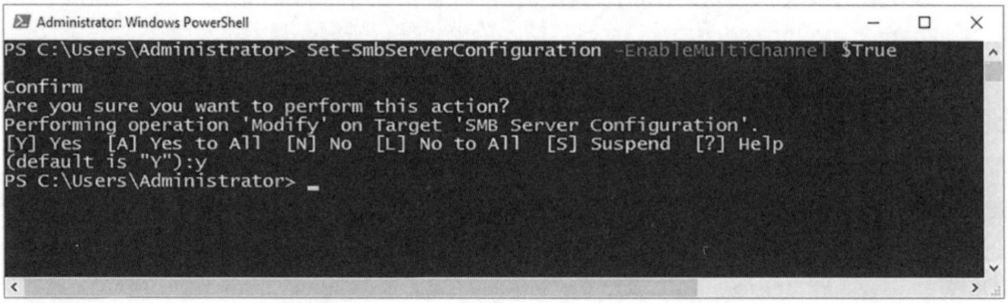

FIGURE 9-4 Set-SmbServerConfiguration

SMB Multichannel must be enabled on both the client and the server for it to be used. If either one of the systems are disabled, then the SMB Multichannel is not used. Configuring a client uses the same parameter, but is set by using the Set-SmbClientConfiguration cmdlet.

Enable and configure Virtual Machine Multi-Queue

Virtual Machine Multi-Queue (VMMQ) uses hardware queues for each virtual machine on the Hyper-V host. This provides a performance increase compared to previous versions of Hyper-V hosts. To enable VMQ on a network adapter, use the Enable-NetAdapterVmq cmdlet. Once enabled, VMQ can be configured by using the Set-NetAdapterVmq cmdlet.

VMQ assists in routing packets for virtual machines on a Hyper-V host. By routing packets to different queues, different processors can process the network traffic for multiple virtual machines, increasing performance.

> *NEED MORE REVIEW? POWERSHELL SYNTAX*
>
> For more information on the VMQ interface, visit *https://technet.microsoft.com/en-us/library/jj130870.aspx*.

Enable and configure Single-Root I/O Virtualization on a supported network adapter

Single-Root IO Virtualization (SR-IOV) provides virtual machines with access to physical PCI Express resources that are on a Hyper-V host. This requires specific supported hardware to be used on the Hyper-V host, and additional drivers to be installed on the virtual machine. SR-IOV can only be used with 64-bit versions of guest operating systems.

SR-IOV uses both Virtual Functions and is associated with a Physical Function. The Physical Function is what is used on the Hyper-V host, and is treated as a PCI-E device. The virtual machine uses Virtual Functions to interact with the physical PCI-E device. A single physical PCI-E device, such as a network adapter with multiple ports, can present each physical port as a different Virtual Function to virtual machines. Figure 9-5 shows the settings of a virtual machine. Both the VMQ and SR-IOV settings can be configured from the Hardware Acceleration options of a virtual machine.

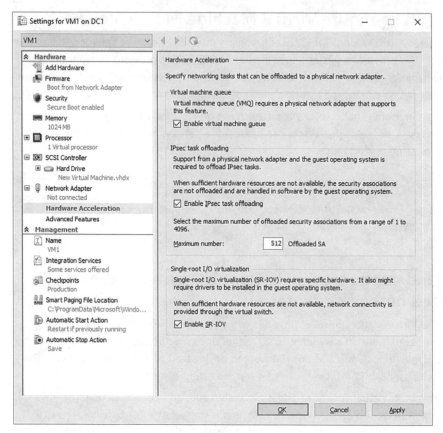

FIGURE 9-5 Virtual Machine Hardware Acceleration Settings

Skill 9.2: Determine scenarios and requirements for implementing Software Defined Networking

In this section, we discuss the scenarios are requirements that are commonly used with SDN. That includes the requirements for using Hyper-V Network Virtualization, Generic Route Encapsulation, and Virtual Extensible LAN encapsulation. We will also discuss new features that can be used with Software Load Balancing to manage different traffic loads. Finally, we will explain how to implement a Windows Server Gateway with different SDN needs, and how to use new firewall policies to manage network traffic.

Determine deployment scenarios and network requirements for deploying SDN

Software-defined Networking (SDN) enables you to virtualize networks by abstracting individual networking components such as IP addresses, ports, and switches. An SDN configuration uses policies to manage how traffic is routed through both physical and virtual networks. Windows Server 2016 provides a few tools to configure and manage a SDN:

- **Network Controller**   New to Windows Server 2016, the network controller centralizes the management, configuration, monitoring, and troubleshooting for infrastructures.
- **Hyper-V Network Virtualization**   This assists in the process of abstracting the software and workload from physical to virtual networks.
- **Hyper-V Virtual Switch**   Provides the connection from individual virtual machines to virtual and physical networks in the infrastructure.
- **RRAS Multitenant Gateway**   Extends a network to Microsoft Azure to provide an on-demand hybrid infrastructure.
- **NIC Teaming**   Combines network adapters to aggregate bandwidth and provide redundancy for underlying physical networks.

A common scenario for an SDN configuration is to integrate with the Microsoft System Center suite to extend the capabilities of the SDN. Some System Center benefits include:

- **System Center Operations Manager**   This enables you to monitor private, hybrid, and public clouds.
- **System Center Virtual Machine Manager**   This enables you to manage virtual machines, networks, and policies that apply to an infrastructure.
- **Windows Server Gateway**   This virtual endpoint enables you to route internal or cloud traffic to the appropriate network. Windows Server Gateway is discussed in more detail later in this chapter.

A typical SDN deployment includes the following components:

- **Management and Hyper-V Network Virtualization**   Logical networks that can be accessed by all Hyper-V hosts. Hyper-V network Virtualization is discussed in detail in the next section.

- **Load balancing networks**   A dedicated network for gateways and software load balancing that can be used for transit, public, private, or GRE networks.

- **RDMA-based storage network**   RDMA is used for storage connections, when a separate VLAN should be defined.

- **Routing**   Virtual IP addresses should be advertised to other networks as necessary by using BGP or another routing protocol. BGP peering can be configured on physical switches or routers with the physical infrastructure.

- **Default gateways**   One default gateway must be defined that can connect to the different networks that have been configured.

- **Network hardware**   The underlying physical network must support the scaling capabilities that the virtual network provides to the cloud services.

Determine requirements and scenarios for implementing Hyper-V Network Virtualization using Network Virtualization Generic Route Encapsulation encapsulation or Virtual Extensible LAN encapsulation

Network virtualization enables you to manage network traffic like managing a virtual machine. Just as many virtual machines can run on a single Hyper-V host, many virtual networks can be connected to provide multiple networks, network isolation, or improved performance.

Hyper-V in Windows Server 2016 supports using network virtualization by using two IP addresses for individual virtual machines. This provides a method to separate the logical and physical network topologies. The Hyper-V switch processes the network traffic to allow communication from the virtual machine to the physical network without additional overhead.

Network virtualization is typically used in these common scenarios:

- **Provide flexible VM placement**   This ensures that you can use a virtual machine on any Hyper-V host regardless of the underlying physical network.

- **Multitenant network isolation**   Network traffic isolation can be defined for tenants, even without using separate VLANs. Network virtualization uses a 24-bit identifier for virtual networks, and does not require any additional configuration on physical networking devices when moving or creating virtual machines.

- **IP address management** Virtual machines that are in different virtual networks can use the same IP address, even if they are on the same physical network.

Network Virtualization Generic Route Encapsulation (NVGRE) is the process of using two IP addresses for a single virtual network adapter. These two IP addresses include:

- **Customer Address (CA)** The IP address that is used by the virtual machine's guest operating system and by the tenant of the virtual machine. This IP address is used for communication with other virtual machines on the same network.

- **Provider Address (PA)** The IP address that is used by the cloud provider and is assigned to a virtual machine by the Hyper-V host. When used with network virtualization, the Hyper-V host encapsulates packets from virtual machines and sends them with the source modified to be the PA address. This ensures that the physical network can route the packet appropriately, and that the Hyper-V hosts deliver responses to the correct virtual machine.

Table 9-1 lists IP addresses that might exist in an example environment.

TABLE 9-1 Example IP address with network virtualization

Server name	CA	PA
Server1	192.168.1.100	10.0.0.1
Server2	192.168.1.101	10.0.0.2
Server3	192.168.1.102	10.0.0.3

Using the information in the above table, when Server1 communicates with Server2, only the CA addresses are used during the communication. These addresses are on a virtual network that are only used by the virtual machines associated with the network. However, when any of the servers communicate with the Internet, the CA is encapsulated by the Hyper-V host. The Hyper-V host then modifies the source IP address of the packet header as the PA. The PA is used on the physical network to exit the virtual network and onto the Internet. When a response is received, it is sent to the PA address. The Hyper-V hosts then translate the PA back to the CA to deliver to the individual virtual machine.

Determine scenarios for implementation of Software Load Balancer for North-South and East-West load balancing

A new feature introduced with Windows Server 2016 is Network Controller. The Network Controller feature provides two APIs: Southbound and Northbound. The Southbound API enables you to communicate with a given network. The Northbound API enables you to communicate with the Network Controller.

The Southbound API enables you to:

- Discover network devices
- Detect network configurations
- Ascertain network topology details
- Push configuration changes to the network infrastructure

The Northbound API enables you to obtain information from the Network Controller to monitor and configure a given network. The Northbound API can be used with:

- Windows PowerShell
- REST API
- Management applications, including System Center

The Network Controller features can be used with Software Load Balancing (SLB) to distribute network traffic based on the policies defined in the load balancer. This includes:

- Layer 4 load balancing for North-South and East-West network traffic
- Internal and external network traffic
- Dynamic IP addresses
- Health probes

An SLB maps virtual IP addresses to the dynamic addresses in an environment. The components of an SLB environment include:

- **Virtual machine Manager**   System Center can be used to manage the Network Controller and SLB.
- **Network Controller**   Deploying the Network Controller feature is a requirement for deploying SLB in an environment.
- **SLB Multiplexer**   Maps and directs traffic so that it is sent to the correct dynamic IP address.
- **SLB Host Agent**   Listens for policy updates from the Network Controller and configures virtual switches with the configured policy.
- **BGP-enabled router**   BGP enables you to route the traffic to and from the SLB Multiplexer.

Determine implementation scenarios for various types of Windows Server Gateways, including L3, GRE, and S2S, and their uses

With Windows Server 2016 and System Center, you can deploy a Windows Server Gateway to for routing in a multitenant environment. Windows Server Gateway supports BGP options, including Local BGP IP Address and Autonomous System Numbers (ASN), List of BGP Peer IP Addresses, and ASN values. This enables a cloud provider to route datacenter traffic between virtual and physical networks to and from the internet.

A RAS Gateway can be used with Hyper-V Network Virtualization to provide several benefits:

- **Site-to-site VPNs**   Connect two networks at different physical locations together over the Internet.
- **Point-to-site VPNs**   Connect individual clients to a corporate network over the Internet.
- **GRE tunneling**   Provide connectivity for tenant virtual networks and external networks.
- **BGP routing**   Uses a dynamic routing protocol to learn subnets and routes that are connected to the RAS gateway.

A RAS Gateway is useful in several scenarios, including:

- **Multitenant gateway**   Virtual networks direct traffic to the RAS gateway. The RAS gateway can then direct the traffic over a site-to-site VPN or other destination based on the packet.
- **Multitenant NAT**   The RAS gateway can also forward the traffic from virtual networks to the Internet, and translate the addresses to publicly routable addresses.
- **Forwarding gateway**   If the virtual networks need access to physical resources on a network, the RAS gateway can forward the traffic to the appropriate resource.

Determine requirements and scenarios for distributed firewall policies and network security groups

A new service with Windows Server 2016 is the Datacenter Firewall. Datacenter firewall provides stateful, multitenant firewall protection at the network layer. Figure 9-6 outlines the how the firewall is used by a Network Controller.

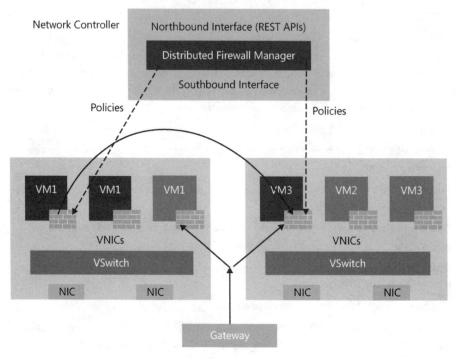

FIGURE 9-6 Virtual Machine Hardware Acceleration Settings

The Datacenter Firewall provides several benefits:

- Scalable and manageable software-defined firewall
- Move virtual networks without effecting tenant networks
- Protect tenant services outside of an operating system

By using a Datacenter Firewall, you can apply firewall policies to virtual machines or sub-nets. Like a network access list, a Datacenter Firewall policy can be configured to look at five key network traffic elements:

- Protocol
- Source port number
- Destination port number
- Source IP address
- Destination IP address

Chapter summary

- Using NIC Teaming with virtual switches and Switch Embedded Teaming
- How to enable Receive Side Scaling
- Using Quality of Service with Data Center Bridging
- Enabling SMB Direct with RDMA
- Enabling VMMQ and SR-IOV on virtual machine network adapters
- Define scenarios for using Software Defined Networking
- Configuring Network Virtualization with Generic Route Encapsulation
- Using Software Load Balancing with Network Controller
- Using a RAS Gateway as a Windows Server Gateway
- Using a Datacenter Firewall for multitenant network protection

Thought Experiment

A cloud provider is planning an expansion of their services. Additional Hyper-V hosts, network resources, storage, and other support components are installed. The cloud provider plans to provide new capabilities to their customers as part of the expansion. These capabilities must include:

- Built-in firewall services for tenant networks
- Tenant networks must support overlapping IP addresses
- Enhanced storage performance.

The provider also plans to use a Software Load Balancer for their network.

Using the above scenario, answer the following questions.

1. What feature should the provider use to protect tenant networks?

2. How can the provide ensure that tenant networks can overlap using the same IP addresses?

3. What technology should the network equipment support to enhance storage performance?

Thought Experiment Answers

1. The provider should use the Network Controller and Datacenter Firewall features to ensure that tenant networks have an additional layer of protection.

2. Network Virtualization with Generic Route Encapsulation (NVGRE) can be used to ensure that tenants can assign IP addresses that might overlap with other virtual networks.

3. Networking equipment should support using RDMA to ensure that storage performance is maximized over the network.

CHAPTER 10

Install and configure Active Directory Domain Services

Organizations around the world use Active Directory Domain Services (AD DS) in their infrastructures to support and manage the users and devices on their networks. In doing so, they benefit from enterprise-grade scalability, security, and manageability. AD DS leverages a hierarchical design structure, enabling administrators to organize user and device objects across multiple containers based on the needs of the business. For the exam, you need to be familiar with the various deployment elements for AD DS, such as the installation and configuration of domain controllers.

Skills in this chapter:

- Install and configure domain controllers

Skill 10.1: Install and configure domain controllers

The first step in implementing AD DS involves installing and configuring a domain controller. In its simplest form, a domain controller is a server running the Windows Server operating system with the AD DS role installed. Depending on the size of an organization, the number of domain controllers supporting AD DS can vary. Considerations like location, security, and redundancy play a major role in the architectural design of AD DS. Imagine you are a system administrator for Wide World Importers. The organization has twelve offices across the globe with 3,500 employees. Four of these offices have limited physical security, but all of them require reliable authentication to the network. In this scenario, you might expect to see redundant domain controllers at each office to improve performance and reliability. The four offices with limited physical security could utilize read-only domain controllers (RODC) to improve logical security.

There are a few different approaches for installing domain controllers, including the creation of a new forest and adding and removing domain controllers from that forest. After installing AD DS, we spend some time reviewing basic configuration tasks, such as how to configure a global catalog server, and transferring the operations master role. By the end of this section you should have a good understanding of these fundamentals and be comfortable walking through the steps.

This section covers how to:

- Install a new forest
- Add or remove a domain controller from a domain
- Upgrade a domain controller
- Install AD DS on a Server Core installation
- Install a domain controller from Install from Media
- Resolve DNS SRV record registration issues
- Configure a global catalog server
- Transfer and seize operations master roles
- Install and configure a read-only domain controller
- Configure domain controller cloning

Install a new forest

The AD DS framework is built using a standardized logical structure. This design enables administrators to organize their domain and domain resources in a format that meets the needs of their business. There are four core components in the Active Directory logical structure that contribute to a forest. These include the following:

- **Organizational Units**   Used for organizing the objects in your Active Directory infrastructure. These are individual containers that enable administrators to structure objects with similar requirements. For example, an organization with multiple offices could have a separate organizational unit for each location. Beneath those containers they have separate organizational units for computers and users. This format enables the administrator to apply Group Policy settings and delegate administrative control on a per-site basis.

- **Domains**   A collection of objects that share a common directory database. Each domain acts as an administrative boundary for the associated objects. A single domain can cover multiple geographical locations and contain millions of objects.

- **Domain Trees**   Consist of multiple domains. Domains that are grouped into trees follow a parent child relationship. In a hierarchical structure, the tree root domain is referred to as the parent domain. Domains joined to the parent domain are referred to as child domains.

- **Forests** Make up a complete Active Directory instance. Each forest acts as a security boundary for the information contained within that Active Directory instance. A forest can contain multiple domains and all objects within.

To get started with AD DS, we first need to install a new forest. In the following example, Wingtip Toys has decided to implement AD DS into their environment. They are using Windows Server 2016 for all their domain controllers. For this exam, you should be familiar with installing a forest using Server Manager and PowerShell.

Install a new forest using Server Manager

In this section, we are going to install a new forest using Server Manager. Follow these steps to complete the installation:

1. Open Server Manager.
2. On the Server Manager Dashboard, click Add Roles And Features.
3. On the Before You Begin page of the Add Roles And Features Wizard, click Next.
4. On the Installation Type page, confirm Role-Based or Feature-Based Installation is selected and click Next.
5. On the Server Selection page, make sure that Select A Server From The Server Pool is selected and your server is highlighted in the list. Click Next.
6. On the Server Roles page, check the box for Active Directory Domain Services. When prompted to add additional features, review the list and select Include Management Tools (If Applicable) is checked. Click Add Features and click Next.
7. On the Features page, click Next.
8. On the AD DS page, click Next.
9. On the Confirmation page, review the list of roles and features to be installed. Refer to Figure 10-1 as a reference. Click Install to begin the installation of AD DS.

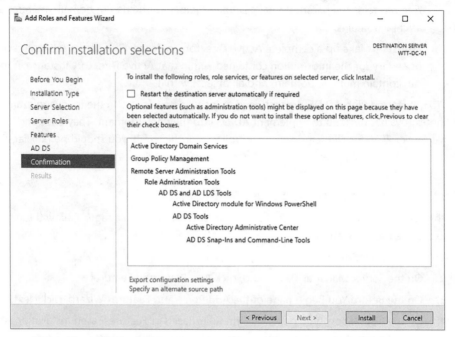

FIGURE 10-1 The Add Roles and Features Wizard shows a list of new roles and features to be installed for AD DS

10. After completing the installation of AD DS, a new warning notification is displayed in Server Manager. Click the notification icon and click Promote This Server To A Domain Controller.

11. On the Deployment Configuration page of the Active Directory Domain Services Configuration Wizard, select Add A New Forest. For the Root Domain Name, type **WingtipToys.local** and click Next.

12. On the Domain Controller Options page, review the default settings for forest and domain functional level. Confirm that Domain Name System (DNS) Server is checked. For the Directory Services Restore Mode (DSRM) Password, type **P@ssw0rd** in the two fields and click Next.

13. On the DNS Options page, note the DNS warning at the top of the wizard. This is expected as this is a new single-server installation of AD DS and we do not currently have a DNS server. Click Next.

14. On the Additional Options page, review the NetBIOS domain name and click Next.

15. On the Paths page, review the default paths for the AD DS database, log files, and sysvol folder. Click Next.

16. On the Review Options page, review the list of configuration options. Click View Script. This opens a text file with the PowerShell commands used to configure AD DS. Copy

the contents of this text file for use in the next section of this objective. Close the text file and click Next.

17. On the Prerequisites Check page, review any warnings displayed in the results pane and click Install. Once installation completes, the server automatically reboots to finish the AD DS configuration.

After completing these steps, you have a new AD DS forest for WintipToys.local that consists of a single domain controller. The first time you log into a new forest, use the WINGTIPTOYS\ Administrator account. Once logged in. you can create additional administrative accounts for managing the objects in the domain.

Install a new forest using PowerShell

In this section, we are going to install a new forest using PowerShell. We utilize the PowerShell script generated in the Server Manager example to assist with this task. Follow these steps to complete the installation:

1. Save the following PowerShell code to a text file under C:\ADDS and name the file ADDSSetup.ps1.

```
Import-Module ADDSDeployment
Install-ADDSForest `
-CreateDnsDelegation:$false `
-DatabasePath "C:\Windows\NTDS" `
-DomainMode "WinThreshold" `
-DomainName "WingtipToys.local" `
-DomainNetbiosName "WINGTIPTOYS" `
-ForestMode "WinThreshold" `
-InstallDns:$true `
-LogPath "C:\Windows\NTDS" `
-NoRebootOnCompletion:$false `
-SysvolPath "C:\Windows\SYSVOL" `
-Force:$true
```

2. Open an elevated PowerShell window.

3. Run the following command to install the Active Directory Domain Services role and all required features:

```
Install-WindowsFeature AD-Domain-Services –IncludeAllSubFeature –
IncludeManagementTools
```

4. Run the following command to run the ADDSSetup.ps1 script:

```
C:\ADDS\ADDSSetup.ps1
```

5. When prompted for the Safe Mode Administrator Password, type **P@ssw0rd**.

6. Review the status messages in the PowerShell window as AD DS is configured on your server. Once the operation completes, the server automatically reboots.

At this point, we have completed the installation and configuration of a new AD DS forest using both Server Manager and PowerShell. Both methods are effective and relatively straight forward, but as with most operations, PowerShell does enable you to automate the installation. In the next section, we walk through the process of adding and removing domain controllers from an existing forest.

Add or remove a domain controller from a domain

As an administrator of AD DS, you occasionally need to retire domain controllers and deploy new ones. This might be due to an operating system update, or possibly due to some recent expansion in your organization. In these situations, it is important to know the process.

Install a new domain controller

In the following example, you are a system administrator for Wingtip Toys. This organization has a healthy AD forest running a single domain. Inside the WingtipToys.local domain, there are three domain controllers located across three geographically dispersed offices. Wingtip Toys has decided to close its Chicago office and open a new location in Washington. You have been tasked with demoting the domain controller in Chicago and deploying a new one in Washington. We start the process by deploying the new domain controller in Washington. Before you begin, you need to set up a new server running Windows Server 2016. Confirm that the server is on your network and can successfully resolve the WingtipToys.local domain. Complete the following steps to install a new domain controller using Server Manager:

1. Open Server Manager.
2. On the Server Manager Dashboard, click Add Roles And Features.
3. On the Before You Begin page of the Add Roles And Features Wizard, click Next.
4. On the Installation Type page, confirm Role-Based or Feature-Based Installation is selected and click Next.
5. On the Server Selection page, highlight Select A Server From The Server Pool, and be sure that your server is highlighted in the list. Click Next.
6. On the Server Roles page, check the box for Active Directory Domain Services. When prompted to add additional features, review the list and confirm that Include Management Tools (If Applicable) is checked. Click Add Features and click Next.
7. On the Features page, click Next.
8. On the AD DS page, click Next.
9. On the Confirmation page, review the list of roles and features to be installed. Refer to Figure 10-1 as a reference. Click Install to begin the installation of AD DS.
10. After completing the installation of AD DS, a new warning notification is displayed in Server Manager. Click the notification icon and click Promote This Server To A Domain Controller.

11. On the Deployment Configuration page of the Active Directory Domain Services Configuration Wizard, select Add A Domain Controller To An Existing Domain. Click the Select option that appears next to the Domain field. When prompted, enter the domain credentials for an account in the wingtiptoys.local domain that is a member of the Domain Admins group. Select the WingtipToys.local domain and click Next.

12. On the Domain Controller Options page, review the default options. Confirm that Domain Name System (DNS) Server and Global Catalog (GC) are checked. For the Directory Services Restore Mode (DSRM) password, type **P@ssw0rd** in the two fields and click Next.

13. On the DNS Options page, click Next.

14. On the Additional Options page, note the default option for Replication and click Next.

15. On the Paths page, review the default paths for the AD DS database, log files, and sysvol folder. Click Next.

16. On the Review Options page, review the list of configuration options. Click View Script. This opens a text file with the PowerShell commands used to configure the new domain controller, which is similar to what we saw when we installed a new forest. Close the text file and click Next.

17. On the Prerequisites Check page, review any warnings displayed in the results pane and click Install. Once the installation is complete, the server automatically reboots to complete the installation.

After completing these steps, the new domain controller is now associated as an object in the WingtipToys.local domain. Open Active Directory Users and Computers from an existing domain controller and confirm that the new server is shown in the Domain Controllers organizational unit. As with the installation of a new forest, adding a new domain controller can also be automated using the PowerShell script output seen in Step 16. Most notably, the Install-ADDSDomainController cmdlet.

Demoting an existing domain controller

Continuing with our task, we now demote the domain controller in the Wingtip Toys Chicago office. For this operation, let's use PowerShell to demonstrate how quickly a domain controller can be demoted. Note that this same procedure can be accomplished in Server Manager using the Remove Roles And Features Wizard. Follow these steps to demote the domain controller using PowerShell:

1. Open an elevated PowerShell window.

2. Type the following command to uninstall the AD DS domain controller role:

```
Uninstall-ADDSDomainController
```

3. When prompted, type the local administrator password for the server.

4. When prompted, type **Y** to complete the operation. Monitor the output shown in the PowerShell window for any warnings or errors. Refer to Figure 10-2 for an example of the expected output. Once complete, the server automatically reboots.

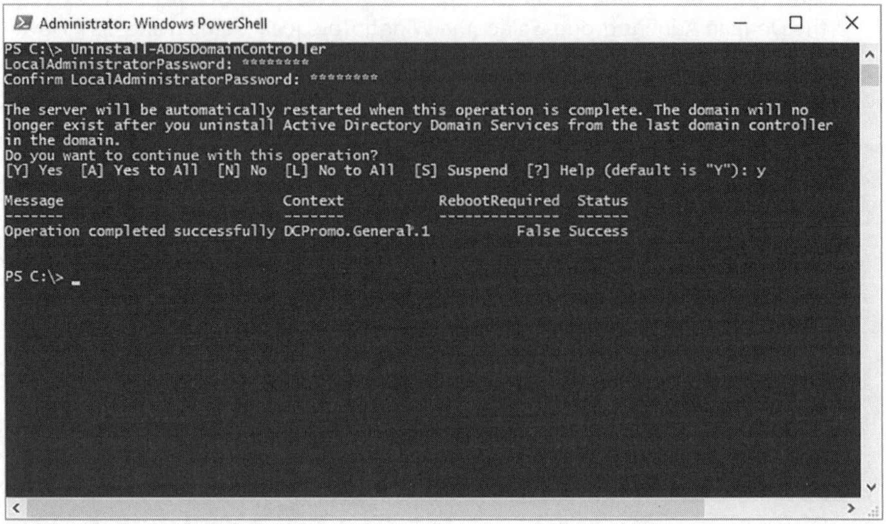

FIGURE 10-2 The Uninstall-ADDSDomainController cmdlet can be used to demote a domain controller from an existing forest.

The process of promoting or demoting a domain controller is something you need to be comfortable with. There are many situations where this can be a required task. Another possible scenario involves upgrading a domain controller to achieve a more current domain functional level, which we discuss in the next section.

Upgrade a domain controller

Once a domain controller is deployed, often they remain untouched, aside from routine maintenance and patches. Of course, there are times where it does become important to upgrade or refresh these servers. One such scenario involves upgrading the functional level for your domain. With each iteration of Windows Server, new features and enhancements are introduced for AD DS. Some of these features are domain-wide, such as the AD recycle bin. However, before you can enable domain-wide features, you must first raise the functional level of your domain. This task involves updating each of the domain controllers in your domain to the latest version of Windows Server and then raising the domain functional level to match.

Imagine you are a systems administrator for Wide World Importers. This organization has a single domain that consists of 18 domain controllers. The domain functional level is currently set to Windows Server 2008 R2 and there is a mixture of operating system versions among the existing domain controllers. Half of the servers are three to four years old and are running Windows Server 2008 R2. The other half are one to two years old and are running Windows Server 2012 R2. Your team has been tasked with upgrading the operating system across all 18 domain controllers to Windows Server 2016, followed by raising the domain functional level to match. There are three approaches to consider when faced with this scenario:

- **In-place upgrade** In-place upgrades of the Windows Server operating system are supported. They also tend to be more cost effective, allowing you to reuse the existing hardware. If you plan to do an in-place upgrade of the operating system, be aware of the updated system requirements for the new operating system version. Also, take into consideration any application compatibility concerns if the domain controller is hosting additional roles for your organization.

- **Demote, upgrade, and promote** If costs are a concern but a fresh installation is preferred over an in-place upgrade, consider demoting the existing domain controller, formatting it, installing the latest version of Windows Server, and promoting it back into the domain. When taking this approach, you still need to consider the system requirements for the newer version of Windows Server, and the lifecycle of the physical hardware you are reusing.

- **Side-by-side upgrade** A side-by-side upgrade is not as cost efficient as the previous two options, but might be mandatory if existing hardware has reached end-of-life or doesn't meet the system requirements for the latest version of Windows Server. In this situation, you would build a new server and promote it as a domain controller. You want to consider the need for new host names, IP addresses, and possibly firewall changes to support the side-by-side upgrade. After a new domain controller is online, you will transition any roles from the existing domain controller, and then demote the existing domain controller.

After reviewing the above options, the best approach for Wide World Importers involves a mixture of side-by-side upgrades and refreshing existing domain controllers. Knowing that a portion of the existing domain controllers are three to four years old, it is safe to assume that the hardware for those domain controllers is reaching end-of-life and should be replaced soon. Whereas the servers that are one to two years old could be demoted, refreshed, and promoted back into the domain.

Install AD DS on a Server Core installation

The first time you install Windows Server 2016, notice that the default installation type is set to Server Core. Server Core is a minimalistic install of the Windows Server operating system. This install type only provides access to certain core server roles, with the option to install additional roles as needed. This type of installation reduces system overhead and greatly improves the security posture of the server. Since its introduction with Windows Server 2008, several enhancements have been made to Server Core, enabling administrators to manage these servers centrally. For example, you can add and manage dozens of Server Core installs from a central management server using Server Manager and PowerShell.

As we mentioned earlier in this chapter, domain controllers are often deployed and then managed from a central location, or through a set of tools that do not require direct access to the server. A Server Core installation is an ideal install in these working conditions, while collecting on the benefits that Server Core provides.

In the following example, we are going to walk through the steps for installing AD DS on a Server Core installation of Windows Server 2016. Let's create a new forest for Wingtip Toys. Before installing AD DS on any server, it is important that we configure the network interface first. There are multiple ways to accomplish this task in Server Core. The Server Configuration tool is one option, which provides you with a basic text interface for configuring core components. You can access the Server Configuration tool by typing sconfig at the command prompt. Another option is to use PowerShell. Let's look at the PowerShell cmdlets used for configuring the network adapter on our server.

1. Log in to your server running Windows Server 2016 Server Core.

2. At the command prompt, type powershell.exe to start PowerShell.

3. Run the Get-NetAdapter command to retrieve a list of available network adapters on your server. Make a note of the adapter name that you are configuring.

4. Run the following command to assign a static IP address, replacing the value for InterfaceAlias with the name of your network adapter:

   New-NetIPAddress -IPAddress 10.0.0.10 -InterfaceAlias "Ethernet"
   -DefaultGateway 10.0.0.254 -AddressFamily IPv4 -PrefixLength 24

5. Run the following command to assign the DNS servers:

   Set-DnsClientServerAddress -InterfaceAlias "Ethernet" -ServerAddresses
   ("10.0.0.1","10.0.0.10")

6. Run the ipconfig /all command and review the IP and DNS settings for your network adapter. Confirm that the values match the assignments set above.

With the network adapter configured, we can now install the AD DS role on this server. To do so, utilize the same PowerShell cmdlets discussed earlier in this chapter.

1. Log in to your server running Windows Server 2016 Server Core.

2. At the command prompt, type powershell.exe to start PowerShell.

3. Run the following command to install the Active Directory Domain Services role and all required features:

   Install-WindowsFeature AD-Domain-Services -IncludeAllSubFeature -
   IncludeManagementTools

4. Run the following command to create the new forest and promote the server to a domain controller:

   Install-ADDSForest -DomainName WintipToys.local

5. When prompted for the Safe Mode Administrator Password, type **P@ssw0rd**.

6. When prompted to continue and allow an automatic reboot, type **Y**.

7. Review the status messages in the PowerShell window as AD DS is configured on your server. Once the operation completes the server automatically reboots.

After rebooting, your server is now an active domain controller in the WingtipToys.local domain. At this point, you have the option of installing the AD DS management tools on a remote server, or downloading the Remote Server Administration Tools (RSAT) for Windows 10 and managing AD from your workstation. As you explore Server Core, familiarize yourself with the sconfig utility. These options are important starting points for managing your Server Core installs.

Install a domain controller from Install from Media

Every Active Directory domain rests on the shoulders of a database. This database varies in size based on the amount of data stored in Active Directory, which is typically dictated by the size of your organization and the number of objects you manage. As your database grows in scale, variables such as replication and bandwidth become increasingly important. These variables are even more important when dealing with WAN connections that have limited bandwidth between remote offices.

In this section, we are going to look at promoting another domain controller, but this time let's use the Install From Media (IFM) feature. IFM is an option presented during the process of promoting a new domain controller that enables you to select a recent database export from your existing domain. Doing so eliminates the need for the new domain controller to replicate a complete copy of the database when it first comes online. Instead, IFM only replicates the recent changes since the last export was created. This method can greatly reduce the replication traffic and deployment time for a new domain controller. In some cases, this might be a mandatory operation depending on a few factors, such as the size of your AD database, the available bandwidth to the remote location, or if you have a short time window to deploy the new domain controller.

There are four types of installation media that can be created. The four types include:

- **Create Full**   This installation media type is used for writable domain controllers or Active Directory Lightweight Directory Services (AD LDS) instances.

- **Create Sysvol Full**   This installation media type is used for writable domain controllers and includes SYSVOL.

- **Create RODC**   This installation media type is used for read-only domain controllers (RODC).

- **Create Sysvol RODC**   This installation media type is used for RODC and includes SYSVOL.

EXAM TIP

For the exam, you should be familiar with each installation media type and the output they provide.

As a systems administrator for Wide World Importers, you are responsible for deploying new domain controllers when the need arises. You work at the corporate headquarters, located in San Francisco, CA. Your manager has just informed you that a new office is set to open in Dublin, Ireland later this year. This is the company's first office in Dublin, with the expectation of future growth. Initially you are limited to a 10 MB WAN link between the new office and the corporate headquarters. In the following example, we walk through the process of exporting the existing AD database, copying it to a new server, and using the IFM option to promote the server to a domain controller.

1. Log in to a domain controller on your domain.

2. Open an elevated command prompt.

3. At the command prompt, run the `ntdsutil` command to start the command-line tool for managing AD DS.

4. Run the `activate instance ntds` command to set NTDS as the active instance.

5. Run the `ifm` command to start the Install from Media process.

6. Run the following command to begin exporting a copy of your AD database and corresponding files. In this example, we are using the create sysvol full media type.

7. `create sysvol full C:\IFM`

Several status messages appear in the command prompt; these provide you with a progress report as the export runs. Once the export has completed successfully you receive a status message, as shown in Figure 10-3. At this stage, you can copy the contents of the IFM directory to a removable media source, or to the drive on the new server before you ship it to its future destination.

```
Administrator: Command Prompt - ntdsutil                          —    □    ×
osoft\Windows NT
Copying C:\IFM\SYSVOL\WingtipToys.local\Policies\{31B2F340-016D-11D2-945F-00C04FB984F9}\MACHINE\Micr
osoft\Windows NT\SecEdit
Copying C:\IFM\SYSVOL\WingtipToys.local\Policies\{31B2F340-016D-11D2-945F-00C04FB984F9}\MACHINE\Micr
osoft\Windows NT\SecEdit\GptTmpl.inf
Copying C:\IFM\SYSVOL\WingtipToys.local\Policies\{31B2F340-016D-11D2-945F-00C04FB984F9}\MACHINE\Regi
stry.pol
Copying C:\IFM\SYSVOL\WingtipToys.local\Policies\{31B2F340-016D-11D2-945F-00C04FB984F9}\USER
Copying C:\IFM\SYSVOL\WingtipToys.local\Policies\{6AC1786C-016F-11D2-945F-00C04fB984F9}
Copying C:\IFM\SYSVOL\WingtipToys.local\Policies\{6AC1786C-016F-11D2-945F-00C04fB984F9}\GPT.INI
Copying C:\IFM\SYSVOL\WingtipToys.local\Policies\{6AC1786C-016F-11D2-945F-00C04fB984F9}\MACHINE
Copying C:\IFM\SYSVOL\WingtipToys.local\Policies\{6AC1786C-016F-11D2-945F-00C04fB984F9}\MACHINE\Micr
osoft
Copying C:\IFM\SYSVOL\WingtipToys.local\Policies\{6AC1786C-016F-11D2-945F-00C04fB984F9}\MACHINE\Micr
osoft\Windows NT
Copying C:\IFM\SYSVOL\WingtipToys.local\Policies\{6AC1786C-016F-11D2-945F-00C04fB984F9}\MACHINE\Micr
osoft\Windows NT\SecEdit
Copying C:\IFM\SYSVOL\WingtipToys.local\Policies\{6AC1786C-016F-11D2-945F-00C04fB984F9}\MACHINE\Micr
osoft\Windows NT\SecEdit\GptTmpl.inf
Copying C:\IFM\SYSVOL\WingtipToys.local\Policies\{6AC1786C-016F-11D2-945F-00C04fB984F9}\USER
Copying C:\IFM\SYSVOL\WingtipToys.local\scripts
Snapshot {4ba174d4-9843-4467-a79b-53223991213b} unmounted.
IFM media created successfully in C:\IFM
ifm: ▄
```

FIGURE 10-3 The ntdsutil command line tool is used to manage Active Directory, including the ability to create installation media for new domain controllers

In this example, we copy the contents of the IFM folder to the root of the system drive on our new server. Upon arrival, the server is powered up and ready to be promoted. The following steps demonstrate walk through promoting a domain controller using the IFM export:

1. Open Server Manager.

2. On the Server Manager Dashboard, click Add Roles And Features.

3. On the Before You Begin page of the Add Roles And Features Wizard, click Next.

4. On the Installation Type page, confirm Role-Based Or Feature-Based Installation is selected and click Next.

5. On the Server Selection page, confirm Select A Server From The Server Pool is selected and your server is highlighted in the list. Click Next.

6. On the Server Roles page, select Active Directory Domain Services. When prompted to add additional features, review the list and confirm that Include Management Tools (If Applicable) is checked. Click Add Features and click Next.

7. On the Features page, click Next.

8. On the AD DS page, click Next.

9. On the Confirmation page, review the list of roles and features to be installed. Refer to Figure 10-1 as a reference. Click Install to begin the installation of AD DS.

10. After completing the installation of AD DS, a new warning notification is displayed in Server Manager. Click the notification icon and click Promote This Server To A Domain Controller.

11. On the Deployment Configuration page of the Active Directory Domain Services Configuration Wizard, select Add A Domain Controller To An Existing Domain. Click Select next to the Domain field. When prompted, enter the domain credentials for an account in the wingtiptoys.local domain that is a member of the Domain Admins group. Select the WingtipToys.local domain and click Next.

12. On the Domain Controller Options page, review the default options. Confirm that Domain Name System (DNS) Server and Global Catalog (GC) are checked. For the Directory Services Restore Mode (DSRM) password, type P@ssw0rd in the two fields and click Next.

13. On the DNS Options page, click Next.

14. On the Additional Options page, check the box for Install From Media, as shown in Figure 10-4. In the path field, enter C:\IFM, where we copied the database export, and click Verify to confirm the files can be accessed. Click Next.

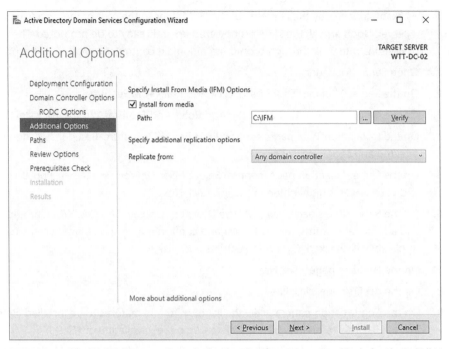

FIGURE 10-4 The Active Directory Domain Services Configuration wizard includes the Install from Media (IFM) feature on the Additional Options page

15. On the Paths page, review the default paths for the AD DS database, log files, and sysvol folder. Click Next.

16. On the Review Options page, review the list of configuration options. Click View Script. Note the additional parameter for InstallationMediaPath. Close the text file and click Next.

17. On the Prerequisites Check page, review any warnings displayed in the Results pane and click Install. Once installation completes the server automatically reboots to complete the installation.

18. After your new domain controller is online, log in and open Active Directory Users and Computers. Compare the contents with an existing domain controller. Confirm that the OU structure, objects, and attributes match across both domain controllers.

At this stage in the chapter we have walked through multiple installation scenarios for promoting a new domain controller. IFM adds some additional flexibility in your deployments, enabling you to reliably deploy domain controllers remotely, with limited saturation to your organization's WAN. These same methods can be used to prepare for larger deployments. For example, an organization that specializes in retail might have hundreds of stores across the globe, each with their own domain controller. Using IFM in this situation can be very beneficial in reducing overhead.

Resolve DNS SRV record registration issues

Throughout this chapter, we have deployed a few domain controllers under different circumstances. One common component among those domain controllers has been DNS. For AD DS to function properly, DNS must be installed and configured correctly. Every environment is different when it comes to DNS, and that plays a major role in the overall health of your AD DS forest.

AD DS relies on SRV records—also referred to as service records. Each record performs a different purpose, such as guiding clients to their nearest LDAP server, or allowing servers to communicate with each other. As the administrator for AD DS, you need to be familiar with these SRV records and how to troubleshoot registration issues. When problems do arise, there are a few resources that you can use to find a solution. Let's look at those now.

- **DNS Manager**. The DNS management console is part of the AD DS management tools. You can explore the SRV records in your domain using DNS Manager. In Figure 10-5, you can see we are looking at the forward lookup zone for WingtipToys.local. In the sites directory, we can confirm that the Ldap and Kerberos SRV records are present for our domain controllers.

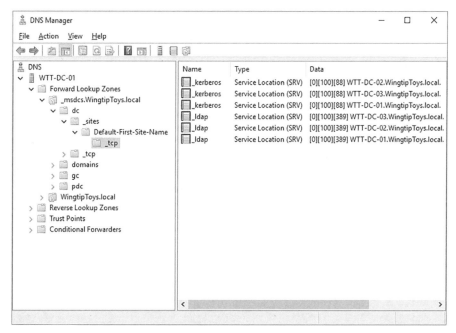

FIGURE 10-5 The DNS Manager management console is an important tool for checking on SRV records

- **Dcdiag**   The dcdiag utility is a command-line tool that provides tests that can assist in troubleshooting issues in your AD DS forest. A DNS test can be initiated from any of your domain controllers by running the following command from an elevated command prompt: dcdiag /test:dns.

- **Ipconfig**   The ipconfig utility provides network-specific information on your windows devices. If DNS is setup to accept dynamic DNS updates, and you suspect a workstation or server has not registered their SRV record, you can run the following command from an elevated command prompt: **ipconfig /registerdns**.

- **Netlogon.dns**   In environments where dynamic DNS is not enabled—and DNS is managed by a separate appliance—you can retrieve the mandatory SRV records from the netlogon.dns file on your domain controllers. This information can be provided to your DNS team so they can ensure it is added. This file is located in the following path: %WinDir%\System32\Config\netlogon.dns.

The DNS health among your domain controllers is an important variable when managing your AD DS environment. For the exam, make sure you are familiar with each of the tools mentioned above. Spend time exploring DNS manager and reviewing the SRV records in your domain.

Configure a global catalog server

In AD DS, the global catalog is designed to improve performance in environments with multiple domain controllers, or sites with limited bandwidth. The global catalog contains partial representation of every object in your AD DS forest. Domain Controllers can be designated as global catalog servers, enabling them to answer global catalog requests. If an application is connected to Active Directory, and that application issues a search to a nearby global catalog server, the search completes faster because it has the necessary information available.

Let's start by determining whether a domain controller has been configured as a global catalog server. There are places we can look for this information. The first location is in Active Directory Users And Computers. If you navigate to the Domain Controllers container, there is a column named DC Type. Domain controllers that have been designated as global catalog servers have a DC type of GC (Global Catalog). In Figure 10-6, you can see that two of our three domain controllers are set up as Global Catalog servers.

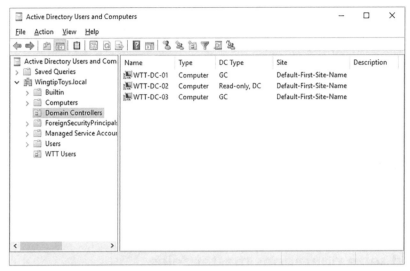

FIGURE 10-6 The Active Directory Users and Computers management console displays the DC type for the domain controllers in your domain

Another location for reviewing the status of a global catalog server is within the Active Directory Sites And Services Management console. To reveal these options, you need to expand sites, followed by the site where your domain controller is assigned. Under the site, expand Servers. With the desired domain controller selected, right-click NTDS Settings and choose Properties. On the General tab of the NTDS Settings properties window, there is a checkbox for designating the global catalog role, as shown in Figure 10-7. If you need to toggle this role on or off, apply the action here and the AD DS topology is updated.

FIGURE 10-7 The Active Directory Users and Computers management console displays the DC type for the domain controllers in your domain

As you promote new domain controllers, you'll notice that the Global Catalog role is checked by default. In most scenarios, having the global catalog on every domain controller in your environment is a positive addition. In rare situations, depending on the AD DS topology, you might find a case in which removing the global catalog role from specific domain controllers might improve the environment. Other considerations include a Read-Only Domain Controller (RODC), which can be designated as a Global Catalog Server. However, not all directory-enabled applications supports connectivity to a Global Catalog Server hosted on a RODC.

> **NEED MORE REVIEW?** **ADDITIONAL DETAILS ON THE GLOBAL CATALOG**
>
> To study more about the global catalog, dependencies, and interactions, visit *https://technet.microsoft.com/library/cc728188(v=ws.10).aspx.*

Transfer and seize operations master roles

AD DS is comprised of five Flexible Single Master Operation (FSMO) roles. These roles are assigned to the domain controllers in your environment. Each role can only be assigned to a single domain controller, but there are no restrictions as to which roles are assigned where. For example, if you have five different domain controllers, you could technically assign each role to a different domain controller. It is also worth noting that RODCs cannot host any of the FSMO roles. Let's look at the function for each role:

- **Schema master**   The schema master role can only be assigned to a single domain controller at any given time. This role is responsible for performing schema updates within AD. After processing a schema update, the schema master replicates the changes to the other domain controllers.

- **Domain naming master**   The domain naming master role can only be assigned to a single domain controller at any given time. This role is responsible for making changes to the forest-wide domain name space within AD.

- **RID master**   The RID master role is responsible for processing relative ID (RID) requests from all domain controllers in your domain.

- **PDC emulator**   The PDC emulator role is responsible for synchronizing time within AD. This role has associations with core security components, such as password changes and account lockouts.

- **Infrastructure master**   The infrastructure master role is responsible for keeping domain references to objects up-to-date. It accomplishes this by comparing its data with the information in the global catalog. Due to its design, it is best to have the infrastructure master role on a domain controller that is not designated as a global catalog server, but does have a strong connection to a global catalog server. If all your domain controllers are designated as global catalog servers, the infrastructure manager role does not operate.

EXAM TIP

You should be familiar with each of the FSMO roles, their individual purpose, and how to transfer the roles to a different DC.

Now that you have a basic understanding of the FSMO roles, let's look at where these roles are installed in your domain.

1. Log in to a domain controller on your domain.
2. Open an elevated command prompt.
3. Run the following command to lookup where each FSMO role is assigned, as shown in Figure 10-8:

```
netdom /query FSMO
```

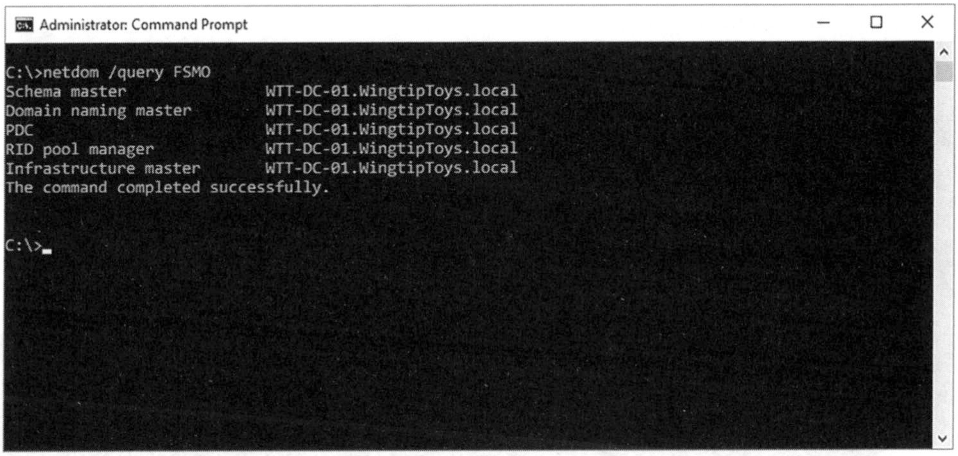

Administrator: Command Prompt
C:\>netdom /query FSMO
Schema master WTT-DC-01.WingtipToys.local
Domain naming master WTT-DC-01.WingtipToys.local
PDC WTT-DC-01.WingtipToys.local
RID pool manager WTT-DC-01.WingtipToys.local
Infrastructure master WTT-DC-01.WingtipToys.local
The command completed successfully.
C:\>

FIGURE 10-8 The netdom utility can assist in identifying where the FSMO roles are assigned in your domain

After you have identified which domain controllers have which FSMO roles assigned, we need to understand the difference between transferring a role and seizing a role.

- **Transfer** Transferring an FSMO role is the preferred operation. You should use the transfer option when the current role holder is operational and can be accessed on the network by the future FSMO owner.
- **Seize** Seizing an FSMO role is undesirable, but might be necessary in disaster recovery scenarios. You should use the seize option when the current role holder is experiencing a failure and is otherwise nonoperational.

Transferring FSMO roles

Transferring and seizing FSMO roles is accomplished using the ntdsutil utility. Figure 10-8 shows that WTT-DC-01 contains all the FSMO roles for the domain. Let's transfer the infrastructure master role to WTT-DC-03.

1. Log in to a domain controller on your domain.

2. Open an elevated command prompt.

3. Type ntdsutil and press enter.

4. Type roles and press enter.

5. Type connections and press enter.

6. Type connect to server WTT-DC-03. Review the output and confirm that the connection was successful.

7. Type q and press enter.

8. Type transfer infrastructure master and press enter. When prompted to confirm the transfer, click Yes. Review the output and confirm that the transfer was successful.

9. Type q to exit FSMO maintenance and q again to exit the ntdsutil.

After the role has been transferred, run the netdom utility again and confirm that the infrastructure master role is now assigned to WTT-DC-03, as shown in Figure 10-9.

FIGURE 10-9 The netdom utility can assist in identifying where the FSMO roles are assigned in your domain.

Seizing FSMO roles

Let's imagine that WTT-DC-03 has suffered a catastrophic failure, which is preventing us from cleanly transferring the assigned FSMO roles. In this example, the domain controller is no longer on the network, so let's use the seize option to recover the role and reassign it to WTT-DC-01.

1. Log in to a domain controller on your domain.

2. Open an elevated command prompt.

3. Type ntdsutil and press enter.

4. Type roles and press enter.

5. Type connections and press enter.

6. Type connect to server WTT-DC-01. Review the output and confirm that the connection was successful.

7. Type q and press enter.

8. Type seize infrastructure master and press enter. When prompted to confirm the transfer, click Yes. Review the output and confirm that the transfer was successful.

9. Type q to exit FSMO maintenance and q again to exit the ntdsutil.

After the role has been seized, run the netdom utility once more and confirm that the infrastructure master role is now assigned to WTT-DC-01

EXAM TIP

For the exam, make sure you understand the differences between the transfer and seize operations.

Install and configure a read-only domain controller

Security is a critical consideration for any organization. The virtual perimeter surrounding your intellectual property requires constant attention and remediation. AD DS contains user accounts, e-mail addresses, passwords, and most importantly, access to resources and services that are intended to be tightly secured. When you review the security of AD DS, one consideration to consider is the physical placement of your domain controllers, and the expected requirements of those servers. Here are a few questions you should consider when reviewing the security of your domain controllers:

1. Is there physical security?

2. Is the domain controller connected to an external network or DMZ?

3. Are non-administrative users requesting access to the domain controller to support internal applications?

The RODC was first introduced with Windows Server 2008. It was designed to address the questions listed above. The features shown in Table 10.1 were introduced with the intention of providing additional security to AD DS and your organization.

TABLE 10-1 RODC security feature chart

Feature	Description
Unidirectional replication	Unlike writable domain controllers, RODCs are designed to replicate changes inbound but not outbound. The other domain controllers in your forest does not replicate changes from an RODC. This improves security by preventing the possibility of a malicious update from replicating outward through your forest.
Special krbtgt account	The krbtgt account prevents a comprised RODC from accessing re-sources at a remote site.
Password Replication Policy (PRP)	The PRP prevents passwords from being cached locally on the RODC. If an RODC is compromised, no account passwords can be obtained.
RODC Filtered attribute set (FAS)	The FAS enables the administrator to assign which applications can replicate data to RODCs. This is accomplished by adding the at-tributes for the application to the RODC FAS and marking them as confidential.

For example, Wingtip Toys has recently expanded into the retail market, with 12 new stores set to open in the next six months. These stores require local domain controllers to support the multiple point-of-sale computers at each location. The physical security of these stores is limited, and in some cases, requires your servers to share some centralized rack space with the joining stores. Based on these requirements you have chosen to promote RODCs at each store. Let's walk through process of promoting a RODC:

1. Open Server Manager.

2. On the Server Manager Dashboard, click Add Roles And Features.

3. On the Before You Begin page of the Add Roles And Features Wizard, click Next.

4. On the Installation Type page, confirm Role-Based or Feature-Based Installation is selected and click Next.

5. On the Server Selection page, confirm Select A Server From The Server Pool is selected and your server is highlighted in the list. Click Next.

6. On the Server Roles page, check the box for Active Directory Domain Services. When prompted to add additional features, review the list and select Include Management Tools (If Applicable). Click Add Features and click Next.

7. On the Features page, click Next.

8. On the AD DS page, click Next.

9. On the Confirmation page, review the list of roles and features to be installed. Refer to Figure 10-1 as a reference. Click Install to begin the installation of AD DS.

10. After completing the installation of AD DS, a new warning notification is displayed in Server Manager. Click the notification icon and click Promote This Server To A Domain Controller.

11. On the Deployment Configuration page of the Active Directory Domain Services Configuration Wizard, select Add A Domain Controller To An Existing Domain. Click Domain field option. When prompted, enter the domain credentials for an account in the wingtiptoys.local domain that is a member of the Domain Admins group. Select the WingtipToys.local domain and click Next.

12. On the Domain Controller Options page, review the default options. Check the box for Read Only Domain Controller (RODC), as shown in Figure 10-10. For the Directory Services Restore Mode (DSRM) password, type **P@ssw0rd** in the two fields and click Next.

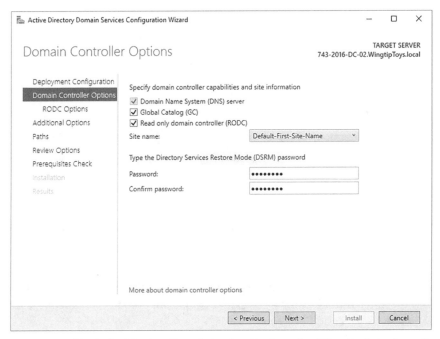

FIGURE 10-10 The Active Directory Domain Services Configuration Wizard includes the option for promoting a RODC on the Domain Controller Options page

13. On the RODC Options page, review the default accounts and groups that replicate passwords to the RODC and those that are denied, as shown in Figure 10-11. Click Next.

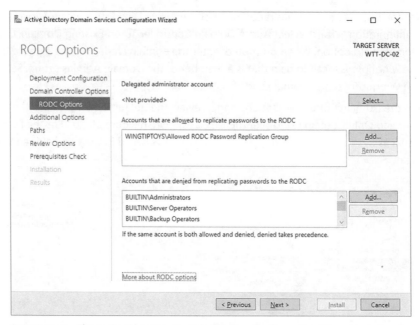

FIGURE 10-11 The Active Directory Domain Services Configuration Wizard includes password replication permissions on the RODC Options page

14. On the DNS Options page, click Next.

15. On the Additional Options page, note the default option for replication and click Next.

16. On the Paths page, review the default paths for the AD DS database, log files, and sysvol folder. Click Next.

17. On the Review Options page, review the list of configuration options. Click View Script. This opens a text file with the PowerShell commands used to configure the RODC. Close the text file and click Next.

18. On the Prerequisites Check page, review any warnings displayed in the results pane and click Install. Once installation completes, the server automatically reboots to complete the installation.

After completing the steps above, you should have a new domain controller in your domain with a DC type of Read-only. Let's connect to this domain controller and see what options are available.

1. Log in to one of your domain controllers.

2. Open Active Directory Users And Computers.

3. In the left pane of the Active Directory Users And Computer Management console, right-click WingtipToys.local and choose Change Domain Controller.

4. On the Change Directory Server dialog window, select the RODC in the list and click OK. Before connecting to the RODC you are presented with a warning stating that write operations are not permitted, as shown in Figure 10-12. Click OK.

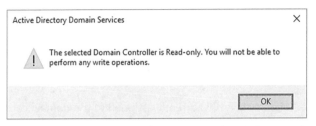

FIGURE 10-12 RODC does not allow you to perform write operations

5. Right-click the Users container. Notice that the option to create new items is not available.

6. Click the Users container. Right-click the Administrator account. Notice the options to update group membership, disable the account, and reset the password are all disabled.

Now that you have deployed an RODC and explored some of the basic functionality, consider the cases where this would make sense in your environment. The RODC is very effective at preventing changes to your existing AD DS forest. However, be cautious in your deployments. I had a customer that insisted on replacing all the writable domain controllers with RODCs at each of their remote offices. This quickly introduced a lot of management overhead. Changes could only be made on the writable domain controllers at the central office. This affected replication when multiple changes needed to be made. Offices were thousands of miles apart and operated in different time zones. These domain controllers were all racked in secure locations, so the RODC topology didn't make sense for this environment.

Configure domain controller cloning

Prior to Windows Server 2012, it was an unsupported practice to use any form of duplication to deploy a new domain controller. This included operations like cloning the VHD of an existing domain controller. Doing so could severely affect your AD DS infrastructure. This has since changed with the introduction of Windows Server 2012 and subsequent releases of Window Server. Under the right circumstances, administrators can now clone an active virtual domain controller, enabling them to do consistent deployments, in rapid succession if needed.

Before you can clone a virtual domain controller, you must meet the following requirements:

- The target domain control must be running a Windows Server 2012 or later.
- The administrator performing the cloning operation must be a member of the Domain Admins group.

- The domain controller containing the PDC emulator role must be online during the cloning process and

- The hypervisor for the domain controller must support VM-Generation ID.

With these prerequisites in mind, let's walk through the process of cloning an existing virtual domain controller. In this example, let's use Hyper-V for our hypervisor.

1. Log in to the source domain controller in your domain. This is the domain controller that we plan on cloning. In this example, the name of our domain controller is WTT-DC-02.

2. Confirm that the PDC emulator role is not currently assigned to this domain controller. To do so, run the following command from an elevated command prompt:

   ```
   netdom /query FSMO
   ```

3. Open an elevated PowerShell window.

4. Add the source domain controller to the AD security group: Cloneable Domain Controllers security group in AD. To do so, run the following command:

   ```
   Add-ADGroupMember -Identity "Cloneable Domain Controllers" -Members "WTT-DC-02$"
   ```

5. Confirm that the source domain controller does not have any applications or services installed that are not compatible with cloning. To do so, run the following command:

   ```
   Get-ADDCCloningExcludedApplicationList
   ```

6. If any items appear in the application list, they need to be removed from the domain controller or added to a CustomDCCloneAllowList.xml before you can proceed with cloning. To create the CustomDCCloneAllowList.xml, run the following command:

   ```
   Get-ADDCCloningExcludedApplicationList -GenerateXML
   ```

7. Create a new clone configuration file for the source domain controller. To do so, run the following command and review the output for any warnings or errors:

   ```
   New-ADDCCloneConfigFile -CloneComputerName "WTT-DC-03" -SiteName Default-First-Site-Name -IPv4Address 10.0.0.15 -IPv4DefaultGateway 10.0.0.254 -IPv4SubnetMask 255.255.255.0 -IPv4DNSResolver 10.0.0.1,10.0.0.15 -Static
   ```

8. Shutdown the source domain controller.

At this point we have prepared the source domain controller for cloning by granting it access in the directory, validating the running services, and creating a configuration file. Next let's clone the VM by first exporting a copy of the source domain controller and re-importing it. Because we are using Hyper-V, let's utilize PowerShell for these steps.

1. Open an elevated PowerShell window on your Hyper-V host.

2. Run the following command to export a copy of your source Domain Controller.

   ```
   Export-VM -Name WTT-DC-02 -path D:\VMExports
   ```

3. Run the following command to import the new virtual machine

```
Import-VM -Path "<XMLFile> -Copy -GenerateNewId -VhdDestinationPath D:\WTT-
DC-03
```

Once the import has completed, power on the new virtual machine. Be sure to leave the source domain controller powered off during this time. When you start the new virtual machine, it initially runs under the context of the source domain controller until the cloning process has completed, at which point you can restore the source domain controller to active duty.

When the new domain controller powers up for the first time the cloning process triggers automatically. This process utilizes the cloning configuration file that we created earlier in this section. The boot sequence displays a simple percentage to indicate how far along the cloning process is, as shown in Figure 10-13.

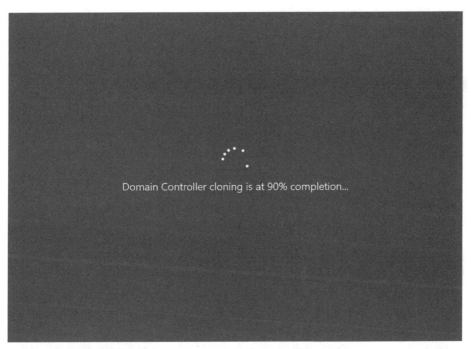

Domain Controller cloning is at 90% completion...

FIGURE 10-13 The domain controller cloning process starts automatically

Once the cloning process has completed, log in to your new domain controller. Open Active Directory Sites and Services on your new domain controller. Navigate to the Default-First-Site-Name site and look in the Servers directory. Confirm that all three domain controllers are present. At this stage, you can power on your source domain controller that was previously left offline.

In preparation for the exam, familiarize yourself with the PowerShell cmdlets used to generate the custom application list XML and cloning configuration XML. Be prepared to answer questions related to prerequisites, such as knowing with versions of Windows Server support domain controller cloning.

Chapter summary

- How to install a new forest by using the GUI and PowerShell
- Adding and removing a domain controller
- Upgrading a domain controller
- Using Server Core with AD DS
- Using the Install from Media option to provision a domain controller
- Using DNS SRV records with AD DS
- Configuring a domain controller as a global catalog
- Using FSMO roles in AD DS
- Installing a read-only domain controller
- Configuring domain controller cloning

Thought experiment: Upgrading the forest

In this thought experiment, demonstrate your skills and knowledge of the topics covered in this chapter. You can find answers to this thought experiment in the next section.

You are a systems administrator for Wingtip Toys, an organization with 16 offices around the globe, and an additional 45 stores that specialize in high performance quadcopters and drones. Your team is relatively new to the organization, inheriting a single-domain with a total of 72 domain controllers. A single physical writeable domain controller is present at each retail store, and a mixture of 1-2 domain controllers are present at each office. All the domain controllers are running Windows Server 2008 R2 and the domain functional level is set to match. All the hardware for these domain controllers are reaching end-of-support over the next six months. Your enterprise applications team is also interested in integrating AD DS with their public facing retail web portal. Your manager has added a domain controller refresh to the annual budget. In preparation for this work, he has requested answers to the following questions:

1. There is a concern with the limited physical security at each of the retail stores. What would you recommend for enhancing the logical security of the domain controllers at these locations?

2. System maintenance for the retail stores can only occur after hours, and it is critical that all systems are online before stores open. What is your recommendation for deploying the new domain controllers in this limited timeframe?

3. The main offices are not running a consistent number of domain controllers at each location. What is your recommendation for improving this topology?

4. What type of install would you recommend for the public facing retail web portal?

Thought experiment answers

1. Implementing RODCs at the retail stores helps restrict potential malicious activities if the local domain controller is compromised.

2. Utilizing IFM for the deployment of these new domain controllers enables the team to rapidly deploy the new servers, as well as greatly reducing the replication overhead across the multiple WAN links.

3. To improve reliability and redundancy, each office should utilize two domain controllers. New servers should be deployed to offices that only contain a single domain controller.

4. For the web portal, utilizing a server core installation to host the domain controller improves security and limit downtime for routing patching, due to the reduced number of security patches.

CHAPTER 11

Implement identity federation and access solutions

In this chapter, we discuss the identify management solutions that are provided with Active Directory Federation Services (AD FS). AD FS can also be combined with the Remote Access server role, which can be used to enable a Web Application Proxy (WAP). AD FS can be used to manage federated environments, and enable multi-factor authentication for organizations. Used together with a WAP, clients can be preauthenticated by an application or service before being directed to the application server.

Windows Server 2016 introduces a few new features to AD FS, not all of which are included on the upgrade exam. New features include:

- **Azure multi-factor authentication (MFA)**   Use Azure to enable MFA for an application or server in the organization.

- **Password-less access from devices**   Use Azure AD or Intune MDM policies to enable sign-on and access control based on the compliance status for the device.

- **Sign in using Windows Hello for Business**   This was previously known as Microsoft Passport for Work.

- **Enable sign-in using third-party LDAP**   LDAP v3-compliance directories can be used as a source for authenticating users.

- **Customizable sign-in**   The logon screen for individual applications can be customized for companies or brands.

- **Enhanced auditing**   AD FS in Windows Server 2016 has been streamlined and less verbose to reduce administrative complexity.

- **SAML 2.0 support**   AD FS can be used with InCommon Federations and other SAML 2.0 configurations.

- **Simplified password management**   When federating with Office 365, password expiration notifications can be sent and managed by AD FS when a user is being authenticated.

- **Easier upgrades** Previous versions required exporting a configuration and the importing it to a new farm. AD FS can now be upgraded using the existing farm to introduce the new capabilities in Windows Server 2016.

Skills in this chapter:

- Install and configure Active Directory Federation Services
- Implement Web Application Proxy

Skill 11.1: Install and configure Active Directory Federation Services

In this section, we discuss how to use Active Directory Federation Services (AD FS) to manage federated environments. First, we explain the new upgrade process that can be used with AD FS. We also explain new methods of managing authentication, including access control policies, multi-factor authentication, and device registration. Another new capability with Windows Server 2016 is enabling Windows Hello for Business for Windows 10 devices. Finally, we cover using new integration capabilities with Azure, Office 365, and other LDAP directories.

> **This section covers how to:**
>
> - Upgrade and migrate previous AD FS workloads to Windows Server 2016
> - Implement claims-based authentication, including Relying Party Trusts
> - Configure authentication policies
> - Configure multi-factor authentication
> - Implement and configure device registration
> - Integrate AD FS with Windows Hello for Business
> - Configure for use with Microsoft Azure and Office 365
> - Configure AD FS to enable authentication of users stored in LDAP directories

Upgrade and migrate previous AD FS workloads to Windows Server 2016

To ensure that the new AD FS features introduced in Windows Server 2016 can be used in an AD FS farm, the farm behavior level (FBL) has been introduced to determine which features can and cannot be used. An AD FS farm that is comprised of Windows Server 2012 R2 hosts has an FBL of Windows Server 2012 R2.

FBL works as the domain or forest functional level for Active Directory. When a Windows Server 2016 host is added to a farm, the farm is considered running in a mixed mode. The new features available with Windows Server 2016 cannot be used until the FBL has been raised to Windows Server 2016. The FBL cannot be raised until all Windows Server 2012 R2 servers have been removed from the farm.

Upgrading a farm can be performed by performing in-place operating system upgrades for individual servers, or add and replace servers as necessary. It is not necessary to deploy a new farm or export and import configuration settings to perform an upgrade in the farm.

The overall process of upgrading the farm includes:

1. Add the Windows Server 2016 servers to the existing farm.

2. Configure the AD FS farm properties by using the Set-AdfsSyncProperties cmdlet.

3. Complete the domain and forest preparation for Windows Server 2016.

4. Upgrade the AD FS FBL by using the Invoke-AdfsFarmBehaviorLevelRaise cmdlet.

5. Verify the current farm behavior by using the Get-AdfsFarmInformation cmdlet.

> **NEED MORE REVIEW? UPGRADING AD FS**
>
> For more information on using upgrading AD FS farms, visit: *https://technet.microsoft.com/en-us/windows-server-docs/identity/ad-fs/deployment/upgrading-to-ad-fs-in-windows-server-2016*.

Implement claims-based authentication, including Relying Party Trusts

When adding a Relying Party Trust, you can choose to make the trust claims aware or non-claims aware. Claims aware applications use security tokens as part of the process for authentication and authorization. Non-claims aware applications can be used with a Web Application Proxy (WAP) with Windows Integrated Authentication. Creating a Relying Party Trust can be performed from the AD FS snap-in. Figure 11-1 shows the initial screen of the wizard, selecting claims aware or non-claims aware.

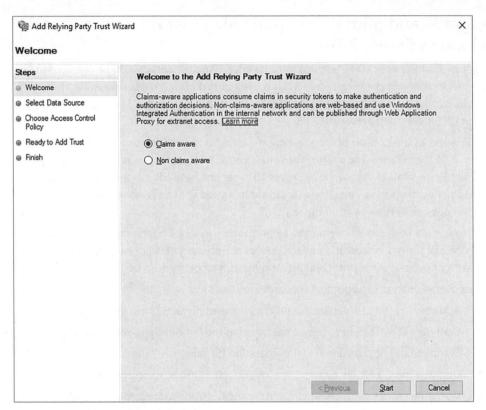

FIGURE 11-1 Add Relying Party Trust

The next step of configuring a relying party trust is to specify the source data for the relying party. This information can be provided in one of three ways:

- From a published source, online or on the network.
- From a federation metadata file.
- Entered manually in the wizard.

Figure 11-2 shows the available options for providing the configuration details.

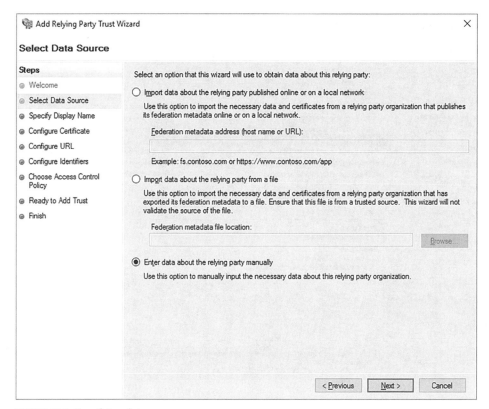

FIGURE 11-2 Specifying data source

When specifying the details manually, the information that is required includes:

- Display name
- Optional certificate
- Federation URLs
- Relying party trust identifiers

After specifying the trust details, the next configuration item is whether to set access control policies. These policies can be configured now, or at a later time. A common access method is to permit everyone, but require multi-factor authentication when the request is external. Figure 11-3 shows selecting an access control policy.

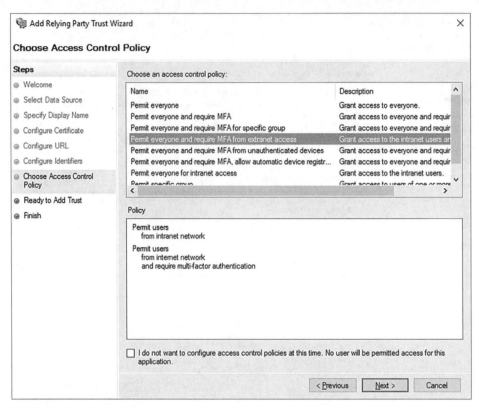

FIGURE 11-3 Specifying data source

Configure authentication policies

Authentication policies, or access control policies as defined in the AD FS management snap-in, define the authentication methods for an application. These policies can be used to define how users or devices can access an application by using AD FS. Figure 11-4 shows the built-in policies from the AD FS management snap-in.

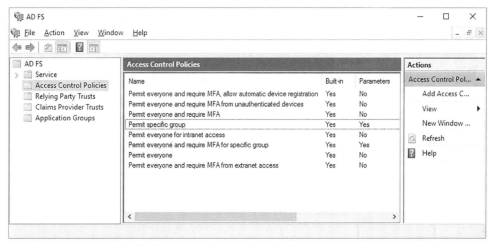

FIGURE 11-4 Access Control Policies

You can also specify a custom access control policy from the AD FS management snap-in. The available options to permit:

- Everyone
- Users
  - From a specific network
  - From specific security groups
  - From devices that have a specific trust level
  - With specific claims in the request
  - And require multi-factor authentication

You can also permit these users or groups with the following exceptions:

- Specific networks
- Specific groups
- Devices with specific trust levels
- Specific claims in the request

Figure 11-5 shows defining a custom access control policy.

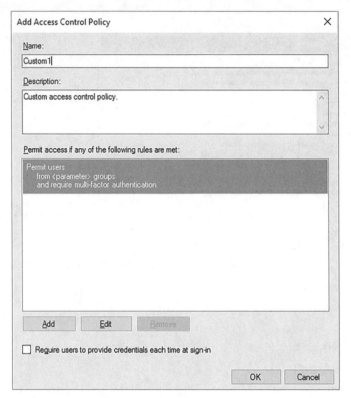

FIGURE 11-5 Custom access control policy

Configure multi-factor authentication

Using Azure multi-factor authentication (MFA) with AD FS has several pre-requisites:

- Azure subscription that includes Azure Active Directory
- Azure multi-factor authentication
    - As of this writing, this is included with Azure AD Premium and the Enterprise Mobility Suite subscription options.
- On-premises AD FS at the Windows Server 2016 Farm Behavior Level
- The on-premises AD FS must be federated with Azure AD
- The Windows Azure Active Directory Module for Windows PowerShell must be installed
- You must have global administrator permissions to modify Azure AD
- You must have Enterprise Administrator credentials to configure the AD FS farm

Overall, the general configuration process for using MFA with Azure includes:

1. Generate a certificate for Azure MFA on each AD FS server.
2. Add the credentials to the Azure MFA Auth-client SPN.
3. Configure the AD FS farm.

Generating a certificate for Azure MFA is completed by running the New-AdfsAzureM-faTenantCertificate cmdlet. This certificate is generated and placed in the local machines certificate store on the AD FS server. The subject name of the certificate is the TenantID for the Azure AD directory.

To add the credentials to the SPN for Azure MFA, obtain the credentials from the generated certificate. Add the credentials by using the New-MsolServicePrincipalCredential cmdlet and specify the GUID for the Azure MFA Auth Client.

Finally, you can configure the AD FS farm by using the Set-AdfsAzureMfaTenant cmdlet. This cmdlet requires the TenantId and ClientId for the Azure subscription. After making the configuration change, the AD FS service must be restarted on each server in the farm. After restarting the service, Azure MFA is available as an authentication method. Figure 11-6 shows using Azure MFA as an authentication method.

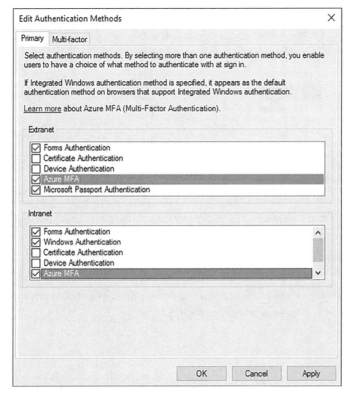

FIGURE 11-6 Authentication methods

Implement and configure device registration

AD FS in Windows Server 2016 enhances device registration to enable sign on and access control based on the compliance status of a device. When users authenticate using a device credential, the device's compliance is re-evaluated to ensure that policies are applied appropriately. This can include:

- Enable access only from devices that are managed and/or compliant
- Enable external access for devices that are managed and/or compliant.
- Require MFA for computers that are not managed or compliant.

Figure 11-7 illustrates using device registration with AD FS. Users and devices can be enrolled by using Azure AD or Microsoft Intune. Both services use Azure AD with Azure AD Connect device write-back. The devices can connect to on-premises services that might also contain conditional access policies, device authentication, or MFA.

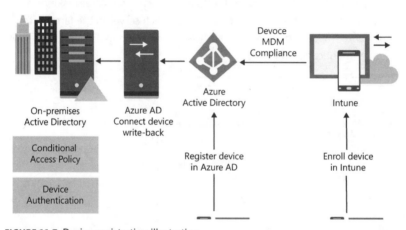

FIGURE 11-7 Device registration illustration

A device's trust level is one of three levels:

- **Authenticated** Devices that have been authenticated are registered in Azure AD, but have not been enrolled in a mobile device management (MDM) policy.
- **Managed** Managed devices are registered devices that are also enrolled in an MDM policy.
- **Compliant** Devices that are compliant are registered and enrolled in an MDM policy. In addition, the device meets the requirements of the MDM policy.

Integrate AD FS with Windows Hello for Business

Windows Hello for Business enables organizations to replace user passwords with a PIN or biometric gestures. AD FS supports these Windows 10 capabilities to provide authentication without needing a password. The general steps to enable Windows Hello with AD FS include:

1. Deploy System Center Configuration Manager with a public key infrastructure.
2. Configure policies settings through Configuration Manager or Group Policy.
3. Configure certificate profiles with smart card sign-in extended key usage.

> *NEED MORE REVIEW?* **CONFIGURING SCCM WITH WINDOWS HELLO**
>
> For a step by step of configuring Configuration Manager with Windows Hello, visit *https://azure.microsoft.com/en-us/documentation/articles/active-directory-azureadjoin-passport-deployment/.*

Configure for use with Microsoft Azure and Office 365

Earlier in this chapter we explained that you can enroll devices in MDM policies through Azure AD and enable MFA with Azure AD. AD FS can also integrate with Azure and Office 365 to send password expiration claims to applications that are federated with AD FS. With Office 365, the password expiration notice can be sent to Exchange and Outlook to notify users that their password soon expires.

As of this writing, these claims are only available for authentication using a username and password, or using Windows Hello for Business. If a user authentication uses window integrated authentication without Windows Hello for Business, then the password expiration is not displayed. Additionally, a password expiration notice is only displayed if the password expires within the next 14 days.

To configure AD FS to enable password expiration claims, add the following claim rule to the relying party trust.

```
c1:[Type == "http://schemas.microsoft.com/ws/2012/01/passwordexpirationtime"]
=> issue(store = "_PasswordExpiryStore", types = ("http://schemas.microsoft.com/
ws/2012/01/passwordexpirationtime", "http://schemas.microsoft.com/ws/2012/01/
passwordexpirationdays", "http://schemas.microsoft.com/ws/2012/01/passwordchangeurl"),
query = "{0};", param = c1.Value);
```

Configure AD FS to enable authentication of users stored in LDAP directories

AD FS in Windows Server 2016 introduces supports for three new LDAP scenarios:

- Third-party LDAP v3 compliant directories
- AD forests that do not have a two-way trust
- AD Lightweight Directory Services (AD LDS)

You can create a connection from AD FS to the LDAP directory by using the New-AdfsLdapServerConnection cmdlet. Figure 11-8 shows creating a new LDAP server connection.

FIGURE 11-8 New-AdfsLdapServerConnection

Then, you can map LDAP attributes to AD FS claims by using the New-AdfsLdapAttributeToClaimMapping cmdlet. For example, you can map name, surname, and displayname fields to the appropriate AD FS claim. Finally, register the LDAP store with the AD FS farm as a claims provider by using the Add-AdfsLocalClaimProviderTrust cmdlet.

Skill 11.2: Implement Web Application Proxy

In this section, we explain how to install and configure a reverse proxy by using the Web Application Proxy (WAP). A WAP is useful for integrating with AD FS and providing access to internal applications. A WAP enables organizations to use either pass-through or AD FS preauthentication in a perimeter network for external users.

This section covers how to:

- Install and configure WAP
- Implement WAP in pass-through mode
- Implement WAP as AD FS proxy
- Integrate WAP with AD FS
- Configure AD FS requirements
- Publish web apps via WAP
- Publish Remote Desktop Gateway applications
- Configure HTTP to HTTPS redirects
- Configure internal and external Fully Qualified Domain Names

Install and configure WAP

While the WAP role service is used with AD FS, the role service itself is a part of the Remote Access server role. Installing the role service is accomplished by using the Add Role or Feature Wizard, or by using Windows PowerShell. Once added, use the Web Application Proxy Configuration Wizard as shown in Figure 11-9 to configure the service.

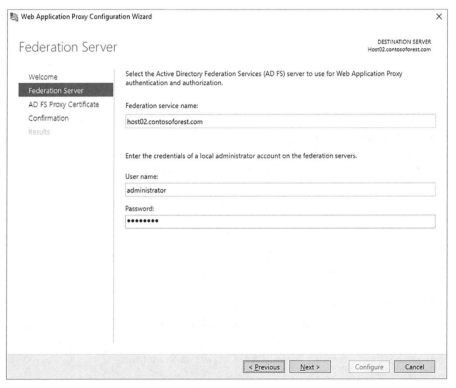

FIGURE 11-9 Web Application Proxy Configuration

As part of the configuration wizard, you connect to the AD FS farm and obtain the certificates that are available and can be used with the Web Application Proxy. Select the desired certificate, as shown in Figure 11-10, and then complete the wizard.

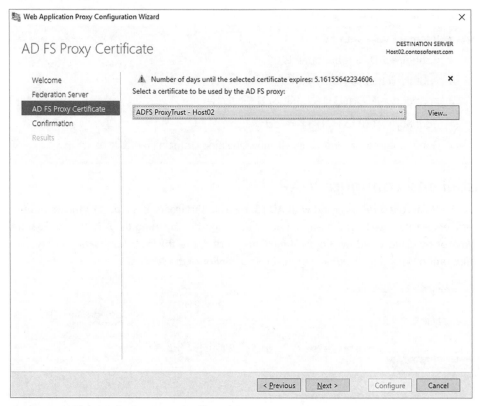

FIGURE 11-10 Web Application Proxy Configuration

Additionally, you can configure the Web Application Proxy by using the Install-WebApplicationProxy cmdlet. The cmdlet must specify the federation service name and certificate thumbprint to be used:

```
Install-WebApplicationProxy -CertificateThumbprint
'A142A369FC60C7984A70A56A17E31228546D85D8' -FederationServiceName 'host02.contosoforest.
com'
```

Implement WAP in pass-through mode

Pass-through mode instructs the WAP to not perform any authentication. All requests that are received by the WAP are automatically forwarded to the destination application. Figure 11-11 shows selecting pass-through as the WAP authentication method.

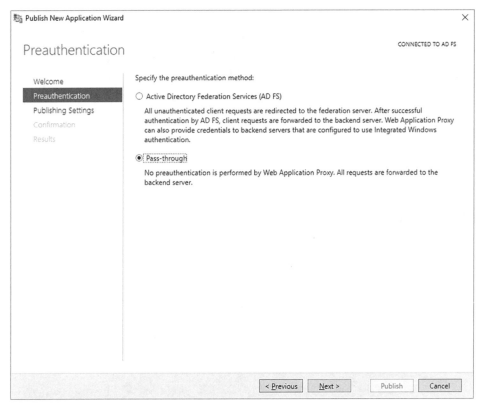

FIGURE 11-11 Publish New Application Wizard

Alternatively, you can use the Add-WebApplicationProxyApplication cmdlet and specify PassThrough for the ExternalPreAuthentication parameter.

```
Add-WebApplicationProxyApplication -BackendServerURL 'https://app1.contosoforest.com/'
 -ExternalCertificateThumbprint '1a2b3c4d5e6f1a2b3c4d5e6f1a2b3c4d5e6f1a2b'
-ExternalURL 'https://app1.contosoforest.com/' -Name 'App1 (no preauthentication)'
-ExternalPreAuthentication PassThrough
```

Implement and integrate WAP as AD FS proxy

There are two sections of the skills that include using WAP with AD FS, which we combine for this section. Figure 11-10 also shows the other pre-authentication option for WAP, which is AD FS. If the WAP receives a request that is not authenticated, then the request is redirected to the AD FS farm. After being authenticated by AD FS, the request is then sent to the backend application. If the client is using Windows integrated authentication, then the WAP can forward the credentials to the backend application.

Figure 11-12 shows the supported clients that can be used with an AD FS proxy, including:

- **Web and MSOFBA**   Authenticates web apps, including Microsoft Office.
- **HTTP Basic**   New for Windows Server 2016, this is used for clients that do not support HTTP redirect, such as Exchange ActiveSync.
- **OAuth2**   Windows Store apps or Office clients that support OAuth2 authentication.

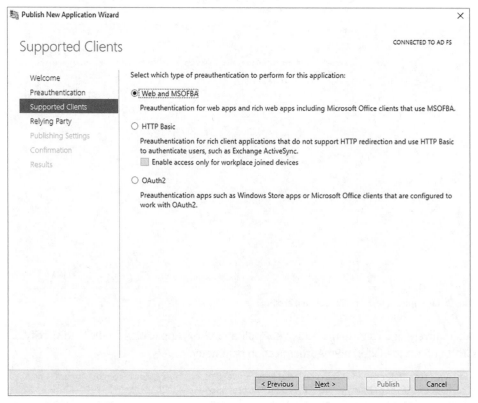

FIGURE 11-12 Supported clients

Configure AD FS requirements

The only requirement for using a WAP with AD FS is that a farm is configured with a relying party trust. Without a relying party trust, you are not able to publish an application to be used with the WAP.

Publish web apps via WAP

Publishing an application is performed from the Remote Access Management Console by using the Publish New Application Wizard. When publishing an application, you must specify specific information for the application:

- Preauthentication method
- Supported clients
- Relying party trust
- Publishing settings

Figure 11-13 shows the publishing settings that must be defined for an application.

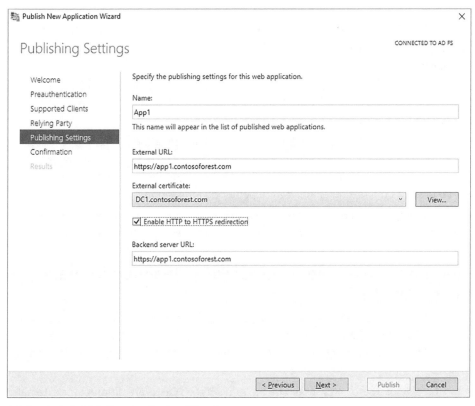

FIGURE 11-13 Publish New Application Wizard

Alternatively, you can use the Add-WebApplicationProxyApplication cmdlet to publish an application.

```
Add-WebApplicationProxyApplication -BackendServerUrl 'https://app1.contosoforest.com'
-ExternalCertificateThumbprint '2FC38D0224B0A6412F450A95972711179878708B0'
-EnableHTTPRedirect:$true -ExternalUrl 'https://app1.contosoforest.com'
-Name 'App1' -ExternalPreAuthentication ADFS -ADFSRelyingPartyName 'AD FS'
```

Publish Remote Desktop Gateway applications

Publishing a Remote Desktop Gateway (RDG) enables you to restrict access to the RDG and add a layer of pre-authentication using a WAP. This is especially useful for enabling MFA with RDG. The process of publishing a RDG through a WAP depends on whether the RD Web Access and RD Gateway are configured on the same server or different servers. Using one server enables you to only publish the root FQDN. Using different servers means that you must publish two directories separately.

As with other published applications, you must create a relying party trust using the FQDN of the RDG. You can then publish the root of the site in the WAP. You must also disable the HttpOnly cookie property in the WAP for the published application.

> **NEED MORE REVIEW?** **PUBLISHING RDG WITH WAP**
>
> For a step by step of publishing an RDG with a WAP, visit *https://technet.microsoft.com/ en-us/library/dn765486.aspx.*

Configure HTTP to HTTPS redirects

Windows Server 2016 and WAP introduces a new capability to automatically redirect user requests from unsecure HTTP to secure HTTPS connections. The redirection setting is controlled per published application, and is simply enabled or disabled for the application. Figure 11-14 shows the setting enabled for a published application.

When using the Add-WebApplicationProxyApplication cmdlet, the EnableHTTPRedirect parameter accepts either $True or $False to enable or disable redirecting client requests.

Configure internal and external Fully Qualified Domain Names (FQDNs)

As shown in Figure 11-13, there are two FQDN addresses that are configured with an application. The External URL is the FQDN that external users request access to when attempting to access an application. The backend server URL is the FQDN of the internal resource where the application is available.

In most scenarios, these URLs should be the same. If the FQDNs are different for external and internal requests, then URL translation must also be configured to ensure requests are redirected correctly. To enable URL translation, use the Set-WebApplicationProxyApplication cmdlet.

```
Set-WebApplicationProxyApplication -ID AppID -DisableTranslateUrlInRequestHeaders:$False
```

Chapter summary

- Using the Farm Behavior Level in AD FS to determine features
- Creating a relying party trust for claims-based authentication
- Configuring access control policies for AD FS
- Using multi-factor authentication with AD FS
- Understanding device registration with AD FS
- Integrating Windows Hello for Business with AD FS
- Using third-party LDAP with AD FS
- Installing and configuring a Web Application Proxy
- Using pass-through or AD FS modes of a WAP
- Publishing applications through a WAP
- Publishing Remote Desktop Gateways through WAP
- Redirecting user requests to be secure with HTTPS
- Understanding the external and backend URLs with WAP

Thought Experiment

An organization has an existing Windows Server 2012 R2 AD FS farm. They plan to upgrade the farm to Windows Server 2016. After the upgrade, they also plan to implement Azure MFA with their applications. The organization does not currently have any additional configuration software in their environment. The MFA solution must also work with biometric options. After the upgrade, they plan to centralize user requests by using a reverse proxy. All user requests must be secured.

Using the above scenario, answer the following questions.

1. How should the organization complete the upgrade?
2. What additional software should the organization use to integrate Azure MFA?
3. What technology should the organization use to enable biometric MFA?
4. How should the organization ensure that all requests are secure?

Thought Experiment Answers

1. The organization should perform individual upgrades to raise the Farm Behavior Level of the AD FS farm. They should not reinstall AD FS and export the configuration.

2. They should use System Center Configuration Manager to simplify the configuration and management of Azure MFA.

3. Windows Hello for Business should be used to ensure that biometric authentication can be used with the published applications.

4. They should set the WAP to redirect all HTTP requests to HTTPS for each published application.

Index

A

F

M

N

O

P

Q

R

About the author

 CHARLES PLUTA is a technical consultant and Microsoft Certified Trainer (MCT) who has authored several certification exams, lab guides, and learner guides for various technology vendors. As a technical consultant, Charles has assisted small, medium, and large organizations deploy and maintain their IT infrastructure. He is also a speaker, staff member, or trainer at several large industry conferences every year. Charles has a degree in Computer Networking, and holds more than 25 industry certifications. He makes a point to leave the United States to travel to a different country once every year. When not working or traveling, he plays pool in Augusta, Georgia.